Explaining Pakistan's Long-Run Growth

Moazam Mahmood • Rabia Ikram

Explaining Pakistan's Long-Run Growth

A Keynesian Model in Seven Essays

Moazam Mahmood
Department of Economics
Lahore School of Economics
Lahore, Pakistan

Rabia Ikram
Department of Economics
Lahore School of Economics
Lahore, Pakistan

ISBN 978-3-031-86676-0   ISBN 978-3-031-86677-7   (eBook)
https://doi.org/10.1007/978-3-031-86677-7

© The Editor(s) (if applicable) and The Author(s), under exclusive license to Springer Nature Switzerland AG 2025

This work is subject to copyright. All rights are solely and exclusively licensed by the Publisher, whether the whole or part of the material is concerned, specifically the rights of translation, reprinting, reuse of illustrations, recitation, broadcasting, reproduction on microfilms or in any other physical way, and transmission or information storage and retrieval, electronic adaptation, computer software, or by similar or dissimilar methodology now known or hereafter developed.

The use of general descriptive names, registered names, trademarks, service marks, etc. in this publication does not imply, even in the absence of a specific statement, that such names are exempt from the relevant protective laws and regulations and therefore free for general use.

The publisher, the authors and the editors are safe to assume that the advice and information in this book are believed to be true and accurate at the date of publication. Neither the publisher nor the authors or the editors give a warranty, expressed or implied, with respect to the material contained herein or for any errors or omissions that may have been made. The publisher remains neutral with regard to jurisdictional claims in published maps and institutional affiliations.

This Palgrave Macmillan imprint is published by the registered company Springer Nature Switzerland AG.

The registered company address is: Gewerbestrasse 11, 6330 Cham, Switzerland

If disposing of this product, please recycle the paper.

Acknowledgements

The authors would like to thank Muzzna Maqsood and Seemab Sajid for their tremendous research support for the whole book project, Maheen Pracha for her invaluable editing, Wyndham Hacket Pain for his gracious publishing, Syed Kalim Hyder Bukhari for the kind provision of national income accounts data on behalf of the State Bank of Pakistan, and the International Monetary Fund's Islamabad office for sharing documentation on loan agreements with Pakistan.

Competing Interests   The authors have no competing interests to declare that are relevant to the content of this manuscript.

Contents

1 Explaining Pakistan's Long-Run Growth: A Keynesian Model in Seven Essays   1
   1.1   Introduction   1
   1.2   Policy Implications   5
   1.3   The Structure of the Book   5

Part I   An Analytical Framework to Examine Growth of Output Over Time   9

2 Four Properties of Growth Models: A Preamble   11
   2.1   Introduction to the Problem of Growth   11
   2.2   Four Properties of Growth Models   13
   2.3   The Analytical Structure of the Book   19
   References   26

3 Two Properties of Growth Models: General Equilibrium and Theoretical Consistency   29
   3.1   The First Property: The Need for General Equilibrium Analysis   29
   3.2   The Second Property: The Need for Internal Consistency in the Theoretical Argument of the Model   45
   References   58

4 The Third and Fourth Properties of Growth Models: The Need for an Equilibrium Solution and a Non-corner One, Requiring In Turn a Mathematically Equilibrating Model — 61
4.1 Introduction and Recap — 61
4.2 The Third Property: The Need for an Equilibrium Solution for Output and its Rate of Growth over Time, and Preferably Not a Corner One — 64
4.3 The Fourth Property: The Need for a Mathematically Equilibrating Model — 85
References — 96

5 The Keynesian Mum Equation — 99
5.1 The Keynesian Mum Equation — 99
5.2 The Global Context of a Model of Aggregate Demand for Output — 100
5.3 The Keynesian Macro Model — 103
5.4 The Derivation of the Keynesian Mum Equation, with Consumption and Investment as Substitutes — 104
5.5 Completing the Full Keynesian Mum Equation — 107
References — 109

Part II Explaining Long-Run GDP Growth for Pakistan — 111

6 Application of a Keynesian General Equilibrium Model to Analysing Growth of Output Over Time for Pakistan — 113
6.1 The Pattern of Long-Run GDP Growth in Pakistan — 113
6.2 A General Theoretical Framework to Analyse GDP Growth in Pakistan — 119
6.3 Theoretical Framework for This Essay — 121
6.4 Three Fundamental Propositions About GDP Growth in Pakistan — 122
6.5 Data — 124
6.6 Is There an Observable, Discrete and Significant Drop in GDP Growth? — 125
6.7 Which of the Keynesian Macro Aggregates Explain This Drop in GDP Growth? — 126

	6.8	Are the Phases of Growth Investment-Led or Consumption-Led?	130
	6.9	Conclusions	132
		References	133
7	**Analysing Pakistan's Investment Growth Over Time**	137
	7.1	The Narrative for the Growth of GDP and Investment	137
	7.2	The Pattern of Long-Run Investment Growth in Pakistan	139
	7.3	Literature Reviewing the Supply-Side and Demand-Side Determinants of Investment	140
	7.4	Theoretical Framework	143
	7.5	Data Description	147
	7.6	Supply-Side Determinants Explaining the Drop in Investment Growth	147
	7.7	Testing the Supply-Side Propositions	151
	7.8	Demand-Side Determinants Explaining the Drop in Investment Growth	161
	7.9	Testing the Demand-Side Propositions	162
	7.10	Conclusion	175
		References	176
8	**The Role of Policy Reforms and the Regulatory Policy Environment in Explaining the Behaviour of Public Investment in Pakistan**	179
	8.1	Implications of the Argument Established in Essays 5 and 6	179
	8.2	Literature Review	181
	8.3	Data	184
	8.4	Part 1: Explaining the Behaviour of Public Investment Over Time	185
	8.5	Part 2: The Impact of the Policy Reforms of the 1990s on the Power Sector	194
	8.6	Part 3: The Role of the Regulatory Policy Environment in Explaining the Drop in GDP Growth and Aggregate Investment	202
	8.7	Policy Mis-sequencing as an Explanation for the Behaviour of Private Investment to Substitute for Public Investment	214

8.8 *Summing Up the Book's Theory and Empirics*	218
8.9 *Policy Implications*	222
Appendix: Definitions of Variables	222
References	224

Index 227

List of Figures

Fig. 3.1	Neoclassical model: Partial equilibrium only in the labour market	31
Fig. 3.2	The Keynesian cross	34
Fig. 3.3	Production function parables	41
Fig. 3.4	Choice of technique	54
Fig. 3.5	Capital re-switching	57
Fig. 4.1	Harrod-Domar model disequilibrium	71
Fig. 4.2	The Feldman model	83
Fig. 4.3	The Harrod Domar model's K/Y ratio	90
Fig. 4.4	The Keynesian multiplier	95
Fig. 6.1	GDP growth in Pakistan	114
Fig. 6.2	Dummy regression for testing a known break date	125
Fig. 6.3	Structural break in real GDP growth series for 1973 to 2017	126
Fig. 6.4	Drop in investment growth	127
Fig. 6.5	Correlating GDP growth to growth in the macro aggregates	129
Fig. 6.6	Estimates of the MPC	132
Fig. 7.1	Investment growth	139
Fig. 7.2	Structural break dummy regression for growth in GDP, investment and savings	153
Fig. 7.3	Investment and savings shares as percentages of GDP	154
Fig. 7.4	Trend regression of share of investment as percentage of GDP	156
Fig. 7.5	Trend regression of share of savings as percentage of GDP	156
Fig. 7.6	Trend regression of share of inflows as percentage of GDP	157
Fig. 7.7	Regression result for growth of investment, savings and inflows	159

Fig. 7.8	Regression showing relationship between growth of savings and inflows	160
Fig. 7.9	Two-sample t test for growth in public investment	165
Fig. 7.10	Shares of total investment, public investment and private investment as percentage of GDP	166
Fig. 7.11	Trend regression of share of investment as percentage of GDP	169
Fig. 7.12	Trend regression of share of public investment	169
Fig. 7.13	Trend regression of share of private investment	170
Fig. 7.14	Two-sample t test for share of public investment	171
Fig. 7.15	Regression of growth of investment, growth in public investment and growth in private investment	172
Fig. 7.16	Regression showing relationship between growth of private investment and growth of public investment	174
Fig. 8.1	Time-series plot and trend break in public investment, productive sector investment and administrative services sector investment as share of output (GDP)	187
Fig. 8.2	Growth of productive sector investment, 1973–2019	187
Fig. 8.3	Public investment, by sector (PKR million)	188
Fig. 8.4	Growth in public investment in electricity	189
Fig. 8.5	Dummy regression to identify direction of change	192
Fig. 8.6	Growth contributions using growth regression	192
Fig. 8.7	Log total energy generation GWh (public + private)	199
Fig. 8.8	Estimated average generation cost for public versus private sectors, 2006–2023	200
Fig. 8.9	EPP, CPP and PPP	201
Fig. 8.10	Loans taken by Pakistan from IMF	206
Fig. 8.11	Observed fiscal deficits, revenues and expenditures as percentage of GDP	207
Fig. 8.12	Dummy regression to identify direction of change	208
Fig. 8.13	Development, current and total expenditures as percentage of GDP	209
Fig. 8.14	Dummy regression to identify the direction of change	210
Fig. 8.15	Targeted fiscal deficit by IMF versus observed fiscal deficit, 1980–2016	212
Fig. 8.16	Dummy regression to identify direction of change	213
Fig. 8.17	Impact of capital outflows on savings and investment (as percentage of GDP)	216

LIST OF BOXES

Box 2.1	The Keynesian Mum Equation	20
Box 3.1	The Classical and Neoclassical Models	32
Box 3.2	Keynesian Model of Aggregate Demand	35
Box 3.3	The Samuelson-Swan-Solow Production Function	46
Box 3.4	The Re-Switching Problem	51
Box 4.1	Harrod-Domar Model Full-Employment Conditions	65
Box 4.2	The Harrod-Domar Model's Knife Edge	72
Box 4.3	Savings and Investment	75
Box 4.4	The Neoclassical Solution to the Harrod-Domar Model's Second Problem of Full-Employment Equilibrium	78
Box 4.5	The Feldman Model	82
Box 4.6	The Lahore School of Economics Modelling Lab's Income Distribution Model	86
Box 4.7	Harrod-Domar Versus Keynes	91
Box 4.8	The Kahn-Keynes Multiplier	94
Box 5.1	The Keynesian Mum Equation	101
Box 5.2	Theoretical Propositions for Keynes's Model	105
Box 6.1	The Keynesian Mum Equation Revisited	119
Box 6.2	Empirical Estimation Model for Growth	128
Box 6.3	MPC and the Determination of GDP	131
Box 7.1	Supply-Side Determinants of Investment	144
Box 7.2	Demand-Side Determinants of Investment	146
Box 7.3	Estimating Savings	148
Box 7.4	Test for a Structural Break in the Growth of Savings and Inflows	151

Box 7.5	Trend Analysis for the Shares of Supply-Side Variables in Output	155
Box 7.6	Analysis of the Investment Growth Variable in Relation to Supply-Side Growth Variables	158
Box 7.7	The Relationship Between the Supply-Side Determinants, Savings and Inflows	160
Box 7.8	A Structural Break Test at a Known Break Date for All Explanatory Demand-Side Variables	163
Box 7.9	Using Trend Regressions to Examine the Shares of the Demand-Side Variables in Output	167
Box 7.10	Analysis of the Investment Growth Variable in Relation to Demand-Side Growth Variables	173
Box 7.11	Empirical Model to Test the Relationship Between Public Investment and Private Investment	175
Box 8.1	Classification of Productive Sector and Administrative Services Investments	185
Box 8.2	Econometric Tests in Essay 7	189
Box 8.3	Components of CPP and EPP	201
Box 8.4	The Aggregate Demand Equation Recalled	204
Box 8.5	Fiscal Variables as Shares of Output	207

List of Tables

Table 3.1	Capital re-switching	56
Table 4.1	Harrod-Domar model initial conditions	67
Table 4.2	Harrod-Domar model equilibrium conditions	68
Table 4.3	Harrod-Domar model corner solution	84
Table 7.1	Structural break test for real public investment growth	164
Table 8.1	Structural break test for break date in year 1992 ± 1	191
Table 8.2	Public and private source-wise energy generation (GWh)	196
Table 8.3	Source–wise energy generation (GWh)	197
Table 8.4	Estimated average generation cost for public versus private sectors, 2006–2023	200

CHAPTER 1

Explaining Pakistan's Long-Run Growth: A Keynesian Model in Seven Essays

1.1 Introduction

This is a book about explaining the behaviour of output and its growth over time. To explain this behaviour, the book deliberates over a choice among three fundamental models—the Samuelson-Swan-Solow neoclassical model, the Harrod-Domar model and the Keynesian model—to choose one fit for purpose.

The criteria for goodness of fit are four mathematical properties of these growth models. The first desirable property is a notion of general equilibrium based on multiple markets, rather than partial equilibrium based on just one market. The second desirable property is theoretical consistency. The third useful property is the need for an equilibrium solution, and one that is not an extreme corner solution with a low probability of occurring. The fourth property is entailed in giving a non-corner equilibrium solution through an equilibrating relationship within the model.

These mathematical properties are not desirable in economic models for mathematical rigour but rather for economic intuition—to give results that track and explain the behaviour of macro variables better. We have had to contend with some mathematical rigour, however, in this deliberation on modelling.

The model chosen for meeting these four mathematical properties is the Keynesian model. It is just a bit better on all four counts. The proof of the pudding (and the model) is of course in the number it comes up with.

© The Author(s), under exclusive license to Springer Nature Switzerland AG 2025
M. Mahmood, R. Ikram, *Explaining Pakistan's Long-Run Growth*, https://doi.org/10.1007/978-3-031-86677-7_1

Its credibility lies in its explanation of observed behaviour. In this sense, this is a modeller's book—certainly not a mathematician's book. A search for a better number, which gives a better explanation of observed behaviour. This is perhaps too Popperian for pure theorists, but it is how we have chosen to argue.

The chosen Keynesian model of aggregate demand has been used to explain the observed behaviour of Pakistan's long-run growth of gross domestic product (GDP). The period chosen is from 1973 to 2019. Prior to 1972, the country comprised another part, now Bangladesh. A more consistent set of national income accounts and macro aggregates becomes available only after 1972. We observe here that Pakistan's GDP growth over the long run between 1973 and 2019 is marked by a statistically significant hiatus at approximately 1992. Pre-1992, GDP growth on trend approximated 6 per cent per annum. Post-1992, GDP growth drops on trend to approximately 4 per cent per annum. These observed trends require an explanation.

An adapted Keynesian model explains this observed hiatus in GDP growth very well. The Kahn-Keynes multiplier explains output growth on the left-hand side of an equation, as a function on the right-hand side of the macro aggregate of investment times a multiplier (k). The multiplier k is given by the marginal propensity to consume (MPC) and therefore ultimately by the macro aggregate of consumption. However, the two macro aggregates of investment and consumption are not simply additive complements as the national income identity seems to present them. This is because investment, for Keynes, is a function not of the rate of interest but of the supply of loanable funds, which are savings. Thus, if investment goes up, savings go up. Savings plus consumption are equal to income. Then, if savings go up, consumption must come down. Therefore, given the multiplier k, investment and consumption become not complements but trade-offs instead.

This theoretical model says that output on the left-hand side of the equation will be determined on the right-hand side by both investment and consumption, not as complements but as trade-offs. If investment goes up, consumption will go down. Therefore, the impact of rising investment on output will be traded off by the multiplier k going down because consumption and the MPC will go down. Conversely, the impact of falling investment on output will be traded off by the multiplier k going up because consumption and the MPC will go up.

Applied to the hiatus in Pakistan's GDP growth after 1992, this model shows that pre-1992, high GDP growth is explained by high investment growth, paired with a low MPC, while post-1992, lowered GDP growth is explained by lowered investment growth, paired with a higher MPC. Thus, Pakistan's higher GDP growth pre-1992 was investment-led while lower GDP growth post-1992 has been consumption-led.

The book then traces the causality of these trends in investment and consumption. It finds that high total investment pre-1992 was due to high public investment. The drop in total investment in 1992 was due to a significant drop in public investment. This is further traced to a drop in the productive sectors, particularly power generation. However, we observe that private investment remained fairly constant over both sub-periods, pre-1992 and post-1992.

This begs the Ricardian hypothesis that if public investment was high pre-1992 and private investment was crowded out by public investment, then post-1992, as public investment dropped, why did private investment not rise to substitute for it? This requires us to pursue two causal chains: one to explain the drop in public investment and the other to explain the inability of private investment to substitute for public investment.

The causal chain to explain the drop in public investment, especially in productive sectors such as power, is sought in a set of domestic policy reforms to the regulatory policy environment. These have been to reduce the fiscal deficit. The causal chain to explain the inability of private investment to rise and substitute for the drop in public investment is sought in a simultaneous set of exogenous policy reforms to the regulatory policy environment. These have been to open up the capital account. This has yielded a case of policy mis-sequencing, leading to unplanned outcomes.

The drop in public investment post-1992 is explained through government expenditures. Government expenditures are a function of revenues and budget deficits set out in a Keynesian analytical macro framework. Government expenditures are observed to drop significantly post-1992. We see that this drop is based on a significant fall in fiscal deficits post-1992, while tax revenues remain constant between the two periods.

Clearly, the Pakistan government, forced by the need to reduce the budget deficit, did this by reducing government expenditures rather than raising tax revenues. The reduction in budget deficits, leading to a reduction in government expenditures, is further observed to be based on a cut in government development expenditures rather than in government recurrent expenditures. Since development expenditures expand the capacity for public goods while recurrent expenditures are on existing capacity, it is the drop in development expenditures that enables the observed drop in public investment in productive sectors such as power generation.

The fundamental question then becomes what kind of regulatory policy environment influenced the observed drop in budget deficits. Pakistan has seen a succession of loan agreements with the International Monetary Fund (IMF), whose conditionality appears to have become tighter over time, particularly after 1991. This has been the impetus for domestic policy reforms to reduce runaway fiscal deficits.

The liberality or austerity of the regulatory policy environment is captured well by the size of the agreed budget deficit decided between the IMF and the Pakistan government. These agreed budget deficits are seen to drop after the 1991 agreement and for all subsequent agreements. The agreed budget deficits are also seen to be well correlated with the observed budget deficits. The regulatory policy environment, heavily influenced by domestic policy reforms to reduce fiscal deficits, became significantly more austere post-1992, leading to the chain of causality through reduced government expenditures to reduced public investment. However, these domestic policy reforms explain only the drop in public investment. They do not explain why private investment did not pick up post-1992 to compensate for the drop in public investment.

To explain why private investment remained constant over the whole period examined from 1973 to 2019, and did not pick up post-1992, we invoke a second set of policy reforms to the regulatory policy environment: exogenous policy reforms to open up the capital account. Enacted simultaneously with the domestic policy reforms, the opening up of the capital account in 1991—and more fully by 1994—led to the onset of significant capital outflows.

Beginning at about 1 per cent of GDP, these capital outflows had risen to about 3 per cent of GDP by 2022. Public investment dropped by about 5 per cent of GDP post-1992, coming up to 2019. With private investment constant on trend at about 10 per cent of GDP over the whole long-run period from 1973 to 2019, the drop in public investment reduced total investment by 5 per cent of GDP. Private investment did not fill this gap of 5 per cent of GDP because by 2022, it was sending near 3 per cent of GDP into capital outflows.

1.2 Policy Implications

This is not a book about policy, being more preoccupied in explaining the behaviour of macro aggregates, based on a picky search for models that might serve better. However, there are some logical implications of the causality that explains the drop in GDP growth in Pakistan post-1992. There are two causal chains: one for public investment and one for private investment. One clear policy option is to fund an increase in public investment and productive sector investment to enhance total investment and output growth.

This first policy option should in theory be based on enhancing tax revenues to enhance public investment without raising the observed fiscal deficits. Pakistan has not followed this option as tax revenues have fallen. The second policy option is to raise private investment. In the short to medium term, this can only be done by reducing capital outflows by closing the capital account.

The existential question for Pakistan's economy is how to raise its very low investment as a share of GDP, which has now slumped to 15 per cent. A balanced growth path is clearly needed—one that incentivizes private investment and increases public investment to enhance total investment. Therefore, if private investment is shy in the shorter run, public investment must be increased to increase total investment. Again, a balance is needed in funding public investment both from increasing revenues and prudent increases in the public deficit.

1.3 The Structure of the Book

The book is structured into two parts. Part I, which sets up the analytical framework of the book, comprises four essays. The first essay (Chap. 2) is a theoretical preamble, setting out the four properties of growth models identified as useful in an analytical framework to examine the growth of output over time. These four properties are:

1. The need for general equilibrium analysis
2. The need for internal consistency in the theoretical argument of the model
3. The need for an equilibrium solution for output and its rate of growth over time, and preferably not a corner one
4. The need for a mathematically equilibrating model.

These four properties are identified in the first essay and examined in the second and third essays (Chaps. 3 and 4). The three essays end up giving in Essay 4 a Keynesian general equilibrium model to analyse the growth of output over time (Chap. 5).

Part II of the book uses this Keynesian general equilibrium model to analyse and explain the trajectory of GDP growth in Pakistan over the long run of the last 50 years. It does this over the next three empirical essays.

Essay 5 finds that a Keynesian aggregate demand model, adapted to estimate growth over time, explains Pakistan's GDP growth trajectory very well (Chap. 6). The application of this adapted Keynesian model to Pakistan's GDP growth trajectory identifies two primary determinants of growth. Pre-1992, high GDP growth of 6 per cent per annum is shown by the model to be led by high investment growth, paired with low consumption growth. Post-1992, lower GDP growth of 4 per cent per annum is shown by the model to be led by high consumption growth, paired with low investment growth.

Pursuing causality, Essay 6 then explains the determinants of investment and consumption (Chap. 7). This high growth of aggregate investment pre-1992 is in turn explained by the high growth of public investment, paired with fairly constant growth in private investment. The low growth of aggregate investment post-1992 is shown to be due to low growth in public investment, still paired with constant growth in private investment.

The search for the last mile in causality implies explaining the behaviour of public investment, its high growth boosting aggregate investment growth and output growth pre-1992, and its low growth lowering aggregate investment growth and output growth post-1992. Essay 7 shows that this last mile in causality closes the Keynesian loop. It brings in a third determinant of output in the Keynesian 'mum' equation: government expenditures (Chap. 8).

The results from running government expenditures as a function of taxation and budgetary deficits shows that pre-1992, high government expenditures are based on high deficits, while post-1992, low government expenditures are based on low budget deficits. The Pakistan government appears to have been unable to raise tax revenues over this long-run period of the past 50 years. It has based high GDP growth pre-1992, of 6 per cent per annum, on the high growth of aggregate investment, based on high public investment, based in turn on high budgetary deficits. Post-1992, the lower growth of 4 per cent per annum has been based on the lower growth of aggregate investment, based on lower growth of public investment, based in turn on lower budgetary deficits. The post-1992 regulatory environment under IMF conditionality appears to have reduced targeted deficits—and with them, observed deficits.

The drop in aggregate investment, based on the drop in public investment post-1992, still leaves unexplained the inability of private investment to pick up and substitute for the drop in public investment. Essay 7 then concludes by tracing this inability of private investment to rise post-1992 to a classic case of policy mis-sequencing. Domestic policy reforms to reduce the budget deficit post-1992 through a reduction in public investment coincided unfortunately with policy reforms to liberalize the capital account, thereby enabling significant capital outflows. Thus, private investment did not fulfil its Ricardian role of substituting for public investment, keeping its domestic investment constant, but raising its investment abroad significantly.

PART I

An Analytical Framework to Examine Growth of Output Over Time

CHAPTER 2

Four Properties of Growth Models: A Preamble

2.1 INTRODUCTION TO THE PROBLEM OF GROWTH

Examining growth in the macroeconomy requires a prior analytical framework. Much importance lies in such a framework. The mid-1900s saw keen contention between alternative models, primarily between the neoclassical growth model—the Samuelson-Swan-Solow production function—and the Keynesian model of aggregate demand. A third contender, the Harrod-Domar model of growth, was intended to enhance the Keynesian model of aggregate demand. These are the essential workhorse models that have been taught to generations of students and their theory brought to bear on analysing output growth in the macroeconomy.

The bells and whistles of derivatives or precursors of these models do not detract from the fundamentally unique theoretical contentions of each. In the case of the neoclassical Samuelson-Swan-Solow production function, Swan (1956) introduced a putty-clay model, Solow (1956) developed a model that avoids the use of capital and Samuelson (1966) presented a surrogate production function. The aggregate demand model originally developed by Keynes (1936) is accompanied by a significant critique of the neoclassical production function's use of the concept of capital, led by Sraffa (1961) and Robinson (1967).

Sraffa, of course, proposed a model of the production of commodities by means of commodities as an alternative to the notion of homogeneous capital. Pasinetti (2007) has contributed further to this line of research.

© The Author(s), under exclusive license to Springer Nature Switzerland AG 2025
M. Mahmood, R. Ikram, *Explaining Pakistan's Long-Run Growth*,
https://doi.org/10.1007/978-3-031-86677-7_2

Lewis (1954) and Kaldor (1966, 1967, 1972) should be regarded as providing less quantitative determinants of output growth and more qualitative insights into manufacturing-led growth (see also Mahmood, 2018). The instability problem in the Harrod-Domar model (Harrod, 1948) led to several solutions, such as Solow (1956, 1957), Hahn and Matthews (1964) and Robinson (1953, 1962, 1967).

Despite the insights of this collateral and satellite body of models, the essential economic causality in determining output growth remains distinct to the three models posited as unique and fundamental: the Samuelson-Swan-Solow production function, the Keynesian model of aggregate demand and the Harrod-Domar model of growth. Each uniquely determines output growth theoretically. Importantly, this uniqueness has made these three models the standard workhorse models for global output growth models. For example, the United Nations' global forecasts for output growth by its Department for Economic and Social Affairs utilize both an aggregate demand model and a production function.

There is a broader causal divide between the neoclassical and Keynesian models. The Samuelson-Swan-Solow production function is considered to place the causality of growth as exogenous to the model. In this view, the two major causal variables of growth—labour and capital—are given exogenously. Labour inputs are determined by demographic growth, which is considered exogenous to the model. Capital inputs are also given to the model and solved for within it.

The Keynesian model of aggregate demand places the causality of growth endogenously within the model. That is, the macro aggregates of demand are determined within the model and the model solves for them. Curiously, the Harrod-Domar model, given its Keynesian DNA, also places the causality of growth as exogenous to the model. This is because its main driver of growth, savings, is given to the model and so the model does not solve for it. Indeed, the Samuelson-Swan-Solow production function emerged in the criticism of, and to solve for, the instability of the Harrod-Domar model.

However, the contention in this book is not the lineage of these models, but rather their theoretical robustness, internal consistency, economic intuition and empirical verification. Therefore, these economic models will be examined precisely for the economic arguments they make, the internal consistency of these arguments and the economic intuition they offer. Based on these criteria, a model can be chosen to provide a broad analytical framework to analyse and explain growth, and then tested empirically for a specific country.

For this project, the chosen country is Pakistan. Therefore, the model-based analytical framework must explain Pakistan's long-run growth from 1973 to 2017, which has experienced a significant drop in gross domestic product (GDP) growth over this period. The causal factors behind this drop need to be explained to find policy remedies. Hence, the theoretical and empirical goodness of fit of the adopted analytical framework will be tested by providing a causal explanation for the observed drop in Pakistan's GDP growth in the long run.

2.2 Four Properties of Growth Models

The conceptual framework of this book is based on choosing a model to examine output growth over time out of the three candidate models: the Samuelson-Swan-Solow production function, the Keynesian model of aggregate demand and the Harrod-Domar model of growth. These models are judged for four properties, arguably considered most useful for models of output growth:

1. The need for general equilibrium analysis
2. The need for theoretical consistency
3. The need for an equilibrium solution—and one that avoids a corner solution
4. The need for a mathematically equilibrating model

2.2.1 The Need for General Equilibrium Analysis

The choice of an analytical framework for this project must begin with the notion of and need for general equilibrium. The notion of general equilibrium analysis is seen in contrast to partial equilibrium analysis, which is the analysis of one market. Thus, an explanation can be sought for a phenomenon in one market. The analysis can also proceed further, seeking an explanation for the phenomenon in multiple markets, that is, general equilibrium analysis. Using this criterion to define general equilibrium gives a clear need for it. Analysis of a phenomenon based on multiple markets will clearly be more comprehensive than an analysis based on a single market.

This is an Orwellian notion of general equilibrium where one market is bad and multiple markets are better.

The argument for general equilibrium analysis, using this criterion of markets, is best made not by Arrow (1962) and Debreu (1970, 1975), but by Keynes (1936) in his setting out the model of aggregate demand, which needs to be examined. This need for general equilibrium analysis gives the first requirement in the search for an analytical framework to explain growth of output.

As outlined above, three workhorse models explain output growth in general equilibrium to a lesser or greater degree. One model that explains output growth in general equilibrium is the neoclassical Samuelson-Swan-Solow production function. The Arrow-Debreu intertemporal general equilibrium is deliberately not considered in this project because it focuses on explaining and proving the existence of equilibrium. It does not focus on explaining the causality of output growth, whereas the Samuelson-Swan-Solow production function seeks to provide the causal factors that explain output growth. The Harrod-Domar model also explains output growth in general equilibrium.

Both the Samuelson-Swan-Solow production function and Harrod-Domar model use three markets: the market for goods, the market for capital and the market for labour. The Keynesian model of aggregate demand uses far more markets to determine the growth of output. The model solves for output in the goods market, determined by aggregate demand given in turn in the private goods market, public goods market, money market, tradeables market and the market for global capital flows. Thus, by the criterion of general equilibrium, the Keynesian model offers a more comprehensive analytical framework for determining output growth than the Samuelson-Swan-Solow production function or the Harrod-Domar model of growth.

2.2.2 The Need for Theoretical Consistency

The choice of an analytical framework for this project also requires theoretical consistency in the candidate model adopted. The Samuelson-Swan-Solow production function encounters a problem of aggregating heterogeneous capital. This issue is known as the Cambridge capital controversy, which was debated between the University of Cambridge in the UK and largely MIT in Cambridge, Massachusetts, in the US (Harcourt, 1976).

In theory, the need to aggregate heterogeneous capital should affect all models that utilize the capital market to determine output. This would allow the Cambridge capital controversy to be relegated to a curiosum, a storm in a teacup. However, the need to aggregate heterogeneous capital goods particularly affects the neoclassical Samuelson-Swan-Solow production function for two reasons. First, this model serves as both a theory for determining output and a theory for determining the distribution of income. This leads to a significant inconsistency or circularity in the causal argument (Robinson, 1967). Second, it prevents a unique equilibrium in the capital market due to Wicksell effects (Wicksell, 1898, 1907).

The need to aggregate heterogeneous capital goods also affects the Harrod-Domar model of growth. It encounters an instability problem and its Solow solution requires an adjustment in the quantity of capital used. However, the quantity of capital used must also be a function of the interest rate used for aggregation, resulting in an inconsistency in the model.

Finally, the Keynesian aggregate demand model avoids the problem of aggregating capital on two counts, as Eatwell and Milgate (2011) show. First, even if it needs to aggregate heterogeneous capital, it does not rely on this aggregation to determine the distribution of income between capital and labour. Second, Keynesian investment is not a function of the interest rate. Therefore, the quantity of capital is not determined by the interest rate.

2.2.3 The Need for an Equilibrium Solution—And One that Avoids a Corner Solution

The choice of an analytical framework for this project requires a model that provides an equilibrium solution for determining output growth. Ideally, the equilibrium should not be a corner solution, meaning that it should not yield extreme values. The probability of such corner solutions is mathematically and statistically low.

The Samuelson-Swan-Solow production function does provide an equilibrium solution for output growth and does not suffer from the problem of corner solutions, which would be unlikely in economic theory and intuition. However, it is weaker in terms of theoretical consistency and is limited to three markets.

The Harrod-Domar model of growth has a well-studied problem of instability. First, its equilibrium solution for the growth rate of output must coincide with an exogenously given growth rate for the labour force.

Second, its equilibrium solution must coincide with a warranted rate of growth of output. Otherwise, the model becomes perverse and cycles away from a stable equilibrium. Neoclassical attempts to address this instability problem led Solow (1956) to propose his own production function. Hahn and Matthews (1964) found the problem of the warranted growth rate of output to be unfixable. Robinson (1953, 1962, 1967) argued that the model works a fortiori but not a priori.

This project raises two issues with the Harrod-Domar model of output growth: (a) the need for an equilibrium solution that avoids corner solutions, and (b) proposing the Keynesian model of aggregate demand as a solution to both problems.

Neoclassical attempts to fix the instability problem in the Harrod-Domar model focus on adjusting the capital-output ratio. Other attempts focus on adjusting the savings rate. However, the argument here is that adjusting the savings rate cannot be done under the assumption of ceteris paribus conditions, where the capital-output ratio remains unchanged. If the ceteris paribus condition is removed and the savings rate is allowed to affect the capital-output ratio, then, under certain conditions, an equilibrium solution may not exist. Furthermore, under these conditions, if the Harrod-Domar model does cycle to an equilibrium, it is likely to yield corner solutions with extreme values.

This project identifies the tendency of the Harrod-Domar model to cycle towards corner solutions as a result of the mathematical lack of an equilibrating variable. The argument then delves into the authors' experiences of current quantitative modelling. Simply put, mathematical macro models need to posit variables in an equilibrating relationship; otherwise, the model will not find equilibrium or, if it does, it may be a corner solution with extreme values that lack theoretical or intuitive justification.

To support this argument for equilibration, the book considers the experiences of two mathematical models. One model was initiated by the International Labour Organization (2016) with Francis Cripps. This has been developed further and completed and is now being run at the Modelling Lab at the Lahore School of Economics (see Mahmood et al., 2022). This model, playfully referred to as the 'Frankenstein model', aims to avoid corner solutions in the distribution of income between capital and labour. Another model is the Feldman-Mahalanobis model, which underlies Soviet state planning and serves as a lesson in postgraduate modelling, highlighting corner solutions between capital goods and consumer goods (Mahalanobis, 1953).

2.2.4 A Mathematically Equilibrating Model

The need of the hour is a mathematically equilibrating model that can determine output and its growth over time. This model should provide an equilibrium solution and one that is not limited to a corner solution. The Harrod-Domar growth model, the Frankenstein model and the Feldman-Mahalanobis model emphasize the importance of achieving a non-corner equilibrium. Greater internal theoretical consistency that affects the Samuelson-Swan-Solow production function is also necessary. Additionally, there is a need for a general equilibrium model that can capture the causal relationship between output growth determined in multiple markets.

As explained above, both the Samuelson-Swan-Solow production function and Harrod-Domar growth model are limited to three markets: goods, capital and labour. Comparatively, the Keynesian model of aggregate demand is a tad more theoretically consistent than the Samuelson-Swan-Solow production function, which struggles with the aggregation of heterogeneous capital to support its theory of income distribution. The Keynesian model of aggregate demand posits a causal relationship for determining output growth in five markets: private goods, public goods, money, tradeables, and global capital flows, which makes its search for causality more comprehensive than the Samuelson-Swan-Solow production function and the Harrod-Domar model. However, the decisive criterion for adopting the Keynesian model of aggregate demand, to explain the causality of output growth, is that it is a mathematically equilibrating model. It provides an equilibrium solution for determining output and its growth, while the equilibration ensures that the solution is not limited to a corner solution.

2.2.4.1 The Mathematically Equilibrating Relationship Between Investment and Consumption in the Keynesian Model

The Harrod-Domar model is rooted in Keynesian economics and based on the Keynesian model of aggregate demand. Its purpose is to depict the expansion of capacity over time, which is determined by savings and the capital-output ratio. However, the posit here is that savings and the capital-output ratio move together. Thus, mathematically, they are the same variable, capital, which, in the model, does not have an equilibrating relationship with any other variable. Therefore, capital can keep increasing over time, either yielding a model that may not cycle towards equilibrium or giving a corner equilibrium solution of extreme values for capital.

This corner solution for the Harrod-Domar model is mirrored in the Feldman-Mahalanobis model, where capital goods keep expanding to extreme values at the expense of consumer goods. Keynes's model of aggregate demand provides a strong equilibrating relationship for the expansion of capital. Since the model's cycling away from equilibrium is avoided, a corner solution is avoided, and capital cannot expand to extreme values.

This distinction is crucial because the Keynesian model of aggregate demand sets out a number of macro aggregates that contribute to the overall aggregate demand for output in what we refer to in this book as the Keynesian 'mum' equation[1] (Mahmood et al., 2022). One of these aggregates is capital investment, which is mathematically balanced with the macro aggregate of consumption. This equilibrium is achieved through the Kahn-Keynes multiplier, which facilitates the trade-off between investment and consumption (Kahn, 1931). Incorporating this trade-off, embedded in the Kahn-Keynes multiplier, prevents the aggregate demand model from cycling away from equilibrium. It also ensures that neither investment nor consumption reaches extreme values in a corner solution.

2.2.4.2 *A Return to General Equilibrium: The Multiplicity of Markets in Keynesian General Equilibrium, Offering a Multiplicity of Growth Paths*

Returning full circle to the need for more comprehensive general equilibrium in models of growth of output, the criteria used here for defining general equilibrium is multiple markets, as opposed to partial equilibrium, identified by a single market. Thus, the greater the number of markets included in an output growth model, the larger the net cast for determining the causality of output and its growth over time. The Samuelson-Swan-Solow production function, for instance, incorporates three markets: for goods, capital and labour. As the output of goods produced is the variable to be explained on the left-hand side of the equation, this leaves two markets to explain causality in determination of output on the right-hand side.

Similarly, the Harrod-Domar model aims to explain output growth on the left-hand side of its equation. In this case, only the capital market is left to explain causality on the right-hand side. However, the requirement for stability, which dictates that the growth of output on the left-hand side of

---

[1] See Essay 4 for an explanation of this euphemism.

the equation must equal the rate of growth of the labour force, mathematically places the labour market on the right-hand side. Therefore, both the Samuelson-Swan-Solow production function and the Harrod-Domar model utilize two markets to explain causality in determining output growth: the capital market and the labour market.

In contrast, the Keynesian model of aggregate demand employs a larger number of markets to explain causality in determining output and its growth over time. Within the Keynesian mum equation framework, output is represented on the left-hand side of the equation. On the right-hand side, causality for determining output demand can be sought in the private goods market, the public goods market, the capital market for investment, the tradeables market for exports and imports, and the market for global capital flows. While the labour market is not explicitly included in the Keynesian model, it is derived from Okun's law, which will be discussed further in the book.

As a result, the Keynesian model gives five markets in which to pursue causality in determining output and its growth time. To explain country growth over time, or indeed global growth over time, this Keynesian model gives five possible growth paths. Output growth can be driven by private consumption, private investment, government consumption and investment, exports or global capital flows. Additionally, there can be combinations of these growth paths and, importantly, over time there may be a transition from one growth path to another. This richness and comprehensiveness make the Keynesian model a valuable tool for estimating and explaining output growth over time.

2.3 The Analytical Structure of the Book

These four properties of growth models give the analytical structure of the book. Part 1 deliberates on the analytical framework to examine the growth of output over time. Part 2 applies this conceptual framework to explain long-run GDP growth in Pakistan over the past 50 years.

2.3.1 *Part 1: An Analytical Framework to Examine Growth of Output Over Time*

Part 1 comprises four essays. This first essay has been a theoretical preamble, setting out the four properties of growth models, identified as useful in an analytical framework to examine growth of output over time. These four properties are:

1. The need for general equilibrium analysis
2. The need for internal consistency in the theoretical argument of the model
3. The need for an equilibrium solution for output and its rate of growth over time—and preferably not a corner one
4. The need for a mathematically equilibrating model

These four properties have just been identified in this introductory essay. The proverb for China's modernization from 1978 was crossing a river by feeling the stones underfoot. These four properties will be examined, and the river crossed, in the second and third essays. Property 1 on the need for general equilibrium analysis and property 2 on the need for theoretical consistency in models of output growth will be examined in the second essay. The third essay delves into property 3 on the need for an equilibrium solution, preferably not a corner one, and property 4, emphasizing the requirement for a mathematically equilibrating model. These three essays should allow the development of a Keynesian general equilibrium model for analysing the growth of output over time, in the fourth essay.

2.3.2 Part 2: Application of a Keynesian General Equilibrium Model to Analysing Growth of Output Over Time for Pakistan

Part 2 of the book uses a Keynesian general equilibrium model to analyse and explain the trajectory of GDP growth in Pakistan over the long run of the last 50 years. It does this over three essays.

The Keynesian general equilibrium model adopted is derived from the Keynesian mum equation, which sets out output on the left-hand side of the equation, to be determined by the macro aggregates on the right-hand side of the equation. In the workhorse model adopted, these macro aggregates are the usual suspects: consumption, investment, government expenditure, exports and imports, as given in Box 2.1, Eq. (2.1):

Box 2.1 The Keynesian Mum Equation

$$Y = C + I + G + X - M \quad (2.1)$$

$$\Delta Y / Y = \Delta C / C + \Delta I / I + \Delta G / G + \Delta NX \quad (2.2)$$

This mum equation gives the level of output and its determining macro aggregates for one point in time, $t0$. To capture growth in these variables, that is, the change over time from $t0$ to $t1$, each variable is converted into a growth variable. This is given by the growth in the variable between $t0$ and $t1$ as a share of its original value at $t0$ as given in Eq. (2.2). Growth in output on the left-hand side of the equation is to be explained on the right-hand side by growth in consumption, growth in investment, growth in government expenditure and growth in net exports.

The workhorse mum equation is adapted into more complex derivations over the course of Essays 5, 6 and 7 as the dependent variable to be explained on the left-hand side, which also changes its determinants on the right-hand side of the equation.

In the first empirical essay, Essay 5, the fundamental variable to be explained on the left-hand side of the equation is output growth. The growth version of the mum equation, given by Eq. (2.2), is used to analyse GDP growth in Pakistan observed from 1971 to 2019. We find that GDP growth drops significantly on trend from 1992 by nearly 2 per cent per annum. Before 1992, trend GDP growth approximates 6 per cent per annum, dropping to approximately 4 per cent per annum after 1992. The fundamental question posed by this observed long-run trend in GDP growth in Pakistan is what explains the discrete and significant drop in growth post-1992.

The adapted Keynesian general equilibrium model explains the change in GDP growth on the left-hand side of the equation through five sets of determinants on the right-hand side. These determinants include consumption, investment, government expenditures, exports, imports and global capital flows (incorporated through the balance of payments, as elaborated in Essay 5).

The model provides a clear answer. Before 1992, high GDP growth of 6 per cent on trend is driven significantly by investment, while after 1992, lower GDP growth of 4 per cent on trend is driven significantly by consumption. This dichotomy between investment-driven growth and consumption-driven growth is explored further in Essay 5, using the Kahn-Keynes multiplier.

The Kahn-Keynes multiplier places output on the left-hand side of the equation, to be explained by two determinants on the right-hand side: investment and the multiplier k. This equation is dynamized from a static model for growth, as elaborated in Essay 5. The multiplier k functions to make investment and consumption in the Keynesian model equation, trade-offs. While these two macro aggregates, as the major drivers of output growth, are nominally additive on the right-hand side of the equation, through the complexity of the multiplier k, they become trade-offs.

It is this Kahn-Keynes multiplier that explains the trajectory of observed GDP growth in Pakistan very well, by making the macro determinants of GDP growth, investment and consumption, into trade-offs. High GDP growth before 1992 is driven by high investment growth paired with low consumption growth. On the other hand, low GDP growth after 1992 is driven by low investment growth paired with high consumption growth. This strongly vindicates the use of the generic Keynesian general equilibrium model of aggregate demand and its more elaborate adaptations.

Essay 5 finds that a Keynesian aggregate demand model adapted to estimate growth over time, explains Pakistan's GDP growth trajectory very well. The plurality of causal variables on the right-hand side of the equation are the advantage of the model in determining output growth on the left-hand side of the equation. Further, the nuance of the model through the Kahn-Keynes multiplier (k) posits investment and consumption as trade-offs rather than simply additive.

The application of this adapted Keynesian model to Pakistan's GDP growth trajectory identifies two primary determinants of growth. Prior to 1992, high GDP growth of 6 per cent per annum was driven by high investment growth, paired with low consumption growth. In contrast, post-1992, lower GDP growth of 4 per cent per annum was driven by high consumption growth, paired with low investment growth. Pursuing causality, Essay 6 then must explain the determinants of investment and consumption. Mathematically, this requires manipulating the Keynesian mum equation to place investment on the left-hand side and deriving the causal determinants on the right-hand side. A similar manipulation is performed to place consumption on the left-hand side. However, given the trade-off relationship between investment and consumption in the Keynesian model, and as this relationship is empirically demonstrated in Essay 5, it is sufficient to focus solely on investment.

Essay 6 mathematically derives the trade-off between investment and consumption, supporting the pursuit of investment as a single variable. The major variable then to be explained is investment growth. Investment growth is now posited to be a function of both supply-side and demand-side determinants. To capture these determinants, a model with two equations is proposed.

For the supply side, mathematical derivations yield investment on the left-hand side of the equation, to be causally determined on the right-hand side of the equation by the supply variables of domestic investment, net capital inflows and the budget deficit. Again, this equation is formulated in growth terms. The equation serves as a test to determine whether savings and inflows are additive, as observed in many developing countries, or substitutes, as suggested by Griffin and Enos (1970). On the demand side, the mathematical derivation posits that aggregate investment on the left-hand side is determined by the budget deficit on the right-hand side.

To refine the model, aggregate investment is decomposed into private investment and public investment. Thus, aggregate investment on the left-hand side of the equation is posited to be determined on the right-hand side of the equation by private investment and public investment. This splits the demand-side equation into two: the demand for private investment and the demand for public investment. The demand for private investment is then posited to be explained by the demand variable of public investment. This tests the theorem of Ricardian equivalence, which argues that aggregate investment relies on private investment rather than public investment, and further that private investment is in turn crowded out by public investment (Ricardo, 1821). Alternatively, the Keynesian model makes aggregate investment reliant on both private investment and public investment as complement and additive factors. Furthermore, private investment is not crowded out by public investment and may even be crowded in.

The results of running the supply equations for Pakistan show that there was high growth in aggregate investment prior to 1992, which was driven by an increase in inflows. However, after 1992, there was a decline in inflow growth, leading to a slump in aggregate investment growth. The results of running the demand equations for Pakistan are even more significant and compelling. They reveal that pre-1992, there was high growth in aggregate investment, mainly due to an increase in public investment. Conversely, post-1992, there was a decline in public investment growth, resulting in a slump in aggregate investment.

Private investment remained relatively constant during both periods, pre-1992 and post-1992, and was not affected by either the high growth of public investment before 1992 or the low growth of public investment after 1992. These findings support the Keynesian model, which suggests that public investment stimulates aggregate investment, as opposed to the

Ricardian equivalence theory, which argues that private investment is crowded out by public investment.

Essay 6, along with Essay 5, are Maynard redux, applying an adapted Keynesian mum equation to explain the trajectory of long-run GDP growth in Pakistan. Pre-1992, high GDP growth of 6 per cent per annum, on the left-hand side of the equation, is explained by the determinants on the right-hand side of the equation—high investment growth paired with low consumption growth. This high growth in aggregate investment can be further explained by the high growth of public investment, with relatively stable private investment. On the other hand, the equation suggests that the low growth of aggregate investment after 1992 can be attributed to the low growth of public investment, while private investment remained constant.

The quest to determine the causality behind public investment behaviour is crucial. We have observed that high growth in public investment before 1992 led to increased aggregate investment growth and output growth, while the low growth of public investment after 1992 resulted in a decrease in aggregate investment growth and output growth. Essay 7 demonstrates that this causality completes the Keynesian loop by introducing government expenditures as a third determinant of output in the Keynesian equation.

Public investment is associated with government expenditures in two components. In the first part of Essay 7, public investment is explained on the left-hand side of the equation by two components on the right-hand side of the equation: public investment in productive sectors and public investment in administrative services. The component of productive sectors under public investment can be further divided into sectors of the real economy, such as manufacturing. Similarly, the component of administrative services can be broken down into subcategories.

In the second part of Essay 7, public investment is taken as a function of aggregate government expenditure. Government expenditure from the Keynesian mum equation is then the variable to be explained on the left-hand side of the equation. On the right-hand side of the equation, the determinants of government expenditure are taxation, including all government revenues as explained in the essay, and the budget deficit. The equation is considered additive in nominal terms. The budget deficit becomes a key variable reflecting the liberality or austerity of the regulatory environment in the country—whether it is more lenient or strict.

Having been under 22 International Monetary Fund loan agreements during the 50-year period examined here, Pakistan has experienced increasing austerity over time.

Government expenditures can be further broken down into two categories. There are development expenditures, which aim to expand existing capacity, such as in the energy, education and healthcare sectors. Recurrent expenditures, on the other hand, are meant to maintain existing capacity. When analysing public investment as a function of its productive and administrative components, we find that the high growth of public investment before 1992 was mainly due to the substantial growth of investment in productive sectors. Conversely, the low growth of public investment after 1992 can be attributed to the limited growth of investment in these productive sectors. When examining the breakdown of public investment in productive sectors, the electricity and manufacturing sectors are identified as significant contributors.

Analysing government expenditures in relation to taxation and budget deficits reveals that high government expenditures before 1992 were driven by high deficits. However, after 1992, low government expenditures were accompanied by low budget deficits. Tax revenues, on the other hand, remained relatively constant throughout both periods. The decline in government expenditures after 1992 can be attributed to a decrease in the development component of these expenditures, which aligns with the previous finding of a drop in public investment in productive sectors.

We can conclude therefore that the Government of Pakistan has struggled to increase tax revenues over the past 50 years. In the period before 1992, high GDP growth of 6 per cent per year was achieved through high aggregate investment, which was driven by substantial public investment funded by large budget deficits. In contrast, the lower growth rate of 4 per cent per year after 1992 can be attributed to a decrease in both aggregate investment and public investment, which in turn resulted from lower budget deficits.

The regulatory environment after 1992, influenced by International Monetary Fund conditionality, seems to have led to reduced targeted deficits and observed deficits. The adopted Keynesian general equilibrium model allows us to consider this complex and interconnected causality. It also highlights three policy needs. First, private investment has remained stagnant over the past 50 years, as have tax revenues. The sequencing of policies is crucial in this context. Second, short-term policy measures should focus on increasing tax revenues, which would enable higher levels of public investment and stimulate GDP growth. Third, efforts should also be made to implement long-term policy incentives to encourage significant increases in private investment.

REFERENCES

Arrow, K. J. (1962). The economic implications of learning by doing. *The Review of Economic Studies, 29*(3), 155–173.
Debreu, G. (1970). Economies with a finite set of equilibria. *Econometrica, 38*(3), 387–392.
Debreu, G. (1975). Four aspects of the mathematical theory of economic equilibrium. In *Proceedings of the international congress of mathematicians* (Vol. 1, pp. 65–77). Canadian Mathematical Congress.
Eatwell, J., & Milgate, M. (2011). *The fall and rise of Keynesian economics*. Oxford University Press.
Griffin, K. B., & Enos, J. L. (1970). Foreign assistance: Objectives and consequences. *Economic Development and Cultural Change, 18*(3), 313–327.
Hahn, F. H., & Matthews, R. C. O. (1964). The theory of economic growth: A survey. *The Economic Journal, 74*(296), 779–902.
Harcourt, G. C. (1976). The Cambridge controversies: Old ways and new horizons—Or dead end? *Oxford Economic Papers, 28*(1), 25–65.
Harrod, R. (1948). *Towards a dynamic economics: Some recent developments of economic theory and their application to policy*. Macmillan.
International Labour Organization. (2016). *Modelling growth and employment for the G20 countries*. Unpublished manuscript. International Labour Organization.
Kahn, R. F. (1931). The relation of home investment to unemployment. *The Economic Journal, 41*(162), 173–198.
Kaldor, N. (1966). Marginal productivity and the macro-economic theories of distribution: Comment on Samuelson and Modigliani. *The Review of Economic Studies, 33*(4), 309–319.
Kaldor, N. (1967). *Strategic factors in economic development*. Cornell University Press.
Kaldor, N. (1972). The irrelevance of equilibrium economics. *The Economic Journal, 82*(328), 1237–1255.
Keynes, J. M. (1936). *The general theory of employment, interest, and money*. Macmillan Cambridge University Press, for Royal Economic Society.
Lewis, W. A. (1954). Economic development with unlimited supplies of labour. *The Manchester School, 22*(2), 139–191.
Mahalanobis, P. C. (1953). Some observations on the process of growth of national income. *Sankhyā: The Indian Journal of Statistics, 12*(4), 307–312.

Mahmood, M. (2018). *The three regularities in development: Growth, jobs and macro policy in developing countries*. Springer.

Mahmood, M., Chaudhry, A. A., Malik, A. T., & Sajid, S. (2022). *Revised estimates of growth FY2022: State of the Pakistan economy*. Lahore School of Economics.

Pasinetti, L. L. (2007). *Keynes and the Cambridge Keynesians: A 'revolution in economics' to be accomplished*. Cambridge University Press.

Ricardo, D. (1821). *On the principles of political economy and taxation* (3rd ed.).

Robinson, J. (1953). The production function and the theory of capital. *The Review of Economic Studies, 21*(2), 81–106.

Robinson, J. (1962). *Essays in the theory of economic growth*. Springer.

Robinson, J. (1967). Growth and the theory of distribution. *Annals of Public and Cooperative Economics, 38*(1), 3–7.

Samuelson, P. A. (1966). *The collected scientific papers of Paul a. Samuelson* (Vol. 2). MIT Press.

Solow, R. M. (1956). A contribution to the theory of economic growth. *The Quarterly Journal of Economics, 70*(1), 65–94.

Solow, R. M. (1957). Technical change and the aggregate production function. *The Review of Economics and Statistics, 39*(3), 312–320.

Sraffa, P. (1961). Production of commodities by means of commodities. *Science and Society, 25*(2), 139–156.

Swan, T. W. (1956). Economic growth and capital accumulation. *Economic Record, 32*(2), 334–361.

Wicksell, K. (1898). *Interest and prices: A study of the causes regulating the value of money*. Macmillan.

Wicksell, K. (1907). The influence of the rate of interest on prices. *The Economic Journal, 17*(66), 213–220.

CHAPTER 3

Two Properties of Growth Models: General Equilibrium and Theoretical Consistency

The first essay was a theoretical preamble, introducing the four properties of growth models identified as useful in an analytical framework for examining growth of output over time.

These four properties are:

1. The need for general equilibrium analysis
2. The need for internal consistency in the theoretical argument of the model
3. The need for an equilibrium solution for output and its rate of growth over time—and preferably not a corner one
4. The need for a mathematically equilibrating model.

In searching for such an analytical framework, this essay examines the first two properties.

3.1 The First Property: The Need for General Equilibrium Analysis

The choice of an analytical framework for this project must begin with the notion of, and the need for, general equilibrium. The concept of general equilibrium is more often associated with the intertemporal general equilibrium set out by Arrow (1962) and Debreu (1970, 1975), who focus on providing proof of the existence of equilibrium in a competitive market economy.

The notion of general equilibrium and the need for general equilibrium analysis, however, are posited by Keynes (1936). This notion is based on markets and best seen when comparing the classical and neoclassical theoretical models with the Keynesian model. The classical and neoclassical models can be represented by Pigou (1937), while the Keynesian model emerges in its entirety in *The General Theory of Employment, Interest and Money*. The economic debate is conceptually intuitive, but multiple markets do need to be elaborated mathematically.

3.1.1 The Classical and Neoclassical Models

The objective of a model of the economy is to determine an equilibrium level of employment and output. Both the classical and neoclassical models are based on Say's law, according to which the supply of output creates its own demand. This law should apply to the goods market for output, but its causality lies in the labour market.

In the labour market, given in Fig. 3.1 and Box 3.1, employment (N) is given by demographics. The money wage (W) adjusts to the demographics. Thus, the supply of labour (Ls) is a positive function of the money wage (W). As the money wage (W) increases, it brings forth an increase in labour supply (Ls). Box 3.1 gives the needed maths, showing this as Eq. (3.1). The demand for labour (Ld) is also a function of the money wage (W), as in Eq. (3.2), which, in an equilibrating labour market, makes employment (N) a function of the money wage (W), as in Eq. (3.3).

If there is a demographic increase in the labour force and labour supply (Ls), this will drive down the money wage (W) in Fig. 3.1 from W1 to W2. The drop in the money wage (W) will increase labour demand (Ld) till it matches the increased labour supply (Ls) to give full employment (Nf). The crucial equation that enables this classical-cum-neoclassical equilibrium at full employment (Nf) in the labour market is Eq. (3.2) in Box 3.1, where labour demand (Ld) is a negative function of the money wage (W). As the money wage (W) falls, labour demand (Ld) goes up to give full employment (Nf). Full employment (Nf) in the labour market gives a full-employment level of output (Yf) in the goods market. In this

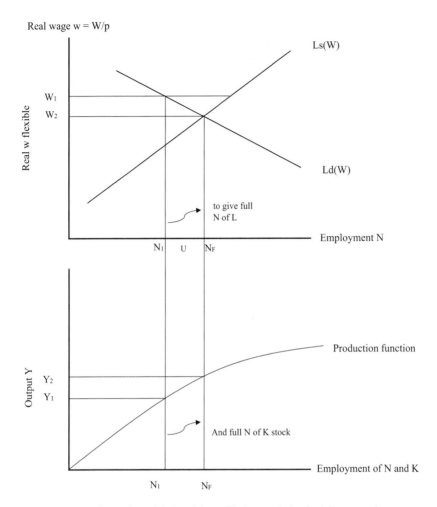

Fig. 3.1 Neoclassical model: Partial equilibrium only in the labour market

model, it is the labour market that determines the level of employment (N) and thereby output (Y). The causal variable in the labour market that enables Say's law of full employment (Nf) is the flexibility of the money wage (W).

> **Box 3.1 The Classical and Neoclassical Models**
> Say's Law: The supply of output (Ys) creates its own demand (Yd).
> Lmkt: Employment gives by demographics to which the money wage (W) adjusts.
>
> $$\text{Ls} = +\text{fn}(W) \tag{3.1}$$
>
> $$\text{Ld} = -\text{fn}(W) \tag{3.2}$$
>
> $$N = -\text{fn}(W) \tag{3.3}$$
>
> So, if Ls↑, W↓ to match Ld.
> Ergo, full employment (Nf) in the Lmkt.

3.1.2 The Keynesian Model of Aggregate Demand

In this classical-cum-neoclassical model determining employment (N) and output (Y), the goods market plays no causal role. All causality lies in the labour market. Thus, this very abstract model, presented here as a heuristic device, relies on causal equilibrium in only one market—for labour.

The Keynesian model of aggregate demand is based on three essential points of departure from the classical-cum-neoclassical model. The first, which concerns the debate here on the notion of general equilibrium, is the structural lack of aggregate demand (ΣD) in the economy. The economy does not generally operate on the production possibility frontier, but below it.

The second point of departure, which is essential but more orthogonal to the immediate debate here on general equilibrium, is the existence of nominal rigidities in the labour market, where workers will resist a cut in their nominal/money wage (W), for instance, through long-run wage contracts. Thus, wages and prices will not adjust immediately to clear the market and return to full employment (Nf).

The third point of departure, also essential, concerns the money market and the third property of growth models—on the need for an equilibrium solution (see Essay 3). It is worth noting here the Keynesian posit—that in the money market, investment (I) being made equal to savings (S) is an accounting identity. Thus, investment is not equalised to savings by the interest rate (r) in equilibrium. It is just true by definition. Savings decisions are made by households, while investment decisions are made by firms. Ergo, decisions by separate agents need not coincide and ex ante savings (S) need not equal ex ante investment (I).

3.1.3 Aggregate Demand and the Need for General Equilibrium in Multiple Markets

The Keynesian model seeks to explain departures from full-employment equilibrium (Nf) in the labour market, explaining the persistence of long-run unemployment (U), which gives an equilibrium solution in the labour market at less than full employment (Nf) with the existence of long-run unemployment (U). However, this Keynesian equilibrium is not determined only in the labour market, unlike the classical-cum-neoclassical models.

Keynes (1936) posits the notion of aggregate demand, where aggregate demand (ΣD) for employment (N) and output (Y) is based in multiple other markets in addition to the labour market. Principally, these are the markets for private goods, public goods, capital investment, tradeables (exports and imports) and global capital flows. However, to simplify the Keynesian argument, aggregate demand for employment and output can be causally determined in just two markets—the labour market and goods market—in contrast to the classical-cum-neoclassical models, where employment and output are causally determined in only one market, the labour market. For Keynes (1936), employment (N) in the labour market becomes a function of aggregate demand for output (ΣDY) in the goods market.

Figure 3.2 brings in the labour market from the classical-cum-neoclassical model given in Fig. 3.1 and adds a Keynesian goods market from A-level textbooks. Box 3.2, giving the Keynesian maths, makes employment (N) in the labour market a function of aggregate demand for output (ΣDY) in the goods market, in Eq. (3.4).

This Keynesian notion of aggregate demand (ΣDY) introduces two new notions: the notion of macro, which is the level of the whole economy, and the notion of micro, which is the level of the firm. It also introduces the notion of general equilibrium, which is the notion of multiple markets, captured here for simplicity by the goods market in addition to the labour market.

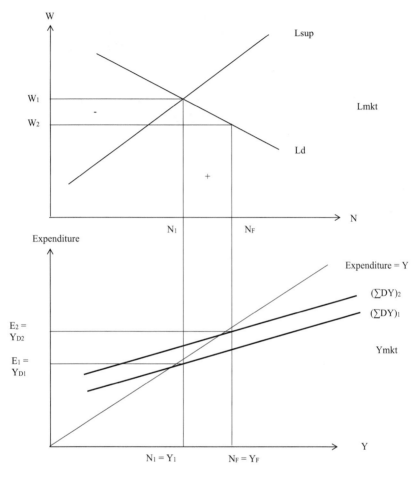

Fig. 3.2 The Keynesian cross

For Keynes (1936), the need arises for both new notions: macro and general equilibrium. Here, the labour market gives the micro level of the firm, which can be defined as partial equilibrium—equilibrium in just one market. Multiple markets, in addition to the labour market, given by the markets for private goods, public goods, capital investment, tradeables and global capital flows, give the macro level of the economy, which can be defined as general equilibrium. For the determination of employment,

Box 3.2   Keynesian Model of Aggregate Demand
The Keynesian model of aggregate demand (ΣD) is based on:

Lmkt and Ymkt

where N in Lmkt will be a function of ΣD in the goods market

$$\text{where } N = \text{fn}\left(\Sigma DY\right) \tag{3.4}$$

This defines a macro level of the economy, where there can be a lack of structural aggregate demand (ΣD) for output (Y).

So, the micro level of the firm in just the Lmkt is defined as partial equilibrium.

The macro level of aggregate demand (ΣDY) for Y is in two markets for labour (L) or goods (Y).

At the micro firm level in partial equilibrium of one market for L, Ld is a function of the real wage (W):

$$\text{Ld} = -\text{fn}\left(W\right) \tag{3.5}$$

Therefore, at the micro level, we have partial equilibrium in Lmkt. if W falls, Ld can rise.

But at the macro level of the economy, in general equilibrium of two markets, Lmkt and Ymkt

$$\Sigma DY = \text{fn}\left(Y\right) \tag{3.6}$$

If W falls, Y falls, C falls for Y in Goodsmkt

$$\therefore \left(\Sigma DY\right) \text{ will fall}$$

Ergo: No point in cutting W in Lmkt because ΣDY falls, so if ΣDY falls why would Ld increase even if this L is now available at a cheaper W?

Alternative policy: to increase (ΣDY).

(*continued*)

Box 3.2 (continued)

At the macro level of general equilibrium, Eq. (3.4) holds.

Now, relaxing the heuristic assumption of the goods market representing all other markets gives full equilibrium where (ΣDY) is contributed to by:

- Private goods market (C) through consumption
- Public goods market (G) through government expenditure
- Capital market for investment through (I)
- Tradeables market through X and M (NX)
- Global capital flows through capital account KA = NX.

This gives the Keynesian mum equation for ΣDY:

$$\Sigma D_Y = C + I + G + X - M \tag{3.7}$$

$$\text{And}\,(X - M) = \text{NX} = \text{CF} \tag{3.8}$$

$$\Sigma D_Y = C + I + G + \text{CF} \tag{3.9}$$

Reduced form:

$$\Sigma D_Y = C + I \tag{3.10}$$

Where:

$$\Sigma D_Y = \left(\text{mpc}(Y - T),\ \text{MEC},\ r\right) \tag{3.11}$$

If $W\downarrow$, then

$$Y = W + \pi \tag{3.12}$$

Then $\pi\uparrow$

$$\text{mpc}(W) > \text{mpc}(\pi) \tag{3.13}$$

Therefore, mpc falls

$$\therefore \Sigma D_Y \text{ falls}$$

Keynesian general equilibrium is represented here in reduced form as requiring equilibrium in two key markets, for labour and goods, as opposed to determination of employment in the classical-cum-neoclassical partial equilibrium, which requires equilibrium in just one market, for labour.

At the micro level of the firm, partial equilibrium in the labour market is given for the classical-cum-neoclassical function in Eq. (3.2) in Box 3.1, where demand for labour (Ld) is a negative function of the money wage. The causal factor determining employment in the labour market is a flexible money wage (W). As the money wage (W) drops, employment (N) increases, as in Eq. (3.3) in Box 3.1—not yet distinguishing between money wages (W) and real wages (w), given by the money wage (W) divided by the price level (p).

For Keynes (1936) too, at the micro level of the firm, partial equilibrium in the labour market can be given by a function similar to the classical-cum-neoclassical one. In Fig. 3.2 and Box 3.2 in Eq. (3.5), labour demand is a negative function of the money wage: as the money wage (W) drops, employment (N) increases. So, at the micro level of the firm in partial equilibrium, the Keynesian model agrees with the classical-cum-neoclassical model: as the money wage (W) drops, employment (N) increases.

However, Keynes (1936) does not place causality for the determination of employment at the micro level of the firm in partial equilibrium or in the labour market. Instead, he introduces the macro level of the economy by adding to the labour market, the goods market, which represents in reduced form multiple other markets, as listed earlier. Causality for the determination of employment (N) for Keynes (1936) then lies in the goods market.

Specifically, demand for employment in the labour market is based on demand for goods in the goods market. Only if there is demand for goods in the goods market will there be demand for labour in the labour market to produce these goods. If not, there will be no demand for labour in the labour market to produce any goods, no matter how low the money wage (W). This demand for goods in the goods market, which is the reduced form for multiple other markets, then becomes an aggregate of demand for goods across all these multiple markets: it becomes the aggregate demand for output (Y) or (ΣDY).

Figure 3.2 and Box 3.2, giving the maths, attempt to capture this notion of aggregate demand for output and its causality in determining employment (N). Figure 3.2 relates the micro labour market that the firm faces to the macro goods market that the economy faces. In the micro labour market, employment (N) is causally determined by the money wage (W). A reduction in the money wage (W) increases the demand for labour by the firm. In just this micro labour market, the classical-cum-neoclassical and Keynesian models agree—that the demand for labour, and therefore employment (N), is a negative function of the money wage (W), as in Eq. (3.2) for the classical-cum-neoclassical model in Box 3.1 and Eq. (3.5) for the Keynesian model in Box 3.2.

The macro goods market that the economy faces is in the second quadrant of Fig. 3.2. It is given by the Keynesian cross familiar from A-level texts. The vertical axis shows aggregate expenditure across all markets in the economy. The horizontal axis shows aggregate output and employment across all markets of the economy. Aggregate expenditure gives effective demand for output (Y), which is called aggregate demand for output (ΣDY). As aggregate demand for output increases from (ΣDY)1 to (ΣDY)2 on the vertical axis, it brings forth an increasing supply of output from Y1 to Yf on the horizontal axis. As output increases from Y1 to Yf, the employment needed to produce this output increases from N1 to Nf (full employment).

The maths for this Keynesian model is given in Box 3.2 in Eq. (3.4), which is for the macro goods market that the economy faces. Employment (N) now becomes a positive function of aggregate demand for output (ΣDY). Thus, for Keynes (1936), at the micro level, the firm's demand for labour (Ld) is indeed a negative function of the nominal wage (W), as in Eq. (3.5) and in agreement with the classical-cum-neoclassical model. At the macro level of the goods market, however, the economy's demand for employment (N) becomes a positive function of aggregate demand for output (ΣDY) in the goods market (read: all markets in the economy).

Keynes's (1936) argument of why micro-level cuts in the wage in the partial equilibrium of the labour market will not increase employment at the macro level in the general equilibrium of the goods market is the very argument for general equilibrium. At the micro level, a cut in the money wage (W) will lower the cost of labour, allowing the firm in theory to hire more workers, thereby increasing employment (N). In Fig. 3.2, the money wage W1 falls to W2, allowing the firm to increase its employment from N1 to Nf. Repeated across all firms in the labour market, this reduction in the money wage (W) allows the labour market to go from an unemployment level of N1Nf to full employment at Nf.

However, for Keynes, the demand for employment (N), according to Eq. (3.4) in Box 3.2, cannot come from just the partial equilibrium of the labour market itself. Rather, it must come from the general equilibrium of the goods market (all other markets). The demand for employment (N) in the partial equilibrium of the labour market must come from the general equilibrium of the aggregate demand for goods in the goods market (read: aggregate demand for goods across all other markets).

Box 3.2 elaborates on this Keynesian notion of employment (N) as a function of aggregate demand for output (ΣDY) in the goods market. Equation (3.4) already expresses the first half of the notion, making employment (N) a positive function of aggregate demand for output (ΣDY). Equation (3.6) now makes aggregate demand for output (ΣDY) a function of the goods market (Y).

The question is why? Why do the general equilibrium Eqs. (3.4) and (3.6) in Box 3.2 supersede the classical-cum-neoclassical partial equilibrium Eq. (3.3) in Box 3.1 and Keynes's own Eq. (3.5) in Box 3.2? There is a simple answer in one iteration (call it a static answer) and a more complex answer in the second iteration (a more dynamic answer).

3.1.4 Keynes's Static Argument for Aggregate Demand

Keynes (1936) has a well-known static argument for general equilibrium Eqs. (3.4) and (3.6) in Box 3.2 of the demand for labour in the labour market being causally determined by the demand for goods in the goods market. This supersedes the partial equilibrium Eq. (3.3) in Box 3.1 and Eq. (3.5) in Box 3.2 of the demand for labour in the labour market being causally determined by the money wage in the labour market.

This can be seen in Fig. 3.2, which shows that a cut in the money wage in the labour market from W1 to W2 can theoretically increase the demand for labour in just the labour market from N1 to Nf. However, consider labour's income, given by the wage bill, which is initially the rectangle W1N1 (the prevalent money wage W1 times the employment level N1). A cut in the money wage along the normally downward-sloping demand curve for labour to W2 will reduce labour's income. The wage bill at W2 now falls within the rectangle W2Nf. There is a loss in the wage bill by the rectangle W1W2N1 and a gain in the wage bill by the rectangle N1NfW2, which gives us a net loss. This net loss will reduce aggregate demand for goods (ΣDY) in the goods market. Firms will then not expand employment in the labour market—even if wage costs are lower—because of lack of demand for goods (ΣDY) for them to produce.

The important point to note here is not the comprehensiveness of the Keynesian argument (which comes with some caveats as explained below), but that the result is obtained only by introducing general equilibrium. Partial equilibrium, based on just the labour market, gives an entirely different causality for the determination of employment in the money wage (W). General equilibrium, based on the addition of the goods market representing multiple other markets, gives a radically different causality for the determination of employment (N) in aggregate demand for output (ΣDY), thereby transforming conceptual frameworks and models for good.

3.1.5 Keynes's Dynamic Argument for Aggregate Demand

The static theory of aggregate demand makes the novel point that a drop in the nominal wage (W) will reduce labour's income, leading to a fall in aggregate demand (ΣDY) in the goods market and in turn to a fall in employment (N) in the labour market. This is the primary argument for the Keynesian Eqs. (3.4) and (3.6) in Box 3.2, that employment (N) is a positive function of aggregate demand for output (ΣDY) in the goods market (Y).

The loss in labour's income, as described above, is based on one iteration in Fig. 3.2. In the first iteration, in the labour market, the nominal wage drops from W1 to W2, with employment remaining constant at N1. This gives a loss in the wage bill of W1W2N1. The classical-cum-neoclassical function given by Eq. (3.3) then kicks in, with employment (N) being a negative function of the nominal wage (W). As a result, the drop in the nominal wage from W1 to W2 gives firms an incentive to expand their employment from N1 to Nf, which increases the wage bill by W1N1Nf.

Note that there is (a) a net loss in labour's income (based on the wage effect of a gross loss due to the fall in the nominal wage from W1 to W2), given by the rectangle W1W2N1, and (b) a gross gain (based on the increase in employment from N1 to Nf), given by the rectangle W2N1Nf. This results in a net loss in the wage bill of the wage effect being greater than the employment effect—that is, rectangle W1W2N1 is greater than rectangle W1N1Nf.

This is simply saying that the net loss in labour's income due to the drop in the nominal wage depends on the elasticity of demand for employment with respect to the nominal wage. If the labour demand curve Ld were flatter, with a higher elasticity of demand for employment with respect to the wage, the negative wage effect would be smaller than the

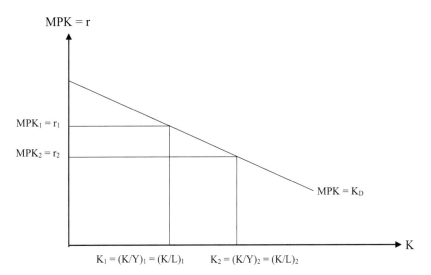

Fig. 3.3 Production function parables

positive employment effect. That is, in Fig. 3.2, the rectangle W1W2N1 would be smaller than rectangle W1N1Nf. This gives a net increase in labour's income, validating the classical-cum-neoclassical argument and invalidating the Keynesian argument. This can be seen in Fig. 3.3.

Alternatively, if the labour demand curve Ld were steeper, with a lower elasticity of demand for employment with respect to the nominal wage, then the negative wage effect would be greater than the positive employment effect. That is, in Fig. 3.3, the rectangle W1W2N1 would be greater than the rectangle W1N1NF. This gives a net decrease in labour's income, thereby invalidating the classical-cum-neoclassical argument and validating the Keynesian one. This makes Keynes's (1936) argument—based on the drop in the nominal wage leading to a loss in labour's income—somewhat arbitrary and dependent on the shape and elasticity of the labour demand curve Ld.

In the first iteration of the economic cycle, the nominal wage drops from W1 to W2 in the labour market and employment remains constant at N1. The classical-cum-neoclassical model argues for a simultaneous expansion of employment by firms from N1 to Nf. However, after the drop in the nominal wage, a second iteration needs to be considered before firms' reflex action to expand employment. Examining this requires us to relax the reduced form of the goods market (Y) representing all other markets and set out the Keynesian mum equation.

3.1.6 The Keynesian Mum Equation

Equation (3.6) in Box 3.2 says that aggregate demand for output (ΣDY) is based on the goods market (Y), which represents all other markets. For Keynes (1936), these are principally the market for private goods, given by private consumption (C); the market for public goods, given by government expenditure (G); the market for capital investment (I); and the market for tradeables, given by exports (X) and imports (Y).

Expanding Eq. (3.6) to include all these other markets explicitly gives the Keynesian 'mum' equation, learnt at mum's knees. Aggregate demand for output (ΣDY) is a positive function of the demand for private goods (C), public goods (G), capital investment (I) and exports (X) minus demand for imports (M). This Keynesian mum equation is given as Eq. (3.7) in Box 3.2.

The term for net tradeables, net exports (NX), is given by exports minus imports in Eq. (3.8) in Box 3.2. Net exports (NX) are also equal to net capital outflows (CF), as given by the same equation. This adds one more market to the general equilibrium of the Keynesian mum equation—that of the market for global capital flows, given by Eq. (3.9). Equation (3.7) then gives the Keynesian general equilibrium in multiple markets. The problem at hand is determining employment (N) in the labour market. Here, the classical-cum-neoclassical model determines employment (N) in partial equilibrium in just the labour market, causally determined by the nominal wage (W), as given in Eq. (3.3) in Box 3.1.

In contrast to the classical-cum-neoclassical partial equilibrium determination of employment (N) in just the labour market, Keynesian general equilibrium causally determines employment (N), in aggregate demand for output (ΣDY), based on multiple key markets in Eqs. (3.7) and (3.9) in Box 3.2. These are given by the markets for private goods (C), public goods (G), capital investment (I), tradeables (NX) and global capital flows (CF).

This is the full Keynesian mum equation, giving general equilibrium in five markets. To examine the determination of employment (N) through the classical-cum-neoclassical causal variable of the nominal wage (W), the Keynesian model then abstracts from the full mum equation with five markets to just two markets (for private goods, given by consumption, and for capital investment, given by investment). The aggregate demand for output (ΣDY) is now a function of these two determinants: C and I, as in Eq. (3.10) in Box 3.2.

Keynes (1936) also argues that the determinant of consumption (C) is based on the marginal propensity to consume (MPC) out of disposable income—income (Y) minus taxes (T). He makes the determinant of investment (I) dependent on the marginal efficiency of capital (MEC). This is a complex notion, which for purposes of argument here, although lacking the purity of original Keynesian intent, can be taken as the rate of return (ROR) on investment (I). The equation of the marginal efficiency of capital (MEC) to the cost of borrowing, given by the market rate of interest (r), determines investment (I).

This reduced form of the Keynesian mum equation now makes aggregate demand for output (ΣDY) a function of three determinants: (a) the marginal propensity to consume (MPC) out of disposable income, (b) the marginal efficiency of capital (MEC) and (c) in relation to the market rate of interest (r). This is given in Eq. (3.11) in Box 3.2. Therefore, employment (N) will also be a function of the aggregate demand for output (ΣDY), which in turn will be a function of the marginal propensity to consume (MPC) and the marginal efficiency of capital (MEC) in relation to the market rate of interest (r).

In this determination of employment (N), consumption (C) is the largest variable relative to investment (I). Therefore, the marginal propensity to consume is the largest determinant of aggregate demand for output (ΣDY) and employment (N). This determinant is allowed to vary then, while assuming ceteris paribus that the marginal efficiency of capital and interest rate remain constant.

Next, we test the classical-cum-neoclassical argument of the impact of a cut in the nominal wage (W) on employment (N). If the nominal wage (W) falls, Keynes (1936) avers, before a knee-jerk expansion in employment, we see the second iteration of a change in the distribution of income (Y). This comprises a wage share (Wshare) plus a profit share (Πshare), as in Eq. (3.12) in Box 3.2. If the nominal wage (W) falls, the wage share (Wshare) will also fall, while the profit share (Π share) will rise.

Keynes (1936) further argues that the marginal propensity to consume (MPC) for lower-income wage earners (MPCW) will be higher than that for higher-income profit earners (MPC Π), as in Eq. (3.13) in Box 3.2.

Then, as the nominal wage (W) falls, the wage share (Wshare) will fall and the profit share (Πshare) will rise. This will reduce the quantum of the marginal propensity to consume from the wage share (MPCW) and increase the quantum of the marginal propensity to consume from the profit share (MPCΠ). In turn, the aggregate marginal propensity to consume (MPC), weighted by the high marginal propensity to consume from the wage share (MPCW), will fall.

As the marginal propensity to consume (MPC) falls, aggregate demand for output (ΣDY) will fall, causing employment (N) to fall. Therefore, according to this Keynesian general equilibrium model, a cut in the nominal wage (W) (in the first iteration) will cause a fall in the marginal propensity to consume (MPC) (in the second iteration), leading to a fall in aggregate demand for output (ΣDY) and a consequent fall in employment (N).

The argument of the impact of a cut in the nominal wage (W) need not end there. As the assumption of ceteris paribus is removed from Eq. (3.11) in Box 3.2, the impact of the fall in the marginal propensity to consume (MPC) must be reckoned on the marginal efficiency of capital (MEC) in relation to the market rate of interest (r) and therefore on investment (I). As the marginal propensity to consume falls, the marginal propensity to save rises reciprocally. As the supply of savings increases, this will tend to lower the market rate of interest (r). This, however, must be examined in relation to the lower demand for investment (I), given lower aggregate demand for output (ΣDY), that is, whether the lower market rate of interest (r), induces higher investment (I), despite the lowered aggregate demand for output (ΣDY), lowering the demand for investment.

This debate between the classical-cum-neoclassical model and the Keynesian model (1936) is not meant here to conclude in a knock-out resolution of the problem. Rather, it is meant as a heuristic device to argue for the need for general equilibrium as a desirable property in growth models. Again, general equilibrium is defined here in Keynesian terms of causality lying in multiple markets rather than the partial equilibrium of a single market, and with more markets being better than fewer markets in which to locate this causality.

That is done admirably by this debate on the determination of employment (N) being based on the nominal wage (W) in a single market for labour, as argued by the classical-cum-neoclassical model, or alternatively on aggregate demand for output (ΣDY) in multiple markets, as argued by the Keynesian model.

3.2 The Second Property: The Need for Internal Consistency in the Theoretical Argument of the Model

The first useful property of a theoretical framework for analysing growth of output is the need for general equilibrium based on multiple markets. Three general equilibrium models defined thus are pre-eminent. The neo-classical Samuelson-Swan-Solow production function is the workhorse didactic model, used to forecast long-run GDP growth.[1] It is based on three markets: for goods, capital and labour. The Harrod-Domar model has a more Keynesian pedigree and has also become a workhorse model for estimating long-run GDP growth. It is initially based on two markets—for goods and capital—but the requirements of a natural rate of growth bring in the labour market. The third model is the Keynesian model of aggregate demand. This is a larger model than the other two, based on five markets: for private goods, public goods, capital investment, tradeables and global capital flows.

The second half of this essay looks at just the neoclassical Samuelson-Swan-Solow production function, for which we test the need for internal consistency in the theoretical argument of the model. This is because it has long been labelled with the theoretical weakness dubbed in the genre as the 'Cambridge capital controversy' (Harcourt, 1976). The other two models are not tainted with this theoretical weakness. Albeit, the Harrod-Domar model has a problem with the third useful property of conceptual frameworks and models—that of reaching an equilibrium solution, and not a corner one. This is examined in Essay 3. Meeting this third property requires a fourth useful property—that of the need for a mathematically equilibrating model. The Keynesian model of aggregate demand is seen to satisfy this fourth property in Essay 3.

3.2.1 The Cambridge Capital Controversy

The second useful property of theoretical frameworks and models is a need for internal consistency in the theoretical argument of the model. The neoclassical Samuelson-Swan-Solow production function has long been tarred with this brush. The model remains, however, a didactic

---

[1] See, for example, the model used by the UN Department for Economic and Social Affairs to determine long-run growth.

workhorse. The question here is whether the theoretical inconsistencies referred to above should be treated as mere curiosums or whether—as bad habits of thought, according to Robinson (1953)—they are more pernicious. The answer must be that if we make an exception for internal consistency in the theoretical argument in one instance, this sets a bad theoretical precedent, allowing more until the exceptions become the rule.

3.2.2 The Neoclassical Production Function

The textbook model for determination of output (Y) and its growth over time remains the neoclassical production function. This is a small general equilibrium model, based on just three markets—for goods, capital and labour. This is the Samuelson-Swan-Solow production function. Box 3.3, giving the maths, shows that output (Y) is a function of capital (K) and labour (L). This production function is illustrated in Fig. 3.3.

Samuelson (1966) derives three key parables from this production function. The marginal product of capital (K), that is, the increase in output (Y) due to a one-unit increase in capital will be equal to the rate of return on capital (K), given by the rate of interest (r). This is given in Box 3.3, where in Eq. (3.14), output (Y) is a function of capital (K) and labour

Box 3.3 The Samuelson-Swan-Solow Production Function

$$Y = \text{fn}(K, L) \tag{3.14}$$

$$\frac{\partial K}{\partial Y} = r \tag{3.15}$$

$$\frac{\partial L}{\partial Y} = W \tag{3.16}$$

$$Y = (\Sigma K * r) + (L * W) \tag{3.17}$$

Where:

$$\Sigma_{i-n} K \text{ value} = (K_i * r) + (K_j * r) + \ldots + (K_n * r) \tag{3.18}$$

(L). The marginal product of capital is given by the term dk/dY, which is equal to r.

This first parable is illustrated in Fig. 3.3. The vertical axis gives the marginal product of capital (MPk) and the rate of return on capital (K), which is the interest rate (r). The marginal product of capital (MPk) slopes downward to reflect decreasing returns to scale. Then, if K1 units of capital are employed, the marginal product of this capital will be MPk1. This marginal product of capital (MPk1), having contributed this to output (Y), will earn its rate of return $r1$.

This has two critical implications for the neoclassical conceptual framework: (a) a quantity of capital is needed to causally determine its marginal product (MPk), which then gives its rate of return, the interest rate (r); and (b) the production function determines output (Y) but also simultaneously determines the distribution of output (Y) by determining the return to capital (r) as the marginal product of capital (MPk).

Samuelson's (1966) second parable is as follows: As a greater quantity of capital is employed (K), the marginal product of capital (MPk) will fall, thus reducing the rate of return to capital (r). This gives a strictly monotonic, inverse relationship between the quantity of capital employed and the rate of return to it, in the interest rate (r).

This monotonic inverse relationship will also apply to the capital-output ratio (K/Y) and the rate of return on capital (r), as shown in Fig. 3.3. If the quantity of capital employed is $K1$ and the capital-output ratio is also $K/Y1$, then the rate of return on this capital will be $r1$. Now, if the quantity of capital employed is increased to $K2$, with a higher capital-output ratio $K/Y2$, then this will lower the marginal product of capital from MPk1 to MPk2. This fall in the marginal product of capital will cause the rate of return on this capital to fall from $r1$ to $r2$. This parable gives the third critical implication for the neoclassical conceptual framework—the strictly monotonic, inverse causal relationship between the quantity of capital (K) employed and its determination of the rate of return to capital (r).

Samuelson's (1966) third parable is that the distribution of income between capital and labour will be determined by the relative scarcities of capital and labour through their marginal products. The price of capital, which is the rate of interest (r), will be given by the marginal product of aggregate capital (ΣK). The price of labour, which is the wage rate (W), will be given by the marginal product of labour (L).

This third parable can also be seen in Fig. 3.3 and Box 3.3. In Fig. 3.3, the aggregated amount of capital employed (ΣK), which is $K1$, causally determines its marginal product (MPk). This marginal product of capital (MPk) is equal to the rate of return on capital ($r1$). The price of capital (r) multiplied by the amount of aggregated capital employed (ΣK) gives the share of capital in total income (Y), as seen in Eq. (3.17) in Box 3.3. Similarly, the price of labour (W) multiplied by the amount of labour employed (L) gives the share of labour in total income, as seen in the same Eq. (3.17). Then, the equation states that the capital share in income plus the labour share in income account for total income earned.

This parable gives the fourth major implication for the neoclassical conceptual framework, which is that the amount of aggregated capital employed (ΣK) determines its price (r) and therefore the share of capital ($\Sigma K * r$) in total income (y), while the amount of aggregated labour (L) determines its price (W) and therefore its share in total income (Y).

The fundamental problem that Wicksell (1907, 1936) recognized early on is that capital is heterogeneous and cannot be aggregated physically, thus requiring some kind of price of capital. This can either be based on the cost of production of this capital or on the present value of the future contribution of this capital to output. Cohen and Harcourt (2003) point out that both these ways of pricing capital require time—and time requires a rate of interest.

3.2.3 The Aggregation of Heterogeneous Capital: Joan and the Production Function

The anecdote recounted by students at the Marshal Faculty of Economics at Cambridge in the early 1970s and younger faculty such as economist Ajit Singh was that Joan Robinson, the doyenne of Keynesian macro, would sit in on neoclassical lectures. As the lecturer drew the neoclassical production function on the board (such as Fig. 3.3), she would ask what the variable on the horizontal axis was. When the reply was 'Capital', she would inquire how this capital was to be measured.[2] This pithy humour sums up the Cambridge capital controversy between the University of Cambridge in the UK and Cambridge Massachusetts, which has raged since Robinson's (1953) seminal article questioning the neoclassical production function (Harcourt, 1976).

[2] Recounted to me by economist Ajit Singh in 2011.

The argument essentially is, and remains, that the neoclassical production function and its powerful parables derived by Samuelson (1966) posit a one-way causality, with the aggregated quantity of capital (ΣK) employed in an economy determining the price of this capital as its interest rate (r). This is done through the aggregated quantity of capital (ΣK) determining the marginal product of capital (MPk), which is equated to the price of capital, given by the rate of interest (r).

The problem, as Wicksell (1907, 1936) notes and Robinson emphasizes (1953), is that capital is heterogeneous. The student of the production function forgets to ask how this heterogeneous capital is to be measured. Before they ever do ask, the student has become a professor, with sloppy habits of thought handed down from one generation to the next. Heterogeneous physical capital goods need to be aggregated across the economy on the horizontal axis of the production function given in Fig. 3.3. A sack of cement needs to be added to a ton of steel, which requires a price for both kinds of physical capital to be aggregated into the total quantity of capital (ΣK).

The price of capital, according to the neoclassical parables, must be given by the interest rate (r). Thus, in Box 3.3, Eq. (3.18) can aggregate three different kinds of capital (Ki, Kj and Kn) only by multiplying each unit of capital by its price (r). Robinson's (1953) point is that the neoclassical production function needs a price of capital, given by the interest rate (r), to be able to aggregate heterogeneous capital goods across the economy. This aggregated value of heterogeneous capital (ΣK) is then used by the production function to causally determine the marginal product of capital (MPk), which is equal to the price of capital, which is the interest rate.

Robinson's (1953) argument then is that there is an unerring circularity in the neoclassical production function, which needs a rate of interest to aggregate heterogeneous capital to causally determine a rate of interest. Sraffa (1961) resonates: of what good is a quantity of capital (since it needs a rate of interest) that cannot be used for its traditional purpose—to determine a rate of interest. The weakness of this circularity in the Samuelson-Swan-Solow production function is added to in the breakdown of the three parables derived by Samuelson (1966).

3.2.4 Choice of Technique, Re-Switching and Capital Reversing

The generalizable result of the Samuelson-Swan-Solow production function is given by Samuelson's (1966) second parable: as a greater quantity of capital is employed (K), the marginal product of capital (MPk) will fall, thus reducing the rate of return to capital, the interest rate (r). This gives a strictly monotonic, inverse relationship between the quantity of capital employed and the rate of return to it. This relationship will also apply to the capital output ratio (K/Y) and the rate of return on capital (r). This monotonicity between capital intensity, given by the capital-output ratio (K/Y) on the horizontal axis of the production function in Fig. 3.3 and the rate of interest (r) on the vertical axis, breaks down.

The essence of this monotonicity is that in Fig. 3.3, a low capital-output ratio like $K/Y1$ will give an unambiguously higher interest rate, $r1$. If more capital is used, raising the capital intensity ratio (K/Y) from $K/Y1$ to $K/Y2$, this will cause the marginal product of capital to fall from MPk1 to MPk2. This means that the price of capital will fall unambiguously from $r1$ to $r2$. This unambiguous, monotonic, inverse relationship between capital intensity and interest rates breaks down. The first step in this argument is that the value of capital will change with the price of capital, which is the interest rate. This is fair enough, but it also raises the question of which interest rate to choose to aggregate heterogeneous capital.

3.2.5 Which Interest Rate to Choose in Aggregating Heterogeneous Capital: Sraffian Pricing

The classical pricing of a good, followed by Sraffa (1961), makes it equal to the cost of production. Box 3.4 takes the example of the aggregate capital of an economy, comprising two heterogeneous capital goods—a truck and a laser. Assume that producing the truck requires twice the capital needed to build a laser. Thus, the production of trucks is twice as capital-intensive as the production of lasers. Then, the cost of producing the truck, given by Eq. (3.19) in Box 3.4, will comprise the wage plus two units of capital. Capital will be priced by a numeraire (to save on messy maths) multiplied by 1 plus the rate of interest (r).

The cost of producing the laser, given by Eq. (3.20) in Box 3.4, will comprise the wage plus one unit of capital—capital, again, being priced by the same numeraire as for trucks multiplied by 1 plus the rate of interest (r). Box 3.4 now assumes values for these parameters in Eqs. (3.19) and (3.20). In the first instance, the wage is taken as $10,000. The numeraire for capital is taken as $10,000. The interest rate is taken in this first instance as 100 per cent. An interest rate of 100 per cent implies that the value of capital (the value of the numeraire for capital) doubles. In the two equations, this makes the bracketed term by which capital is multiplied, equal to (1 + 1).

Box 3.4 The Re-Switching Problem
Samuelson's (1966) choice of technique:

Step 1: The value of capital (K) will vary with its price—the rate of interest

Literature example: Different techniques use different capital intensities (K/Y).

Production of trucks is two times more capital-intensive than lasers.

$$P_T = W * 2K(1+r) \qquad (3.19)$$

$$P_L = W * K(1+r) \qquad (3.20)$$

If:
W = $10,000
K = $10,000
r = 100 % = 1

$$P_T = 10,000 * 2(10,000)(1+1) \qquad (3.21)$$

$$P_T = 50,000$$

$$P_L = 10,000 * 1(10,000)(1+1) \qquad (3.22)$$

$$P_T = 30,000$$

Step 2: Samuelson (1996) on choice of technique

Requirement for Samuelson's second parable:

A fall in the price of capital, given by the interest rate (r), is associated with an increase in capital intensity, given by the capital-output (K/Y) ratio and the capital-labour ratio (K/L).

$$r = -\text{fn}(K/Y) \qquad (3.23a)$$

or

$$r = -\text{fn}(K/L) \qquad (3.23b)$$

(continued)

> **Box 3.4** (continued)
> Samuelson's example of two techniques to produce champagne:
>
> $$\text{Technique } \alpha = 7L(1+r)2 \qquad (3.24)$$
>
> $$\text{Technique } \beta = 2L(1+r)3 + 6L(1+r) \qquad (3.25)$$
>
> Now, if $r = 0$
>
> $$P_T = 10{,}000 + 2(10{,}000)(1+0) \qquad (3.26)$$
>
> $$P_T = 30{,}000$$
>
> $$P_L = 10{,}000 + 1(10{,}000)(1+0) \qquad (3.27)$$
>
> $$P_T = 20{,}000$$
>
> If $\Sigma K = 1T + 1L$
> If $r = 100\%$
> $\Sigma K = \$80{,}000$
>
> Which is simply:
>
> $$\Sigma_{i-n} K \text{ value} = K_i(1+r) \qquad (3.28)$$
>
> $$\Sigma K \text{ value} = K_{t-i}(1+r)^i \qquad (3.29)$$

In this first instance then, the cost of producing a truck (PT) comes out at $50,000 while that of producing a laser (PL) is $30,000. The aggregate value of capital, comprising a truck and a laser, is then $80,000. In the next instance, assume that the rate of interest falls to 0. The cost of producing a truck now falls—with the fall in the price of capital—to $30,000 while the cost of producing a laser now falls to $20,000. The aggregate value of capital is now $50,000. This example yields the simple Eq. (3.28) in Box 3.4, that the aggregated value of heterogeneous capital goods will be equal to the physical quantity of heterogeneous capital goods multiplied by 1 plus the rate of interest (r).

3.2.6 The Assumption of LEETS

Note that the physical quantity of capital, 1K or 2K, still assumes a numeraire for capital—in this example, of $10,000. Like all numeraires, it can be given any value, say 1, in which case the physical quantum of capital for producing a truck is indeed 2K while that for producing a laser is 1K. All that can be said so far, even in measuring the physical quanta of capital, is that these are relative. The production of a truck requires twice the quantum of capital required to produce a laser.

Even measuring the physical quantum of capital must be based on the capital intensity of the technique used to produce that good. Equation (3.28) in Box 3.4 is technique-specific. It says that the aggregate value of capital, as an unknown on the left-hand side of the equation, will be determined on the right-hand side of the equation by the quantum of capital used by the ith technique, multiplied by 1 plus the profit rate r. In the case of a truck, Ki takes the value 2K. In the case of a laser, Ki takes the value 1K.

Using relative capital intensity to measure even the physical quanta of capital used still assumes Robinson's (1953) requirement for a physically homogenous capital good that she mockingly called 'LEETS' ('steel' spelt backwards). The heroic assumption being made is that one unit of LEETS is needed to make a laser while two units of LEETS are needed to make a truck, whereas of course the capital goods needed to produce the laser may well differ from the capital goods needed to produce a truck.

However, to move Samuelson's (1966) parables along, assuming LEETS-like physically homogenous capital goods allows them to be valued by their profit rate, given by the rate of interest (r). This results in the value of capital varying with the physical quantum of capital goods, computed by the relative capital intensities of the choice of technique. In the second step of the argument, it is this variation in the aggregated value of heterogeneous capital that leads to the breakdown of Samuelson's second parable of an unambiguous, monotonic, inverse relationship between capital intensity and the rate of interest.

3.2.7 Capital Re-Switching

Sraffa (1961) and Robinson (1953) both noticed that the valuation of aggregated heterogeneous capital leads to the breakdown of this unambiguous, monotonic, inverse relationship between capital intensity and the rate of interest. This was through the phenomena of re-switching, as anticipated by Wicksell (1907, 1936). Samuelson came to acknowledge the problem in 1966.

Samuelson (1966) uses an Austrian notion of capital, where the productivity of capital is the productivity of time. Capital in this sense is abstention from consumption in favour of future technology, which becomes more roundabout, more mechanized and more productive. An increase in roundaboutness becomes an increase in capital intensity (Cohen & Harcourt, 2003). Samuelson (1966) uses the Sraffian concept of new products made by labour and capital, with capital goods represented by dead labour or the labour embodied in capital. He then posits two alternative techniques to making a product.

Figure 3.4 illustrates these in the form of two techniques for making champagne, using only labour, time and free grapes. In technique α, seven units of labour make one unit of brandy in period $t - 2$. This ferments into one unit of champagne in period t. In technique β, two units of labour make one unit of grape juice in period $t - 3$. This ferments into wine in another period. Six units of labour then process this wine in period $t - 1$, turning it into one unit of champagne in period t.

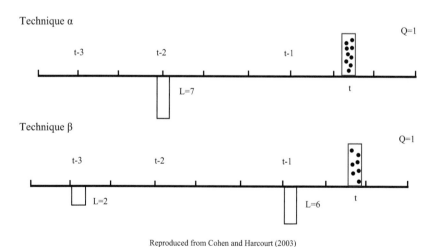

Reproduced from Cohen and Harcourt (2003)

Fig. 3.4 Choice of technique

Since capital is a product of time, as in the Austrian notion adopted by Samuelson (1966), in technique α, the capital that labour works with must be valued in two distinct periods: $t - 2$, which is two periods ago, and t, the current period. The capital to be valued in $t - 2$ accrues over these two periods. There was an abstention from consumption two periods ago, which must be valued at more than the abstention from consumption in period t. Thus, the value of capital in $t - 2$ must be greater than that in period t. This introduction of the notion of time to value capital makes it more complex than the simple Eq. (3.28) in Box 3.4, taken so far to value capital. Equation (3.28) is timeless: it says that the value of capital is based on taking the capital intensity of the ith technique and multiplying it by 1 plus the rate of interest.

Introducing the notion of time implies that the capital intensity of the ith technique is based on the number of periods before t in which the capital was invested and consumption foregone. The capital intensity of the ith technique now becomes the ith period before t. This yields Eq. (3.29) in Box 3.4, where the value of aggregate capital on the left-hand side of the equation is determined on the right-hand side by capital invested i periods before the present period t, multiplied by 1 plus the interest rate, raised to the power i.

For wine-making technique α, the capital invested in $t - 2$ must be valued at 1 plus the interest rate (r) raised to the power 2. This will be greater than the capital invested in t, valued at 1 plus the interest rate (r) raised to the power 1. The value of capital two periods ago, which is consumption foregone two periods ago, will be exponentially that much greater than the value of capital in t, which is consumption just foregone in the current period.

Samuelson's (1966) wine-making by technique α is now captured by Eq. (3.24) in Box 3.4, where seven units of labour work with capital in period $t - 2$. Accordingly, the equation values this technique's capital at 7L multiplied by 1 plus the interest rate (r) raised to the power 2. Technique β is now captured by Eq. (3.25) in Box 3.4, where two units of labour work with capital in period $t - 3$ and six units of labour work with capital in period t. The equation now values this technique's capital at 2L multiplied by 1 plus the interest rate (r) raised to the power 3, plus 6L multiplied by 1 plus the interest rate (r).

Table 3.1 compares the two techniques given in Eqs. (3.24) and (3.25) by plugging in three interest rates, assumed to be 150 per cent, then 75 per cent and then 0 per cent. Plugging in an interest rate of 150 per cent

Table 3.1 Capital re-switching

ρ	Technique α	Technique β
150%	$43.75	$46.25
75%	$21.44	$21.22
0%	$7.00	$8.00

into Eqs. (3.24) and (3.25) gives a cost of production for each technique. At high interest rates above 100 per cent (in this case, 150 per cent), seven units of labour compounded over two periods give a lower cost of production of $43.75 for technique α. Compare this to two units of labour compounded over three periods, giving a higher cost of production of $46.25 for technique β.

However, Table 3.1 also shows that at a lower interest rate of 75 per cent, the cost of production for technique α becomes more expensive at $21.44, compared to technique β at $21.22. At an even lower rate of interest of 0 per cent, technique α becomes cheaper again at $7, compared to technique β at $8. Plotting the two techniques of production in Fig. 3.5 contrasts it to the parables of the production function given by Fig. 3.3.

In Fig. 3.5, technique α is preferred at interest rates above 100 per cent and again at interest rates below 50 per cent. At intermediate interest rates, between 100 and 50 per cent, however, technique β is cheaper. Thus, there is no longer a strictly monotonic, inverse relationship between the quantity of capital per unit of labour (K/L) and the rate of return to it in the rate of interest, as required by the second parable in Fig. 3.3. This relationship between capital intensity (K/L) and the interest rate now zigzags, as in Fig. 3.5. The result is that a capital intensity of $K/L1$ no longer yields one distinct interest rate, but two—of 60 per cent and 100 per cent. This is termed 're-switching' (Cohen & Harcourt, 2003), which breaks down the parable of the production function, that the quantity of capital will determine a unique rate of return in the interest rate (r).

Figure 3.5 also displays capital reversing. A reduction in capital intensity, showing capital becoming scarcer, should raise its rate of return. We see this in Fig. 3.3: when the capital intensity drops from $K/L2$ to $K/L1$, the interest rate rises from $r2$ to $r1$. However, in Fig. 3.5, as the capital intensity drops from $K/L3$ to $K/L2$, the interest rate remains constant at 50 per cent. This dubbed 'capital reversing' (Cohen & Harcourt, 2003).

Both capital re-switching and capital reversing result in multiple equilibria, which means that the causality of the production function—of

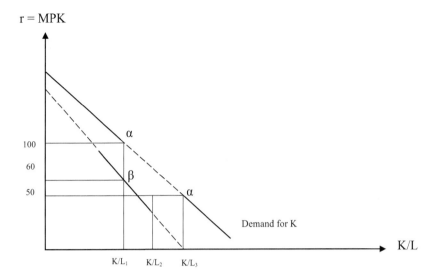

Fig. 3.5 Capital re-switching

going from the quantity of capital to its price—breaks down. Essentially, what breaks down is a neoclassical production function with heterogeneous capital goods, giving a theory of distribution of income between capital and labour—as capital use gets scarcer, its price will rise unambiguously.

The neoclassical production function does not recover from this theoretical inconsistency (Bliss, 1975). Solow (1956) acknowledges that only the one-capital-good case works. Samuelson's (1966) surrogate production function posits heterogeneous capital goods, but these have equal factor proportions, which is tantamount to their becoming one capital good. Neoclassicals such as Hahn (1973) give up on aggregate production functions.

3.2.8 Why Does the Measurement of Aggregating Heterogeneous Capital Not Pose a Theoretical Problem for Non-neoclassical Models?

The question that emerges for growth models is this: why not just aggregate heterogeneous capital using a numeraire, be it the cost of its production discounted for time or even using Sraffa's (1961) Marxian concept of embodied labour? The simple answer is that there is no problem for non-neoclassical models in aggregating heterogeneous capital, using any numeraire. One agreed numeraire is as good as another.

The problem arises only for the neoclassical Samuelson-Swan-Solow production function because it needs to aggregate heterogeneous capital for its value to causally determine the price of capital as its marginal product. This gives a distribution of income between capital and labour—hence the neoclassical conundrum of needing the price of capital to aggregate heterogeneous capital goods, giving the scarcity of capital to causally determine the price of capital as its marginal product. The Samuelson-Swan-Solow production function gives a theory of distribution of income as the marginal product of capital. Other growth models do not do this and non-neoclassical models can therefore blithely aggregate heterogeneous capital goods.

Neoclassical models do retreat to general equilibrium theory, where prices are determined by preferences, endowments and technology. These factors, however, still determine prices through scarcity and approximating marginal products (Cohen & Harcourt, 2003). Thus, the neoclassical model persists with its theory of distribution and is hamstrung by its theoretical internal consistency—unlike non-neoclassical models.

References

Arrow, K. J. (1962). The economic implications of learning by doing. *The Review of Economic Studies, 29*(3), 155–173.

Bliss, C. J. (1975). *Capital theory and the distribution of income.* North-Holland Publishing Company.

Cohen, A. J., & Harcourt, G. C. (2003). Retrospectives: Whatever happened to the Cambridge capital theory controversies? *Journal of Economic Perspectives, 17*(1), 199–214.

Debreu, G. (1970). Economies with a finite set of equilibria. *Econometrica, 38*(3), 387–392.

Debreu, G. (1975). Four aspects of the mathematical theory of economic equilibrium. In *Proceedings of the international congress of mathematicians* (Vol. 1, pp. 65–77). Canadian Mathematical Congress.

Hahn, F. H. (1973). *On the notion of equilibrium in economics: An inaugural lecture.* Cambridge University Press.

Harcourt, G. C. (1976). The Cambridge controversies: Old ways and new horizons—Or dead end? *Oxford Economic Papers, 28*(1), 25–65.

Keynes, J. M. (1936). *The general theory of employment, interest, and money*. Macmillan Cambridge University Press, for Royal Economic Society.

Pigou, A. C. (1937). Real and money wage rates in relation to unemployment. *The Economic Journal, 47*(187), 405–422.

Robinson, J. (1953). The production function and the theory of capital. *The Review of Economic Studies, 21*(2), 81–106.

Samuelson, P. A. (1966). *The collected scientific papers of Paul a. Samuelson* (Vol. 2). MIT Press.

Solow, R. M. (1956). A contribution to the theory of economic growth. *The Quarterly Journal of Economics, 70*(1), 65–94.

Sraffa, P. (1961). Production of commodities by means of commodities. *Science and Society, 25*(2), 139–156.

Wicksell, K. (1907). The influence of the rate of interest on prices. *The Economic Journal, 17*(66), 213–220.

Wicksell, K. (1936). *Interest and prices*. Ludwig von Mises Institute.

CHAPTER 4

The Third and Fourth Properties of Growth Models: The Need for an Equilibrium Solution and a Non-corner One, Requiring In Turn a Mathematically Equilibrating Model

4.1 Introduction and Recap

The first essay was a theoretical preamble, introducing the four properties of growth models identified as useful in an analytical framework for examining growth of output over time.

These four properties are:

1. The need for general equilibrium analysis
2. The need for internal consistency in the theoretical argument of the model
3. The need for an equilibrium solution for output and its rate of growth over time, and preferably not a corner one
4. The need for a mathematically equilibrating model.

In searching for an analytical framework to examine output growth, the second essay examined the first two properties. This third essay examines the third and fourth properties of growth models. The third property is the need for an equilibrium solution for output and its growth rate over time, and preferably not a corner solution. To enable this third property then requires a fourth property—the need for a mathematically equilibrating model.

Below we review the models examined for their mathematical properties so far.

4.1.1 The First Property of General Equilibrium

The choice of an analytical framework for this project begins with the notion of, and the need for, general equilibrium, which is then the first desirable property of growth models. The concept of general equilibrium is more often associated with the intertemporal general equilibrium set out by Arrow (1962) and Debreu (1970, 1975), which focuses on providing proof of the existence of equilibrium in a competitive market economy.

The notion of general equilibrium and the need for general equilibrium analysis, however, are posited by Keynes (1936). This notion of general equilibrium is based on markets and is best seen in comparing on the one hand the theoretical models of the classicals and neoclassicals and, on the other hand, the Keynesian model. The classical and neoclassical models can be represented by Pigou (1937). The Keynesian model comes out in its entirety in *The General Theory of Employment, Interest and Money*.

Both the classical and neoclassical models are based on Say's law—that supply of output creates its own demand. This law should apply to the goods market for output, but its causality lies in the labour market. In this classical-cum-neoclassical model, the market that determines the level of employment (N) and thereby output (Y) is the labour market. The causal variable in the labour market that enables Say's law of full employment (Nf) is the flexibility of the money wage (W). However, Keynes (1936) does not place causality for the determination of employment at the micro level of the firm in partial equilibrium. He does not place this causality in the labour market.

Instead, Keynes (1936) introduces the macro level of the economy by adding to the labour market, the goods market. The goods market represents here, in reduced form, multiple other markets for private and public goods, capital investment, tradeables and global capital flows. Causality for the determination of employment (N), for Keynes, then lies in the goods market. Specifically, demand for employment in the labour market is based on demand for goods in the goods market. Only if there is demand for goods in the goods market will there be demand for labour in the labour market to produce these goods. If there is no demand for goods in the goods market, there will be no demand for labour in the labour market to produce any goods, no matter how low the money wage (W).

This demand for goods in the goods market, which is the reduced form for multiple other markets (for private and public goods, capital investment, tradeables and global capital flows) then becomes an aggregate of demand for goods across all these multiple markets. It becomes aggregate demand for output (Y) or (ΣDY). The first useful property of a theoretical framework or model for analysing growth of output is therefore the need for general equilibrium based on multiple markets rather than partial equilibrium based on a single market.

Three general equilibrium models, defined thus as being based on multiple markets, are pre-eminent:

- The neoclassical Samuelson-Swan-Solow production function is the workhorse didactic model used to forecast long-run gross domestic product (GDP) growth. It is based on three markets: for goods, capital and labour.
- The Harrod-Domar model has a more Keynesian pedigree and has also become a workhorse model for estimating long-run GDP growth. It is initially based on two markets: for goods and capital. The requirements of a natural rate of growth, however, bring in the labour market.
- The third model is the Keynesian model of aggregate demand. This is a larger model than the other two, based on five markets: for private goods, public goods, capital investment, tradeables and global capital flows.

4.1.2 The Second Property of Internal Theoretical Consistency

The second half of Essay 2 considers just the neoclassical Samuelson-Swan-Solow production function. It is tested for the second useful property of analytical frameworks and growth models—that of the need for internal consistency in the theoretical argument of the model—because it has long been labelled with the theoretical weakness dubbed in the genre as the 'Cambridge capital controversy' (Cohen & Harcourt, 2003). The other two models, the Harrod-Domar model and the Keynesian model of aggregate demand, are not tainted with this theoretical weakness.

4.1.3 *The Third and Fourth Properties of an Equilibrium Solution and its Enabling Through a Mathematically Equilibrating Model*

The Harrod-Domar model has a problem with the third property of conceptual frameworks and models—of reaching an equilibrium solution and a non-corner one. This property is examined here in Essay 3. Meeting this third property—of the need for an equilibrium solution that is a non-corner one—requires an enabling fourth property, that of the need for a mathematically equilibrating model. The Keynesian model of aggregate demand is then seen to satisfy this fourth property.

4.2 THE THIRD PROPERTY: THE NEED FOR AN EQUILIBRIUM SOLUTION FOR OUTPUT AND ITS RATE OF GROWTH OVER TIME, AND PREFERABLY NOT A CORNER ONE

4.2.1 *The Harrod-Domar Model*

The Harrod-Domar model has come to be the workhorse model for back-of-the-envelope calculations of GDP growth for generations of students and development economists. Sans caveats and with immaculate assumptions, the model gives a simple, plausible explanation of GDP growth. Putting a pin in these caveats and assumptions for the present, the Harrod-Domar model estimates the rate of growth of output ($Y°$), as given in Box 4.1, as the change in output between two periods, $Yt0$ and $Yt1$, divided by $Yt0$.

Box 4.1 Harrod-Domar Model Full-Employment Conditions

$$Y° = \frac{Y_{t-1} - Y_{t0}}{Y_{t0}} \tag{4.1}$$

$$Y° = \frac{S}{K/Y} \tag{4.2}$$

e.g., $5\% = \dfrac{15\%}{3\%}$.

Full-employment (NF) conditions:

$$(i)\, IF = SF \tag{4.3}$$

because if IF < SF
then D < YF
(ii) For continuous NF,

$$Y° = LF° + (Y/L) \tag{4.4}$$

$$\text{or } Y°f = n + a \tag{4.5}$$

$$(i)\, \text{implies}: Y°w = \frac{S_F}{\left(\dfrac{K}{Y}\right)_W} \tag{4.6}$$

But observed ex-poste, $Y°a$ must be based on observed Sa and observed $\left(\dfrac{K}{Y}\right)_a$

$$\text{i.e., } Y°a = \frac{S_a}{\left(\dfrac{K}{Y}\right)_a} \tag{4.7}$$

This growth rate of output (Y°), as the unknown on the left-hand side of Eq. (4.2) in Box 4.1, is determined by two key macro variables on the right-hand side of the equation. One variable is the savings rate as a share of output (s) in the numerator. The second variable is the capital output ratio (K/Y) in the denominator. This capital-output ratio appears almost as an engineering function at first blush, giving the relationship between output and capital. In the boxed example, a savings rate (s) of 15 per cent, say, with a capital-output ratio (K/Y) of 3 gives an output growth rate (Y°) of 5 per cent.

The Harrod-Domar model is not plagued by the Cambridge capital controversy, unlike the Samuelson-Swan-Solow neoclassical production function, because it does not purport a theory of distribution. Thus, it does not require an interest rate to aggregate capital to derive its marginal product to determine the rate of return on capital. The Harrod-Domar model therefore seems a safer bet for purists. However, it runs into two critical problems: first, in the stability of its equilibrium and, second, in the tendency of this equilibrium to give corner solutions that are extreme values rather than median ones.

4.2.2 The Need for a Stable Equilibrium in the Harrod-Domar Model

The Harrod-Domar model is seen to set out two conditions for full-employment equilibrium (Eltis, 2018):

1. The economy must invest If or the equivalent of full-employment savings (sf) every year. In Box 4.1, this is given by Eq. (4.3). In case full-employment investment (If) is below full-employment savings (sf), effective demand for output will be less than full-employment output (Yf).
2. For continuous full employment (Nf), output growth (Y°) must equal labour force growth (LF°) plus productivity growth [$(Y/L)^\circ$]. In Box 4.1, this is given by Eqs. (4.4) and (4.5).

4.2.3 The Problem of the Warranted Rate of Growth of Output

The first condition is dubbed to give a warranted growth rate of output ($Y^\circ w$), which firms will consider ideal for profit maximization and therefore not want to move away from. The important caveat here is that this is a planned warranted rate of growth. That is, it is an ex-ante objective of firms to meet this equilibrium condition.

This planned, warranted growth rate of output (Y°w) now requires two sub-conditions. The first is that according to Eq. (4.3) in Box 4.1, planned full-employment investment (If) is equal to planned full-employment savings (Sf). The second is that the planned capital-output ratio is warranted $[(K/Y)w]$, that is, the warranted rate of growth of output ($Y°w$) is equal to the warranted rate of savings for full employment (Sf) divided by the warranted capital-output ratio $[(K/Y)w]$. This is Eq. (4.6) in Box 4.1. This is an equilibrium condition in that firms' expectations of profits are met and they will not want to move away from it. Thus, it is a stable equilibrium. However, ex-poste, there will be an observed growth rate of output ($Y°a$). This will be given by an ex-poste observed savings rate (Sa) divided by an ex-poste observed capital-output ratio $[(K/Y)a]$ as given in Eq. (4.7) in Box 4.1.

This ex-poste observed rate of growth of output ($Y°a$) need not equal the warranted growth rate of output ($Y°w$). Therefore, if the ex-ante warranted growth rate of output ($Y°w$) is a condition for stable equilibrium, then the ex-poste observed rate of growth of output ($Y°a$) need not reach this stable equilibrium. Equality between the warranted growth rate of output ($Y°w$) and the observed growth rate of output ($Y°a$) will be coincidental. Robinson (1953) avers that the economy just blunders along.

Worse, the Harrod-Domar model argues that given an initial inequality between the ex-ante warranted growth rate of output ($Y°w$) and the ex-poste observed rate of growth of output ($Y°a$), the inequality, rather than minimizing over successive iterations, will perversely increase. Eltis (2018) illustrates this perverse cycling away of the ex-poste observed growth rate of output ($Y°a$) from the ex-ante warranted growth rate of output ($Y°w$) in Tables 4.1 and 4.2.

Table 4.1 Harrod-Domar model initial conditions

Yr	K stock ($Ki + Ii$)	Y	K/Yr	$I = S/Y$	gw	ga
1	400	100	400	12	3%	3
2	412	103	412	12.36	3%	3
3	424.36	106.9	424.36	12.73	3%	3

Table 4.2 Harrod-Domar model equilibrium conditions

(I = S/r) a	Yr	K stock	Y	K/Yr	I = S/Yw	gw	ga
	1	400	100	400	12	3	3
4.08 * 2 = 8.16	2	412	102	408	12.24	3	2
8.32	3	424.24	104.04	416.16	12.48	3	2
8.48	4	436.72	106.12	424.48	12.73	3	2

Tables 4.1 and 4.2 set out the determination of the warranted rates of growth of output ($Y°w$) and the observed rates of growth of output ($Y°a$) for each year over several years. The required macro aggregates are (a) the capital stock, which is equal to cumulated capital for the year plus last year's investment given by (Ki + Ii); (b) output (Y); (c) the warranted capital-output ratio [($K/Y)w$]; and (d) the savings rate (S), which has to be equal to the investment rate (I), all of which give (e) the warranted growth rate of output ($Y°w$).

Table 4.1 assumes that the ex-ante planned, warranted growth rate of output ($Y°w$) is equal to the ex-poste observed rate of growth of output ($Y°a$), implying a stable equilibrium. Table 4.2 then examines the possibility of the ex-ante planned growth rate of output ($Y°w$) deviating from the ex-poste observed rate of growth of output ($Y°a$), implying a perverse cycling away from stable equilibrium.

Under stable equilibrium, in year 1, the capital stock (Ki + Ii) assumes a value of 400 (Table 4.1). This produces a value of output of 100, giving an ex-ante planned, warranted capital-output ratio [($K/Y)w$] of 400/100 or 4. An ex-ante planned, warranted savings rate (Si) equal to the investment rate (Ii) is assumed at 12 per cent of output. The ex-ante planned, warranted savings rate (Si) divided by the ex-ante planned, warranted capital-output ratio [($K/Y)w$] gives an ex-ante planned, warranted rate of growth of output of 3 per cent for year 1. The ex-ante planned, warranted growth rate of output ($Y°w$) is assumed to be equal to the ex-poste observed rate of growth of output ($Y°a$) at 3 per cent.

In year 2, the capital stock (Ki + Ii) cumulates to 400 from year 1 plus the investment (Ii) from year 1 (of 12), equalling 412. This produces a value of output of 103, giving an ex-ante planned, warranted capital-output ratio [($K/Y)w$] of 4.12. The ex-ante planned, warranted savings rate (Si) equal to the investment rate (Ii) must now be 12.36. This is in order to give the ex-ante planned, warranted rate of growth of output of

3 per cent for year 2, given by the ex-ante warranted savings rate (Si) divided by the ex-ante warranted capital-output ratio [$(K/Y)w$]. This is 12.36/4.12, equalling 3 per cent for year 2. The ex-ante warranted growth rate of output ($Y°w$) will be equal to the ex-poste observed rate of growth of output ($Y°a$) at 3 per cent.

In Table 4.1, the ex-poste observed rate of growth of output ($Y°a$) is equal to the ex-ante warranted growth rate of output ($Y°w$), giving stable equilibrium. The ex-ante planned, warranted capital stock (Ki + Ii) will be just enough to produce the ex-poste observed value of output, keeping the warranted capital stock accumulating through ex-ante planned annual investment (Ii).

Now, take the disequilibrium shown in Table 4.2. In year 1, the ex-ante planned, warranted growth rate of output ($Y°w$) is equal to the ex-poste observed growth rate of output ($Y°a$) at 3 per cent. In year 2, however, the ex-poste observed growth rate of output ($Y°a$) is assumed to fall to 2 per cent, compared to the ex-ante planned, warranted growth rate of output of 3 per cent. Meanwhile, the capital stock (Ki + Ii) keeps accumulating through ex-ante planned, warranted savings (Sw), equal to ex-ante planned, warranted investment (Iw). This ex-ante planned savings equal to investment keeps growing at the warranted rate to produce an ex-ante planned, warranted growth rate of output ($Y°w$).

In Table 4.2, the ex-ante planned, warranted savings rate (Sw), equal to the ex-ante planned, warranted investment rate (Iw) in year 2 is 12.36 per cent. This, divided by the ex-ante planned, warranted capital-output ratio [$(K/Y)w$] of 408 gives the ex-ante planned, warranted growth rate of output ($Y°w$) of 3 per cent.

However, the ex-poste observed growth rate of output ($Y°a$) in year 2 is 2 per cent, thus requiring a lower ex-ante planned, warranted savings rate (Sw) equal to the ex-ante planned investment rate (Iw) of 8.16 per cent. Nor does this gap between (a) ex-ante planned, warranted savings (Sw), equal to ex-ante planned, warranted investment (Iw), required for an ex-ante planned, warranted growth rate of output ($Y°w$) of 3 per cent, and (b) the lower required ex-ante planned, warranted savings rate (Sw), equal to ex-ante planned, warranted investment (Iw), to produce an ex-poste observed growth rate of output ($Y°a$) of 2 per cent decrease over time. Table 4.2 shows the gap increasing over time, from year 2 to year 4.

Herein lies the instability of equilibrium in the Harrod-Domar model. If the ex-post observed growth rate of output ($Y°a$) falls below the ex-ante planned, warranted growth rate of output ($Y°w$), the capital stock (Ki + Ii) will accumulate idle capacity. This will call for the ex-ante planned, warranted savings rate (Sw), equal to the ex-ante planned, warranted investment rate (Iw), to come down. This will in turn reduce aggregate demand for output, further reducing the ex-poste observed growth rate of output ($Y°a$) and increasing the gap between the ex-ante planned, warranted growth rate of output ($Y°w$) and the ex-poste observed growth rate of output ($Y°a$) over time.

The converse applies in symmetry. If the ex-poste observed growth rate of output ($Y°a$) is higher than the ex-ante planned, warranted growth rate of output ($Y°w$), then the capital stock ($K_i + I_i$) will fall short of capacity. This will call for the ex-ante planned, warranted savings rate (Sw), equal to the ex-ante planned, warranted investment rate (Iw), to go up. This will in turn raise aggregate demand for output, further raising the ex-poste observed rate of growth of output ($Y°a$) and increasing the gap between the ex-ante planned, warranted growth rate of output ($Y°w$) and the ex-poste observed growth rate of output ($Y°a$) over time.

The Harrod-Domar model's departure from stable equilibrium—based on a set of macroeconomic aggregates that are ex-ante planned and warranted, and another set of macro aggregates that are ex-poste observed—is perverse. Worse, there appears to be no reason for the ex-ante planned and warranted set of macro aggregates to coincide with the ex-poste observed set of macro aggregates, except coincidence.

Figure 4.1 illustrates the Harrod-Domar model's problem. Steady-state growth is on a knife edge, where the ex-ante planned, warranted rate of growth of output ($Y°w$) is equal to the ex-poste observed rate of growth of output ($Y°a$). This equality must hold only by chance because any deviation from it is not self-correcting and is in fact perverse. If the ex-poste observed rate of growth of output ($Y°a$) is lower than the ex-ante planned, warranted rate of growth of output ($Y°w$), inventories accumulate, signalling investment to fall. This lowers the ex-poste observed rate of growth of output ($Y°a$), which falls further, thereby also increasing the gap between the ex-ante planned, warranted growth rate of output ($Y°w$) and the ex-poste observed rate of growth of output ($Y°a$).

By symmetry, if the ex-poste observed rate of growth of output ($Y°a$) is higher than the ex-ante planned, warranted rate of growth of output ($Y°w$), capacity falls short, signalling investment to increase. This raises the ex-poste rate of growth of output ($Y°a$) further, thereby increasing the gap between the ex-ante planned, warranted growth rate of output ($Y°w$) and the ex-poste observed rate of growth of output ($Y°a$).

$g = \Delta Y/Y$

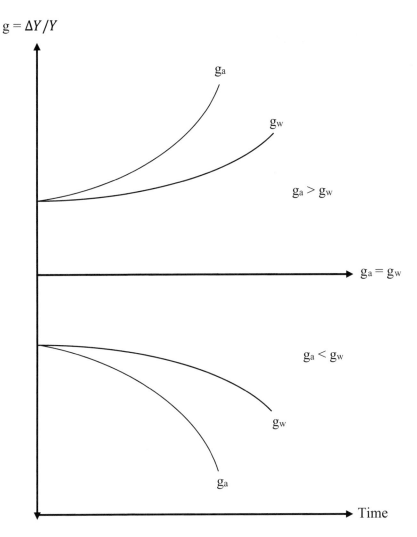

Fig. 4.1 Harrod-Domar model disequilibrium

4.2.4 A Solution to Falling from the Harrod-Domar Knife Edge Into Disequilibrium

The problem of the fall of the ex-poste observed growth rate of output ($Y°a$) from the Harrod-Domar knife edge of ex-ante planned, warranted growth rate of output ($Y°w$) into a perverse veering away from the knife edge, either below or above, has been much examined. The broader consensus from the neoclassical and Keynesian camps is that there is no solution.

Hahn and Matthews' (1964) contention is that the neoclassical attempt to paper the gap between the ex-ante planned, warranted growth rate of output ($Y°w$) and the ex-poste observed growth rate of output does not work. This is because what we require is a crucial assumption about savings and investment. Box 4.2 sets out this necessary condition for a knife-edge equilibrium.

Box 4.2 The Harrod-Domar Model's Knife Edge

$$\text{If } Y°w = \frac{S_w}{(K/Y)_w} \tag{4.8}$$

$$\text{and } Y°a = \frac{S_a}{(K/Y)_a} \tag{4.9}$$

$$\text{and if } Y°w = Y°a \tag{4.10}$$

$$\text{then } Iw = Ia \tag{4.11}$$

$$\text{and } (K/Y)_w = (K/Y)_a \tag{4.12}$$

But if

$$Y°a < Y°w \tag{4.13}$$

$$\therefore \frac{S}{\left(\dfrac{K}{Y}\right)_a} < \frac{S}{\left(\dfrac{K}{Y}\right)_w} \tag{4.14}$$

$$\therefore \Sigma DY \text{ low} \tag{4.15}$$

$$\therefore \text{Inventories } a > \text{Inventories } w$$

$$\therefore \text{Inventories rise} \tag{4.16}$$

(*continued*)

Box 4.2 (continued)

$$\therefore \text{Ia falls} \tag{4.17}$$

$$\therefore Y°a \text{ falls further} < Y°w \tag{4.18}$$

Alternatively:

$$\text{If } Y°a > Y°w \tag{4.19}$$

$$\therefore \frac{S}{\left(\frac{K}{Y}\right)_a} > \frac{S}{\left(\frac{K}{Y}\right)_w} \tag{4.20}$$

$$\therefore \Sigma DY \text{ rises} \tag{4.21}$$

$$\therefore \text{Inventories fall} \tag{4.22}$$

$$\therefore \text{Ia rises} \tag{4.23}$$

$$\therefore Y°a \text{ rise further} > Y°w \tag{4.24}$$

Ergo, knife-edge condition:

$$\text{Ia} = \text{Sw} \tag{4.25}$$

The ex-ante planned, warranted growth rate of output ($Y°w$) is equal to the ex-ante planned, warranted savings share (Sw) divided by the ex-ante planned, warranted capital-output ratio [$(K/Y)w$], as in Eq. (4.8). Similarly, ex-poste observed growth ($Y°a$) is equal to the ex-poste observed savings share (Sa) divided by the ex-poste observed capital-output ratio [$(K/Y)a$], as in Eq. (4.9).

Then, the knife edge is definitionally where the ex-ante planned, warranted growth rate of output ($Y°w$) is equal to the ex-poste observed growth rate of output ($Y°a$), as in Eq. (4.10). This implies that the ex-ante planned, warranted investment share (Iw) is equal to the ex-poste observed investment share (Ia), as in Eq. (4.11). Similarly, the ex-ante planned capital-output ratio [$(K/Y)w$] is equal to the ex-poste observed capital-output ratio [$(K/Y)a$], as shown in Eq. (4.12) and Fig. 4.1.

But what if the ex-poste observed growth rate of output ($Y°a$) happens to fall below the ex-ante planned, warranted growth rate of output ($Y°w$), as in Eq. (4.13)? That is, the ex-poste observed savings share (Sa), divided by the ex-poste capital-output ratio [$(K/Y)a$], falls below the ex-ante planned, warranted savings share (Sw), divided by the ex-ante planned, warranted capital-output ratio [$(K/Y)w$], as in Eq. (4.14).

This will lower aggregate demand for output (ΣYd), allowing inventories to rise, as Eq. (4.16) shows. The consequent drop in ex-poste observed investment will lower the ex-poste observed growth rate of output ($Y^\circ a$) further below the ex-ante planned, warranted growth rate of output ($Y^\circ w$). Thus, the gap between the ex-poste observed growth rate of output ($Y^\circ a$) and the ex-ante planned, warranted growth rate of output ($Y^\circ w$) increases over time, as in Fig. 4.1. This may occur downwards, with the ex-poste observed growth rate of output ($Y^\circ a$) successively falling behind the ex-ante planned, warranted growth rate of output ($Y^\circ w$), or upwards, with the ex-poste observed growth rate of output ($Y^\circ a$) successively rising above the ex-ante planned, warranted growth rate of output ($Y^\circ w$).

The Harrod-Domar model thus falls off the knife edge of equilibrium because of perverse signalling. When the ex-poste observed growth rate of output ($Y^\circ a$) is lower than the ex-ante planned, warranted growth rate of output ($Y^\circ w$), the warranted savings share (Sw) is high. Accumulating inventories, however, signal the ex-poste observed investment rate (Ia) to fall below the warranted savings share, whereas the signal for investors should be to increase ex-poste observed investment to increase the ex-poste observed growth rate of output ($Y^\circ a$) to keep it equal to the ex-ante planned, warranted growth rate of output ($Y^\circ w$). This implies the equilibrium condition for the Harrod-Domar model to remain on the knife edge—that the ex-poste observed investment share (Ia) should equal the ex-ante planned, warranted savings share (Sw), as given in Eq. (4.25) in Box 4.2.

4.2.5 *The Keynesian Dichotomy Between Investment and Savings*

The Harrod-Domar model highlights the crucial equilibrium condition that investors should invest an investment share (Ia) equal to what savers had planned and saved, a savings share (Sw). Else, equilibrium goes awry.

The ex-poste observed investment share (Ia) will definitionally equal the ex-poste observed savings share (Sa). This can be seen in Box 4.3, where output (Y) is equal to consumption (C) and savings (S) in Eq.

> **Box 4.3 Savings and Investment**
> $S_a = I_a$ by definition
> Because
>
> $$Y = C + S \qquad (4.26)$$
> $$I = Y - C \qquad (4.27)$$
> $$\therefore I = S \qquad (4.28)$$
>
> But:
> Sw is not necessarily = Iw
> Because different motives of different agents Ser and Ier.
> *Marshall and Walras*
>
> $$S = -fn(r) \qquad (4.29)$$
>
> If disequilibrium between S and I
> e.g., if $S > I$
> from (4.29), as $S\uparrow$, r will $\downarrow$ $\therefore I \uparrow$
>
> $$\therefore S = I \qquad (4.30)$$
>
> *Keynes*
>
> $$S = +fn(y) \qquad (4.31)$$
>
> As an imputed equation:
>
> $$Y = C + S \qquad (4.32)$$
>
> If disequilibrium between S and I
> e.g., if $S > I$
> From (4.31) as $S\uparrow$, $C\downarrow$, $\Sigma DY\downarrow$
> $\therefore$ demand for $I \downarrow$
> Ergo, no equilibrium between S and I.

(4.26), while investment (I) is equal to output (Y) minus consumption (C) in Eq. (4.27). If, in Eq. (4.26), consumption (C) is taken to the other side and subtracted from output (Y), this will make savings (S) equal to output (Y) minus consumption (C). This makes both savings (S) and investment (I) equal to the same term, output (Y) minus consumption (C), in turn making savings (S) equal to investment (I) in Eq. (4.28). However, this definitional savings (S) equals investment (I) element holds ex-poste for observed values for both terms. This does not imply that the ex-ante planned, warranted savings share (Sw) will end up equal to the ex-poste observed investment share (Ia).

This was precisely Keynes's (1936) bugbear—that the decision to save was made by one agent, the saver, while the decision to invest was made by a different agent, the investor. Since each agent had a different motive, the decision to save need not coincide with the decision to invest.

Sequentially, this dichotomy between savers and investors fits into the Harrod-Domar model. Agents must save first according to their ex-ante planned decisions, giving a warranted savings share (Sw). This gives the supply of loanable funds. Separate agents invest subsequently an ex-poste observed investment share (Ia) from this supply of loanable funds. For Keynes, the demand for investment must be brought into equilibrium with the willingness to save.

4.2.6 The Classical Theory of Equilibrium Between Investment and Savings

This equilibrium between the demand for investment and the supply of savings is, for the classical model, ensured by an equilibrating rate of interest (r) (Keynes, 1936). In Box 4.3, Marshall and Walras's Eq. (4.29) makes savings (S) a negative function of the rate of interest (r). Now, assume a disequilibrium between savings (S) and investment (I), for example, that savings (S) exceed investment (I), as given above.

From the classical Eq. (4.29), as savings (S) increase and accumulate, compared to investment (I), the rate of interest (r) will fall. With the cost of borrowing (r) falling, the demand for investment (I) will rise. This will give an equilibrium of savings (S) equal to investment (I), as in Eq. (4.30).

4.2.7 … and Keynes's Demur

Keynes flips the determinant of savings (S) from Marshall and Walras's rate of interest (r) to income (y), which now gives Eq. (4.31) as an alternative to Eq. (4.29) in Box 4.3. Savings (S) are now a positive function of income (y). An Eq. (4.32) can also be imputed: that income (y) comprises consumption (C) and savings (S).

Now, assume a disequilibrium between savings (S) and investment (I). As in the example above, assume that savings (S) exceed investment (I). From the Keynesian Eq. (4.31) and the imputed Eq. (4.32), as savings rise, consumption (C) must fall. As consumption (C) falls, aggregate demand for output (ΣYd) will also fall. As aggregate demand for output (ΣYd) falls, the demand for investment will also fall.

Ergo, the disequilibrium between savings (S) and investment (I) will persist. With separate decisions by independent agents, Keynes considers that savings (S) being equal to investment (I) is not a necessary condition. In fact, you cannot go from savings (S) to investment (I). Both savings (S) and investment (I) are determined by other variables.

There appears to be no solution to the Harrod-Domar model's problem of equilibrium between the ex-ante planned, warranted savings share (Sw) being equalled by the ex-poste observed investment share (Ia), which would allow the ex-ante planned, warranted growth rate of output ($Y°w$) to equal the ex-poste observed growth rate of output ($Y°a$). If this notion of equilibrium is given up, then as Robinson (1953) observes, the economy blunders from one point to another, with no predicted path.

Without equilibrium, the economy does a drunken walk.

4.2.8 The Neoclassical Solution to the Harrod-Domar Model's Second Problem of Equilibrium

There is a neoclassical solution, but according to Hahn and Matthews (1964), this solves the Harrod-Domar model's second problem of the ex-ante planned, warranted growth rate of output ($Y°w$) also having to equal the rate of growth of the labour force.

Recalling from Box 4.1 above for Box 4.4, the second equilibrium condition for the Harrod-Domar model is the need for full-employment equilibrium. The condition for full-employment equilibrium, now given in Box 4.4 as Eq. (4.33), is that the full-employment growth rate of output ($Y°f$) must equal the rate of labour force growth (LF°). We assume for simplicity that the rate of productivity growth [(Y/L)°] is 0. If we assume disequilibrium with unemployment, this would mean that the required full-employment growth rate of output ($Y°f$) is higher than the observed growth rate of output ($Y°a$), as in Eq. (4.36).

Solow (1956) and Swan (1956) posit a solution to this disequilibrium. This can be presented in the following way: the required full-employment growth rate of output ($Y°f$) is given by the Harrod-Domar model to be

Box 4.4 The Neoclassical Solution to the Harrod-Domar Model's Second Problem of Full-Employment Equilibrium

$$Y_F^\circ = L_F^\circ + \left(Y/L\right)^\circ \qquad (4.33)$$

$$\text{Or } Y_F^\circ = n + a \qquad (4.34)$$

$$\therefore Y_a^\circ = Y_F^\circ = n + a \qquad (4.35)$$

e.g., if $n = 0.5\%$ PA
$a = 1.5\%$ PA
then $Y_F^\circ = 2\%$ PA

$$\therefore Y_A^\circ = Y_F^\circ = 2\% PA$$

Will be the condition for full-employment equilibrium, where the observed growth of output Y_A° is equal to the growth of output for full-employment equilibrium Y_F°.

But if $Y_F^\circ > Y_A^\circ$, there will be unemployment.

$$\text{If } Y_F^\circ > Y_A^\circ \qquad (4.36)$$

Which implies

$$Y_F^\circ = {S_F}\big/{(K/Y)_F} \qquad (4.37)$$

$$Y_a^\circ = {S_a}\big/{(K/Y)_a} \qquad (4.38)$$

$$\therefore {S_F}\big/{(K/Y)_F} > {S_a}\big/{(K/Y)_a} \qquad (4.39)$$

(*continued*)

> **Box 4.4 (continued)**
>
> e.g., $\dfrac{20}{5} = 4\% > \dfrac{20}{10} = 2\%$
>
> i.e., K is higher in relation to L
>
> $\therefore \pi$ low
>
> $\therefore K \downarrow$ to K^*
>
> $\therefore K/\Upsilon \downarrow$ to $\dfrac{5}{1}$
>
> $$\dfrac{20}{5/1} = 4\%$$

the savings share needed for full-employment growth of output (Sf), divided by the capital-output ratio needed for full-employment growth of output $[(K/\Upsilon)f]$, as in Eq. (4.37).

Similarly, the observed growth rate of output ($\Upsilon°a$) will be given by the savings share needed for full-employment growth (Sf), but divided by an observed capital-output ratio $[(K/\Upsilon)a]$, as in Eq. (4.38). This expands Eq. (4.36), using Eqs. (4.37) and (4.38), into Eq. (4.39). Equation (4.39) now says that disequilibrium from a full-employment growth rate of output will be given by the savings share needed for a full-employment growth rate of output (Sf), divided by the capital-output ratio needed for a full-employment growth rate of output $[(K/\Upsilon)f]$, being greater than the savings share needed for a full-employment growth rate of output (Sf), but divided by an observed capital-output ratio $[(K/\Upsilon)a]$.

For Solow (1956) and Swan (1956), the disequilibrium from a full-employment growth rate of output is not caused by the numerators, which are common on both sides of Eq. (4.39), that is, the savings share needed for a full-employment growth rate of output (Sf). Rather, the disequilibrium is caused by the denominators varying on both sides of Eq. (4.39). The denominator on the left-hand side of the inequality is the capital-output ratio needed for a full-employment growth rate of output $[(K/\Upsilon)f]$. The denominator on the right-hand side of the inequality is the observed capital-output ratio $[(K/\Upsilon)a]$.

Solow (1956) and Swan's (1956) solution to restoring equilibrium, making the needed full-employment growth rate of output ($\Upsilon°f$) equal to the observed growth rate of output ($Y°a$), is to allow the observed capital-output ratio $[(K/L)a]$ to vary. This comes to equal the capital-output ratio needed for full employment $[(K/L)f]$.

Box 4.4 takes an example of disequilibrium between the needed full-employment growth rate of output ($Y°f$) and the observed growth rate of output ($Y°a$). If the needed full-employment savings share (Sf) is 20 per cent and the needed full-employment capital-output ratio $[(K/Y)f]$ is 5, then this gives a needed full-employment growth rate of output ($Y°f$) of 4 per cent. The needed full-employment savings share (Sf) is still 20 per cent, but the observed capital-output ratio $[(K/Y)a]$ is 10. This gives a lower observed growth rate ($Y°a$) of 2 per cent.

Thus, the needed full-employment growth rate of output ($Y°f$) of 4 per cent is higher than the observed growth rate of output ($Y°f$) of 2 per cent. Solow (1956) and Swan (1956) would now allow the observed capital-output ratio $[(K/Y)a]$ of 10 to fall to 5, giving a needed full-employment share (Sf), divided by a reduced, observed capital-output ratio $[(K/Y)a]$ of 5, to enable an observed growth rate of output ($Y°a$) to equal 4 per cent. This restores equilibrium between the needed full-employment growth rate of output ($Y°f$) of 4 per cent and the observed growth rate of output ($Y°a$), now also 4 per cent.

The question is, what allows this change in the capital-output ratio, taking the economy from disequilibrium to equilibrium?

Factor price equalization does support this change in the capital-output ratio. Note that in the numerical example in Box 4.4, where the required full-employment growth rate of output ($Y°f$) of 4 per cent is higher than the observed growth rate of output ($Y°a$) of 2 per cent, the observed capital-output ratio $[(K/Y)a]$ is high at 10—higher than the needed full-employment capital-output ratio $[(K/Y)f]$ of 5.

Factor price equalization says that if the quantum of capital is high relative to labour, as with a capital-output ratio of 10, for example, then the profitability of this capital will be low. This will signal a reduction in the quantum of capital, supporting Solow (1956) and Swan (1956). The capital-output ratio will drop in this case from 10 to 5, thereby restoring equilibrium.

4.2.9 What About the Conundrum of the First Harrod-Domar Model Problem of Disequilibrium?

The conundrum that remains is of the ex-ante planned growth rate of output ($Y°w$) being in disequilibrium with the ex-poste observed growth rate of output ($Y°a$) because it is caused by a perverse relationship between the ex-ante planned savings share (Sw) and ex-poste observed investment share (Ia). If the ex-ante planned savings share (Sw) is high, giving a high ex-ante planned growth rate of output ($Y°w$), and the ex-poste observed investment share (Ia) is lower than the planned savings share (Sw), then the ex-poste observed growth rate of output ($Y°a$) will be lower than the planned growth rate of output ($Y°w$).

Here, factor price equalization will not help. This is because if the ex-ante planned savings share (Sw) is higher than the ex-poste observed investment share (Ia), then there will be excess capacity. The price signal will be for the ex-poste observed investment share (Ia) to drop further. This will lower the ex-poste observed growth rate of output ($Y°a$) further, making it lower than the ex-ante planned growth rate of output ($Y°w$).

The disequilibrium becomes perverse, that is, the economy cycles away from equilibrium.

4.2.10 Can We Live with Disequilibrium?

The discussion above leads Robinson (1962, 1967) to ask the fundamental question of whether the notion of equilibrium should be dispensed with, with the economy blundering from one point to another. This question needs to be put into the context of the objective of the enquiry, which is to derive a conceptual framework to analyse the determinants of output growth for their policy implications. If the model does not equilibrate, it can have far-reaching consequences for the economy and its people. One such model that failed to find equilibrium, with huge consequences for the economy and its people, is the Feldman (1928/1964) model, which was applied to the Soviet economy.

4.2.11 The Feldman Model Used for Planning in the Soviet Union

The Feldman (1928/1964) model and its several elaborations[1] on the theory of the rates of growth of national income is set out in a report to the Gosplan Committee in 1929. It was a major planning model on which the Soviet economy was based for a considerable period. The model is based on two sectors (Box 4.5): a consumption goods sector (C goods) and a capital goods sector (K goods). This implies that there are capital goods needed to produce consumption goods, given by K_c, and there are capital goods needed to produce capital goods, given by K_k.

---

[1] See, for example, Ghatak (2003) and Lochner (2008).

> **Box 4.5 The Feldman Model**
> Two sectors:
>
> - C goods
> - K goods
>   K goods needed to produce C goods: K_c
>   K goods needed to produce K goods: K_k
>   Theorem 1
>
> $$Y° = -fn\left(\frac{K_c}{K_K}\right) \qquad (4.40)$$
>
> i.e., as $K_k \uparrow$, $Y° \uparrow$
> Theorem 2
> For steady-state Y:
>
> $$\text{I proportion} = \frac{K_C}{K_K} \qquad (4.41)$$
>
> Now if:
>
> $$I_K = (\Delta K_K + \Delta K_C) \qquad (4.42)$$
>
> This also implies that
>
> $$I_K = \frac{\Delta K_K}{\Delta K_K + \Delta K_C} + \frac{\Delta K_C}{\Delta K_K + \Delta K_C} \qquad (4.43)$$

The model can be set out in two theorems without going into the proofs.

The first theorem is as follows. The growth rate of output ($Y°$) is a negative function of the ratio of K goods needed to produce C goods (K_c) to K goods needed to produce K goods (K_k). This becomes K_c/K_k, as in Eq. (4.40) in Box 4.5. This inverse relationship can also be seen in Fig. 4.2, reproduced here. As the ratio of K goods needed to produce C goods (K_c) to K goods needed to produce K goods (K_c/K_k) goes down, the growth rate of output ($Y°$) rises.

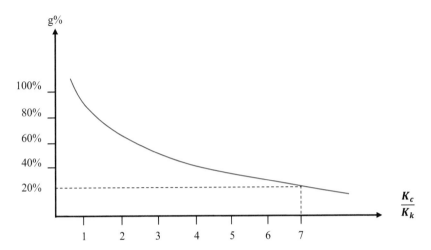

Fig. 4.2 The Feldman model

This is the theorem that gives primacy in policy to the K goods sector over the C goods sector in the early Soviet economy. The argument entailed is that K goods that produce K goods (K_k) give a higher growth rate of output ($Y°$). Hence, the ratio of K goods that produce K goods (K_k) will go up, as will the ratio of K goods to C goods. The ratio of K goods that produce C goods will go down, as will the ratio of C goods to K goods.

This tongue-twisting logic is a grave one, associated with the early Soviet economy, which so prioritized K goods over C goods. The imbalance between K goods and C goods is a first weakness in the model and the economy, by now well highlighted. Of more concern here for modelling is that this theorem gives disequilibrium. If the growth rate of output is to be maximized ($Y°$), then the ratio of K goods that produce K goods (K_k) to K goods that produce C goods (K_k/K_c) can rise without any bounds. This gives a corner solution in Fig. 4.2 towards the origin of the axis, rather than a median solution.

The reason for the Feldman (1928/1964) model to cycle towards a corner solution—of a continually increasing ratio of K goods to produce K goods (K_k) to K goods to produce C goods (K_c), which is K_k/K_c—is that there is no equilibrating variable to constrain this ratio. This lack of an equilibrating equation in the Feldman model as well as the Harrod-Domar model leads to them cycling away from equilibrium and is prone to give corner solutions rather than median ones. It also points to the need for the fourth desirable property in models—the need for a mathematically equilibrating model.

The second theorem of the Feldman (1928/1964) model arguably reinforces the dis-equilibration of the model. It says that steady-state growth requires that investment (I) be allocated in proportion to the ratio of K goods needed to produce C goods (K_c) to K goods needed to produce K goods (K_k), given by K_c/K_k, as in Eq. (4.41) in Box 4.5.

The investment going into enhancing K goods (Ik) will be allocated between additions to K goods to produce K goods (ΔK_k) and additions to K goods to produce C goods (ΔK_c), as in Eq. (4.42). In terms of shares, this allocates the investment into enhancing K goods (Ik) between (a) additions to K goods to make K goods (ΔK_k), out of total additions to K goods [$\Delta K_k/(\Delta K_k + \Delta K_c)$] and (b) additions to K goods to make C goods, out of total additions to K goods [$\Delta K_k/(\Delta K_k + \Delta K_c)$], as given in Eq. (4.43).

The first theorem then says, as illustrated in Table 4.3, that growth of output ($Y°$) will go up as the ratio of K goods to produce K goods (K_k) to K goods to produce C goods (K_k/K_c) goes up. The table shows that as this ratio of K_k/K_c goes up from 0.1 to 1.0, the growth of output ($Y°$) goes up from 4 to 24 per cent.

The second theorem says that to maintain a steady state, the ratio of investment allocated to K goods to make K goods (K_k), out of total additions to K goods, given by $\Delta K_k/(\Delta K_k + \Delta K_c)$, must also go up. For growth of output ($Y°$) to go up from 16 to 24 per cent, this investment ratio for additions to K goods to make K goods, out of total additions to K goods, given by $\Delta K_k/(\Delta K_k + \Delta K_c)$, must now increase from a third share to a half. This gives a corner solution: of the ratio of K goods to make K goods (K_k) to K goods to make C goods (K_c), given by K_k/K_c, reaching 1.

Table 4.3 Harrod-Domar model corner solution

K_K/K_C	$Y°$ where $K/Y = 2.1$	$\dfrac{\Delta K_K}{\Delta K_C + \Delta K_K}$
0.106	4.6	0.096
0.2	8.1	0.167
0.5	16.2	0.333
1.0	24.3	0.500

There is clearly no equilibrating variable in the Feldman (1928/1964) model to constrain the maximization of growth of output (Y^o) by increasing the ratio of K goods to make K goods (K_k) to K goods to make C goods (K_c), given by K_k/K_c, and by correspondingly increasing the investment allocation share for additions to K goods to make K goods out of total additions to K goods, $\Delta K_k/(\Delta K_k + \Delta K_c)$. This explains the need for a mathematically equilibrating model.

4.3 The Fourth Property: The Need for a Mathematically Equilibrating Model

The fourth useful property for a model of growth of output is the need for the model to be mathematically equilibrating. This need, and its solution, now requires some simple modelling. The need is illustrated by an income distribution model borrowed from the Lahore School of Economics Modelling Lab (Mahmood et al., 2024). The solution is a Keynesian model of growth. This Keynesian model now satisfies all four properties needed in growth models: (a) it is a general equilibrium model, (b) it is internally consistent theoretically and mathematically, (c) it provides an equilibrium solution that is not a corner one, and (d) which is only enabled precisely because it is a mathematically equilibrating model.

The essential concept of this Keynesian model, set out in Book II of the *General Theory of Employment, Interest and Money*, is that investment (I) cannot be considered independently of consumption (C). The sole objective of human activity is taken to be consumption (C), so that aggregate demand for output (Y) is a function of present consumption (C) and present provision for future consumption, which is investment (I). Thereby hangs the Keynesian model.

This can be set out beginning with an income distribution model given in Box 4.6. Assuming a closed economy and no government expenditures, output (Y) will be a function of consumption (C) and investment (I), as in Eq. (4.44). Consumption (C) can be taken as a function of the wage bill (W), as in Eq. (4.45), while investment (I) can be taken as a function of profits (Π), as in Eq. (4.46). Output (Y) can also be decomposed into a functional distribution of income, comprising the wage bill (W) plus profits (Π), as in Eq. (4.47). This functional distribution can be parked for the moment till needed.

Box 4.6 The Lahore School of Economics Modelling Lab's Income Distribution Model

$$Y = C + I \tag{4.44}$$

$$C = \text{fn}(W) \tag{4.45}$$

$$I = \text{fn}(\pi) \tag{4.46}$$

$$Y = W + \pi \tag{4.47}$$

Assumptions: $S = I$

$$\text{Then } Y = C + S \tag{4.48}$$

$$\therefore S = Y - C \tag{4.49}$$

$$\text{or } C = Y - S \tag{4.50}$$

Ergo, C and S are trade-offs.
This highlights the need for a mathematically equilibrating model.
Recalling Harrod-Domar's growth model:

$$Y^\circ = \frac{S}{K/Y} \tag{4.51}$$

To maximize Y0, $S\uparrow$
With no equilibrium till:

$$\frac{S}{Y} = 1 \tag{4.52}$$

This is an extreme corner solution because there is no equilibrating variable in the Harrod-Domar growth model in (4.51).
Putting in an equilibrating variable in the distributions model
Assume in Eqs. (4.44), (4.45), (4.46), and (4.47) that (4.45) does not hold, which gives primacy to (4.53)

$$I = \text{fn}(\pi) \tag{4.53}$$

(continued)

> **Box 4.6** (continued)
> So, as $\pi\uparrow$, $I\uparrow$
> With no equilibrium in the model given by (4.54)
>
> $$Y = W + \pi \qquad (4.54)$$
> $$\text{Till } \pi = Y \qquad (4.55)$$
>
> This is a corner solution again like (4.52)
> Now, putting in an equilibrating function by restoring Eq. (4.56)
>
> $$C = \text{fn}(W) \qquad (4.56)$$
>
> Where in a closed-loop model of
>
> $$Y = (\pi) + (W) \qquad (4.57)$$
>
> Now, in general equilibrium given by (4.58)
>
> $$Y = C + I \qquad (4.58)$$
>
> $\therefore$ if $I\uparrow$, $\pi\uparrow$
> But from (4.57), $W\downarrow$
> From (4.56), if $W\downarrow$, $C\downarrow$
> $\therefore$ in general equilibrium in (4.58)
> If $I\uparrow$ but $C\downarrow$, $\bar{Y}$
> Conclusion: I and C equilibrate each other
> I and C are trade-offs

Assuming that savings (S) are equal to investment (I) allows a substitution in Eq. (4.44), making output (Y) now a function of consumption (C) plus savings (S), as in Eq. (4.48). Output (Y) is either consumed (C) or saved (S). This makes savings (S) equal to output (Y) minus consumption (C), as in Eq. (4.49) or consumption (C) equal to output (Y) minus savings (S), as in Eq. (4.50). Therefore, consumption (C) and savings (S) are clear trade-offs. Present consumption (C) is at the expense of savings (S)

and savings (S) are at the expense of consumption (C). This is the main implication of the Keynesian argument, that the fundamental human objective is present consumption (C) or deferring this consumption through savings (S) for investment (I).

4.3.1 Consumption and Savings as Trade-Offs and the Need for a Mathematically Equilibrating Model

Recalling the Harrod-Domar model's growth equation in Box 4.6, growth of output ($Y°$) is a positive function of the savings share (S) divided by the capital-output ratio (K/Y). Assuming the fiction that the savings share (S) is equal to the investment share (I), as the savings share (S) goes up, growth of output ($Y°$) goes up. To maximise growth of output ($Y°$), the savings share (S) must be maximized, which implies that there will be no equilibrium until the savings share (S) has consumed all output, as in Eq. (4.52).

This is paralleled in the Feldman (1928/1964) model, where K goods can exhaust all output, driving out C goods. This is an extreme, corner solution, but is so because there is no equilibrating variable in the Harrod-Domar growth model in Eq. (4.51). It is the savings share in the Harrod-Domar model that needs an equilibrating variable, given by the Keynesian posit of a consumption share.

The extreme corner solution in the Harrod-Domar model results from the savings share (S) spiralling to 1 because it has no equilibrating variable. This equilibrating variable is provided by consumption (C) precisely because consumption (C) and savings (S) are seen above to be trade-offs. This is the major implication of the Keynesian posit of the fundamental human objective being present consumption (C) or deferred consumption (S).

Test-driving this equilibrating model of a savings share trading off against a consumption share is the distribution model borrowed from the Lahore School of Economics' Modelling Lab above. Box 4.6 begins by assuming no equilibrating consumption variable, which knocks out the consumption Eq. (4.45) from the model, leaving a system of three equations. Equation (4.44) gives general equilibrium in two markets, for goods and money, where output (Y) is a function of consumption (C) and investment (I). Equation (4.46) determines investment (I) as a positive function of profits (Π). Equation (4.47) gives the functional distribution of income, with output (Y) comprising the wage bill (W) and profits (Π).

In this non-equilibrating model, the determinant of output (Y) is only investment (I) in Eq. (4.44). Investment (I) is driven up by profits (Π) in Eq. (4.46). Thus, investment (I) and profits (Π) will increase together. Increasing profits (Π) in Eq. (4.47) will not give equilibrium until profits (Π) exhaust all output (Y), as in Eq. (4.55), which is an extreme corner solution, like the Harrod-Domar case given by Eq. (4.52) above. We put in an equilibrating consumption (C) variable to trade off against investment (I) to avoid a corner solution. This equilibration is provided by Eq. (4.45), which determines consumption (C) as a positive function of the wage bill (W).

In this system of four equations, general equilibrium continues to be given by the drivers of consumption (C) and investment (I), with consumption (C) determined by the wage bill (W) and investment (I) determined by profits (Π). Repeating the non-equilibrating first simulation as above, investment (I) and profits (Π) increase together. This should increase Y in the general equilibrium Eq. (4.58). However, from the functional distribution of income Eq. (4.57), as profits increase, the wage bill (W) will drop. Wages now determine consumption (C) in Eq. (4.56), driving down consumption (C).

Back in general equilibrium, while investment (I) will increase, consumption (C) will decrease. Therefore, output (Y) may not increase. Ergo, output (Y) cannot be driven just by increasing investment (I) alone because that will be based on increasing profits (Π) and driving down the wage bill (W). This will in turn reduce consumption (C). Thus, an extreme corner solution is avoided by positing two equilibrating variables—of consumption (C) and investment (I) as the drivers of output (Y).

Consumption (C) and investment (I) equilibrate each other by being trade-offs. This equilibrating simulation has been labelled somewhat whimsically at the Lahore School of Economics' Modelling Lab as 'Frankenstein' because it involved putting a smaller distribution model, as given in reduced form here as Eq. (4.57), into a bigger general equilibrium model, as given in reduced form here as Eq. (4.58) (Mahmood et al., 2024). Keynes's (1936) model offers this trade-off between consumption (C) and investment (I).

4.3.2 The Keynesian Model of Growth

Continuing the convenient fiction that savings (S) are equal to investment (I) and harking back to Box 4.6, output (Y) comprises consumption (C)

and savings (*S*), as in Eq. (4.48). This makes consumption (*C*) and savings (*S*) trade-offs mathematically, as Eqs. (4.49) and (4.50) show. If savings (*S*) are equal to investment (*I*), that makes consumption (*C*) and investment (*I*) trade-offs mathematically. It is this trade-off between consumption (*C*) and investment (*I*) that is offered behaviourally in Keynes's (1936) model of growth.

Sequentially, the Harrod-Domar model is meant to be an extension of Keynes's economics to the long run, bringing in the supply side of capital through savings (*S*) and the capital-output ratio (*K/Y*) to Keynes's theory of aggregate demand for output (ΣY). The Harrod-Domar model is thus based on thrift (Boianovsky, 2015) and obviously so. As elaborated ad nauseum above and illustrated by Fig. 4.3, savings (*S*) equal to investment (*I*), divided by the capital-output ratio (*K/Y*), gives a growth rate of output (*Y°*). Box 4.7 uses an example of a savings share (*S*) of 12 per cent, divided by a capital-output ratio (*K/Y*) of 3, giving a growth rate of output (*Y°*) of 4 per cent.

Increasing the savings share (*S*) will increase the growth rate of output (*Y°*). Therefore, the growth of output (*Y°*) will be maximized by increasing the savings share (*S*) to exhaust all output (*Y*). This gives the now-familiar corner solution, akin to the Feldman model (1928/1964) because there is

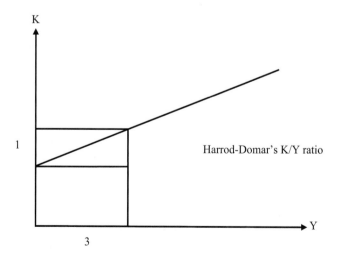

Fig. 4.3 The Harrod Domar model's *K/Y* ratio

4 THE THIRD AND FOURTH PROPERTIES OF GROWTH MODELS: THE NEED... 91

> **Box 4.7 Harrod-Domar Versus Keynes**
> Assumption: $S = I$
>
> $$Y^\circ = \frac{S}{K/Y} \quad (4.59)$$
>
> e.g., $S = 12\%$
>
> $$K/Y = 3$$
> $$\therefore Y^\circ = \frac{12}{3} = 4\%$$
>
> Corner solutions:
>
> $$Y^\circ \text{ max if } S = Y \quad (4.60)$$
>
> Keynes:
>
> $$Y = C + S \quad (4.61)$$
> $$\text{Where } Y = +\text{fn}(C) \quad (4.62)$$
> $$\text{But } Y = -\text{fn}(S) \quad (4.63)$$
>
> Because of the paradox of thrift, which is essentially
>
> $$C = Y - S \quad (4.64)$$
>
> $\therefore$ as $S\uparrow C\downarrow$

no equilibrating variable to bound savings (S) to give a median solution. Thus, the major driver of growth of output (Y°) in the Harrod-Domar model is the savings share (S). There is no equilibrating variable to the savings share (S), thus yielding a corner solution to the Harrod-Domar model.

The Keynesian model disagrees fundamentally with the Harrod-Domar model on both counts. First, savings (S) is not the major driver of growth of output (Y°) in the Keynesian model—consumption (C) is. Second, consumption (C) is the equilibrating variable in the Keynesian model because it trades off with investment, thus avoiding a corner solution. While the Keynesian model may be prior to the Harrod-Domar model, the former avoids a corner solution with a mathematically equilibrating solution based on a trade-off between consumption (C) and investment (I).

4.3.3 The Fundamental Disagreement Between the Keynesian and Harrod-Domar Models on the Role of Savings

Harking back to Keynes's (1936) proposition that the fundamental objective of human activity is present consumption (C) or present provision of future consumption (S), he posits that output (Y) comprises consumption (C) and savings (S), as well established in Box 4.6, Eq. (4.48). For Keynes, aggregate demand for output (ΣY) is first based on consumption (C) but then not based on savings (S). For Keynes, savings depress current consumption (C) and therefore depress current aggregate demand for output (ΣY). Keynes posits two paradoxes to argue this, as explained below.

Bernard Mandeville's 'Fable of the Bees' is an allegorical poem in which is set forth the appalling plight of a prosperous community in which all the citizens take it into their heads to abandon luxurious living and for the state to cut down on armaments in the interest of saving (Keynes, 1936). The paradox of thrift makes this argument explicit, where in Box 4.7, output (Y) is equal to consumption (C) plus savings (S), in Eq. (4.61). This makes consumption (C) a positive function of output (Y), as in Eq. (4.62). However, output (Y) becomes a negative function of savings (S) in Eq. (4.63). The argument is that from Eq. (4.61): consumption (C) is equal to output (Y) minus savings (S), as in Eq. (4.64). Consumption (C) and savings (S) are trade-offs. As savings (S) go up, consumption (C) falls. Therefore, savings (S) depress output (Y).

There is a related parable in Keynes (1936) whereby thrift in an economy based on producing bananas will only lead to rotten bananas, heavy business losses, large unpaid loans and destroyed wealth. Keynes's behavioural argument elaborates thus: savings (S) depress current consumption (C) and therefore depress current aggregate demand for output (ΣY). He uses the example that not having dinner today will not determine having this dinner a year from now or buying boots a year from now. It depresses making dinner today and does not help making dinner a year from now.

Savings (S) should therefore not be seen conceptually as a substitution of current consumption (C) for future consumption. Savings (S) depress current consumption (C) demand. Since future consumption demand is based on current consumption demand (C), savings can depress future consumption demand.

This Keynesian conceptual framework gives two clear postulates. First, consumption C and savings (S) are not complements as in the accounting identity given by Eq. (4.61) in Box 4.7, equalling output (Y). They trade off, with savings (S) depressing consumption (C). Second, as savings (S) increase, they depress consumption (C) and therefore depress output (Y). Ergo, thrift is a 'good' for the Harrod-Domar model but a 'bad' for the Keynesian model. Savings (S) raise output growth ($Y°$) in the Harrod-Domar model but lower output (Y) in the Keynesian model. The Keynesian model thus stands the Harrod-Domar model on its analytical head, doing so through the Kahn multiplier (k).

4.3.4 The Kahn-Keynes Multiplier

In the Harrod-Domar model, the capital-output ratio (K/Y) determines the impact of capital (K) or investment (I) on output (Y). Keynes (1936) too needs to determine the impact of investment (I) on output (Y). We use the two Keynesian postulates given in Box 4.8: (a) consumption (C) and savings (S) are trade-offs, and (b) as savings (S) rise, consumption (C) falls and therefore output (Y) falls. Using investment (I) for savings (S) makes consumption (C) and investment (I) trade-offs. Consumption (C) and investment (I) can be used to equilibrate each other mathematically to give an equilibrium solution for the model, which is not a corner one.

This equilibration is enabled by the Kahn-Keynes multiplier denoted by k. The Kahn-Keynes multiplier (k) gives the impact of investment (I) on output (Y). In Box 4.8, Eq. (4.65) says that output (Y) will be determined by investment (I) times the Kahn-Keynes multiplier (k). The Kahn-Keynes multiplier (k) will be given by the inverse of the marginal propensity to save (MPS), as in Eq. (4.67), or by the inverse of 1 minus the marginal propensity to consume (MPC), as in Eq. (4.66). The MPC plus the MPS must sum up to 1, as in Eq. (4.68).

Box 4.8 gives an example of the working of the Kahn-Keynes multiplier (k). Assuming that the MPC is 0.8 gives an MPS of 0.2. The inverse of the MPS gives a multiplier (k) value of 5. From Eq. (4.65), the impact on

> **Box 4.8 The Kahn-Keynes Multiplier**
> We need to determine the impact of I on Y.
> Postulate 1: C and S are trade-offs
> Postulate 2: ∴ if $S\uparrow - C\downarrow\ Y\downarrow$
> Using I for S
> ∴ C and I are trade-offs
> ∴ C and I equilibrate each other mathematically to give an equilibrium solution that is not a corner one.
> Kahn-Keynes multiplier: k
>
> $$Y = I^* k \qquad (4.65)$$
>
> $$k = \frac{1}{1 - \text{mpc}} \qquad (4.66)$$
>
> $$\text{Or } k = \frac{1}{\text{mps}} \qquad (4.67)$$
>
> Where $\text{mpc} + \text{mps} = 1 \qquad (4.68)$
>
> e.g., If mps = 0.2
> mpc = 0.8
> ∴ $k = \dfrac{1}{1-0.8} = \dfrac{1}{0.2} = 5$
>
> $$\therefore k = -\text{fn}(\text{mps}) \qquad (4.69)$$
>
> $$\therefore k = +\text{fn}(\text{mpc}) \qquad (4.70)$$
>
> The full mum equation of the Keynesian model:
>
> $$Y = C + I + G + X - M \qquad (4.71)$$

output (Y) of any level of investment (I) will be multiplied by the Kahn-Keynes multiplier value of 5.

Since the MPS is in the denominator of the Kahn-Keynes multiplier (k), savings (S), through the MPS, will reduce the value of this multiplier (k), while consumption (C), through the MPC, will raise the value of k. Ergo, the impact on output (Y) for any given level of investment (I) will decrease

4 THE THIRD AND FOURTH PROPERTIES OF GROWTH MODELS: THE NEED...

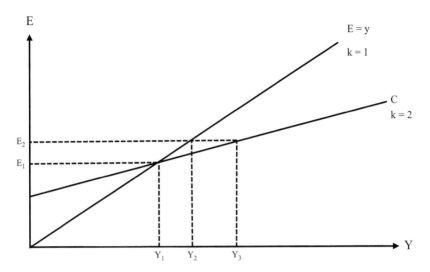

Fig. 4.4 The Keynesian multiplier

if the MPS increases because of the lowered value of the multiplier (k). Alternatively, the impact on output (Y), for the same level of investment (I), will increase if the MPC increases because of the raised value of the multiplier (k).

In Fig. 4.4, the same level of investment (I) increase from E1 to E2, with a smaller multiplier (k) with a value of 1, gives a smaller increase in output from y1 to y2. The same level of investment increase from E1 to E2, but with a higher value of the multiplier of 2, expands output by more—from y1 to y3.

The equilibration in the Keynesian model is provided by the trade-off between consumption (C) and investment (I). Let us assume that the MPS increases, driving down the MPC. As the MPS increases, this will drive up investment (I), leading to an increase in output (Y), which is investment-driven. However, there are two terms determining output (Y) in Eq. (4.65): (a) investment (I) and (b) the Kahn-Keynes multiplier (k). As the MPC falls and the MPS rises, this will reduce the value of the multiplier (k). Consequently, the impact on output (Y) of the increased investment, through the increased MPS, will be reduced by the impact on output (Y) of the value of the multiplier (k) precisely because of the increased MPS and reduced MPC. The equilibration of the Keynesian model to give a solution that is non-corner is provided by the two variables—consumption (C) and investment (I)—being trade-offs.

4.3.5 A General Equilibrium Keynesian Model with Investment-Led Regimes and Consumption-Led Regimes

The conceptual trade-off between investment and consumption in the Keynesian model through the Kahn-Keynes multiplier gives an interesting possibility of characterizing growth in output over time. Output growth can be characterized as investment-driven or consumption-driven.

The full mum equation of the Keynesian general equilibrium model, given as Eq. (4.71) in Box 4.8, makes output (Y) a function of consumption (C), investment (I), government expenditure (G) and net exports ($X - M$). The trade-off between consumption (C) and investment (I) then allows the characterization of output growth to be either investment-driven by I or consumption-driven by C. This can also work in combination with the other drivers of output growth, government expenditure and net exports.

The Keynesian model thus meets the four mathematical properties considered useful for growth models as set out here:

- It is a general equilibrium model, based on equilibrium in multiple key markets.
- It is not tainted by the internal consistency problem that dogs the neoclassical Samuelson-Swan-Solow production function.
- It gives a solution that avoids corner ones, unlike the Harrod-Domar model …
- … because it has a mathematically equilibrating set of variables in the trade-off between consumption (C) and investment (I).

References

Arrow, K. J. (1962). The economic implications of learning by doing. *The Review of Economic Studies, 29*(3), 155–173.

Boianovsky, M. (2015). *Modeling economic growth: Domar on moving equilibrium.* Centre for the History of Political Economy.

Cohen, A. J., & Harcourt, G. C. (2003). Retrospectives: Whatever happened to the Cambridge capital theory controversies? *Journal of Economic Perspectives, 17*(1), 199–214.

Debreu, G. (1970). Economies with a finite set of equilibria. *Econometrica, 38*(3), 387–392.

Debreu, G. (1975). Four aspects of the mathematical theory of economic equilibrium. In *Proceedings of the international congress of mathematicians* (Vol. 1, pp. 65–77). Canadian Mathematical Congress.

Eltis, W. (2018). Harrod-Domar growth model. In *The new Palgrave dictionary of economics* (pp. 5650–5654). Palgrave Macmillan.

Feldman, G. A. (1964). On the theory of the rates of growth of national income. In N. Spulber (Ed.), *Foundations of soviet strategy for economic growth*. Indiana University Press. (Original work published 1928).

Ghatak, S. (2003). *Introduction to development economics*. Routledge.

Hahn, F. H., & Matthews, R. C. O. (1964). The theory of economic growth: A survey. *The Economic Journal, 74*(296), 779–902.

Keynes, J. M. (1936). *The general theory of employment, interest, and money*. Macmillan Cambridge University Press, for Royal Economic Society.

Lochner, L. (2008). Intergenerational transmission. In L. Blume & S. Durlauf (Eds.), *New Palgrave dictionary of economics*. Palgrave Macmillan.

Mahmood, M., Chaudhry, A. A., Sajid, S., & Fatima, A. N. (2024). *State of the Pakistan economy, FY 2023–2024*. Lahore School of Economics.

Pigou, A. C. (1937). Real and money wage rates in relation to unemployment. *The Economic Journal, 47*(187), 405–422.

Robinson, J. (1953). The production function and the theory of capital. *The Review of Economic Studies, 21*(2), 81–106.

Robinson, J. (1962). *Essays in the theory of economic growth*. Springer.

Robinson, J. (1967). Growth and the theory of distribution. *Annals of Public and Cooperative Economics, 38*(1), 3–7.

Solow, R. M. (1956). A contribution to the theory of economic growth. *The Quarterly Journal of Economics, 70*(1), 65–94.

Swan, T. W. (1956). Economic growth and capital accumulation. *Economic Record, 32*(2), 334–361.

CHAPTER 5

The Keynesian Mum Equation

5.1 THE KEYNESIAN MUM EQUATION

The Keynesian model is a model learnt quite literally at my mother's knee as an A-level student—hence the pardonable euphemism of the Keynesian 'mum' equation for the work-horse model:

Aggregate demand for output (ΣY) will comprise the macroeconomic identity of consumption (C), investment (I), government expenditure (G) and net exports ($X - M$), as given in Box 5.1.

This Keynesian mum equation and the Keynesian cross diagram seen in Essay 3, Fig. 4.4, were senior-school reading in Samuelson's (1948) textbook. As Krugman (2018) argues in his preface to the 2018 edition of Keynes's *General Theory of Employment, Interest and Money*, the nifty 45° line may not have been in the book, but the multiplier equation is pristine present.

The significance of the Keynesian mum equation and the whole model it captures is that it explains the level of aggregate demand for output (ΣY), which is based on the four key variables: consumption (C), investment (I), government expenditure (G) and net exports ($X - M$). These represent, in the reduced form of the model, the goods market, the money market and the tradeables market, which is equal to the market for global capital flows. The raison d'etre of the model is to explain the level of employment (N), which is determined by the level of aggregate demand for output (ΣY).

The argument of the Keynesian model is that the level of aggregate demand for output (ΣY) need not be equal to that needed for full employment (Nf), requiring government intervention, through monetary policy, to raise the money supply, and through fiscal policy, to raise the level of consumption (C), investment (I) and direct government expenditure (G).

The notion of full employment (Nf) now becomes a critical heuristic device to explain not just the growth cycle of peaks and troughs in gross domestic product (GDP) over the short run of a year or two, but also long-run cycles of highs and lows in GDP. The Keynesian mum equation goes from being a macroeconomic identity to a behavioural equation explaining the highs and lows in GDP through the variables of consumption (C), investment (I), government expenditure (G) and net exports ($X - M$). This was the point of the model and its efficacy.

5.2 The Global Context of a Model of Aggregate Demand for Output

In a stylized view of the global economy, there have been six major crises in the last century: the Great Depression of the 1930s and 1940s, the Latin American crisis of the 1970s and 1980s, the Asian financial crisis of the late 1990s, the global financial crisis of 2008 stretching to 2016, and the Covid-19 pandemic of 2020 to 2022. The Japanese economy has been in a recession since the mid-1990s.

In the Great Depression, to explain falling output (Y), employment (N) and wages (W), Keynes revised his classically held model to that of the principle of aggregate demand for output (ΣY) to explain the observed falling output (Y), falling employment (N) and falling wages (W). Indeed, in a debate between Keynes and Pigou (Klein, 1947a, 1947b, 1955), the latter's classical model of a cut in the money wage (W) restoring full employment (Nf) became inconsistent. Pigou's quote was: how could labour seek employment if it were demanding a king's ransom in its wages? But the observed fall in the money wage (W) did not manage to restore full employment in the Great Depression. To the contrary, Keynes's (1936) model was to show that a cut in the money wage, even if accepted by labour, would only serve to reduce aggregate demand for output (ΣY), which in turn would reduce employment (N).

> **Box 5.1 The Keynesian Mum Equation**
>
> $$Y = C + I + G + X - M \qquad (5.1)$$
>
> $$C = fn(Y - T) \qquad (5.2)$$
>
> $$I = fn(Y, r) \qquad (5.3)$$
>
> $$G = fn(T + D) \qquad (5.4)$$

The major theoretical and policy battle for aggregate demand for output (ΣY) was fought out in the US, where unemployment had doubled. President Roosevelt was urged by Keynes (1933) in an open letter in the *New York Times* to expand output (Y) to increase employment (N) through three determinants. The first was to increase consumption (C). The second was to increase investment (I) by reducing the interest rate (r). The third was to increase government expenditure (G) by raising the deficit by printing money. All this pretty much gives the Keynesian mum Eq. (5.1) in Box 5.1.

In retrospect, the stop-start policies of Roosevelt only revived aggregate demand for output (ΣY) by 1937, while it took the enhanced expenditure of the Second World War to pull the advanced economies out of the depression. Writing in the shadow of the Great Depression, Samuelson (1948) put the major problem of persistent unemployment at the forefront of his textbook, to be tackled by the Keynesian mum equation. Bowles and Carlin (2020) find the standard supply-demand analysis of price theory relegated to later in the text. The point is that this Keynesian model that guided the golden age of capitalism (Glyn et al., 1988) till the 1970s was not used for the next two crises—the Latin American crisis of the 1980s and 1990s, and the Asian financial crisis of the late 1990s.

In the Latin American crisis, in two large economies—Argentina and Chile—with rising unemployment and falling wages, rather than using counter-cyclical policies, cyclical austerity policies were followed, based on indigenous and multilateral advice (see, for example, Mahmood, 2001). In the Asian financial crisis, the collapse of pegged exchange rates in four major economies—Indonesia, Thailand, South Korea and Malaysia—led to a mushrooming of US dollar-denominated debt, bankrupting firms, raising unemployment and reducing wages. Again, the multilateral advice to these economies was to follow cyclical austerity policies, to run fiscal surpluses and not protect the money wage (Mahmood & Aryah, 2001).

Only in the last two crises—the global financial recession running from 2008 to 2016 and the Covid-19 pandemic running from 2020 to 2022—has the Keynesian model of aggregate demand for output (ΣY) been re-adopted. The global financial crisis was of course triggered by the collapse of securitized subprime mortgages, epitomized by collateralised debt obligations (CDOs) and higher powers of CDOs such as $CDO2$ and $CDO3$, primarily in the US but also in the European Union (EU). This raised the risk on banking asset portfolios, leading to a lending freeze.

The weakness underpinning this risky behaviour in selling NINJA mortgages to people with no incomes, no jobs and no assets, lay in the labour market, with a near-constant real wage in the US, certainly over near two decades (Mahmood, 2009). Given constant purchasing power, the market worked to increase consumption (C) by selling the largest ticket item on the menu—houses, followed by cars.

The demand side of this market model had to be ratcheted up to meet a large supply of investment that crowds into the US and the EU as flights to quality safe havens. However, examination of this market model for advanced economies and its empirical evidence belongs elsewhere. The point in this essay is not to establish conclusive causality for the global financial crisis, but instead to establish the counter-cyclical policy followed.

The International Labour Organization (ILO) (2009, 2010, 2011) among others observes that the global financial recession in 2008 saw a massive fiscal stimulus in the advanced economies and China primarily. This was followed by conventional monetary policy of lowering interest rates to the zero lower bound in the EU and US, further followed by unconventional monetary policy of taking interest rates to the negative territory of −0.7 percent in the EU. This was supported by quantitative easing in both the EU and the US, of buying bonds, beginning with mortgage-backed securities.

Ben Bernanke, chair of the Federal Reserve Bank in the US, honed his counter-cyclical policy response based on the Japanese struggle to raise aggregate demand and counter deflation since the 1990s. The Eurozone's president of the European Central Bank famously vowed monetary policy to do whatever it takes.

The Keynesian model of maintaining aggregate demand for output (ΣY) was also supplemented in the labour markets of advanced economies in the global financial recession through experimental wage subsidies for firms, known as Kuzarbeit in Germany and wage furloughs in the US. The ILO (2011) estimates that for the G20 countries, the impact of the fiscal stimulus on jobs saved or generated was approximately 21 million jobs.

The most notorious exception to these Keynesian counter-cyclical policies to maintain aggregate demand for output (ΣY) is perhaps Greece and to a lesser extent, Spain. Greece's revised national income accounts during the crisis revealed a far higher budget deficit than estimated earlier. Being in the Eurozone, it could not devalue its way out of the crisis by increasing exports, which would increase output (Y), thus shrinking the share of the deficit in a growing GDP. As a result, very harsh austerity policies were imposed on Greece by the European Central Bank to shrink government expenditure (G) by slashing public sector employment and wages. As a result, total employment (N) and the money wage (W) were eroded for the whole economy (ILO, 2010, 2011). The finance minister, Yanis Varoufakis, was eased out as a non-adult for not countenancing this cyclical austerity program.

The most recent global crisis to date, the Covid-19 pandemic, ranging from 2020 to 2022, too, elicited Keynesian counter-cyclical policies. The pandemic shuttered workplaces en masse, delivering a global supply shock in the advanced economies and emerging economies, China being the last emerging economy to come out of formal quarantine protocols in early 2023. Aggregate demand for output (ΣY) was maintained, primarily in the labour market, through wage subsidies and wage furloughs in the advanced economies. China, which followed stricter protocols of quarantining neighbourhoods for longer, also provided meals and groceries. The Keynesian model of aggregate demand for output (ΣY) has thus provided an incisive causality in establishing the determinants of this output and implied a clear genre of counter-cyclical policy over the past century.

This Keynesian model springs pristine from the *General Theory of Employment, Interest and Money*. There are two critical points that it establishes about the model: (a) it is a macro model, and (b) the Keynesian mum equation can be derived from it.

5.3 The Keynesian Macro Model

The concept of macro is introduced by Keynes in the *General Theory of Employment, Interest and Money*. In his preface to the French edition, Keynes (1936, 1942) spells out that the book is concerned with aggregates of variables across the economy. These are the aggregates of income (y), profits (Π), output (Υ), employment (N), investment (I), savings (S) and consumption (C).

These are not the income (y), profits (Π), output (Υ), employment (N), investment (I), savings (S) and consumption (C) of firms or households. These are the aggregates for the economy. Since the aggregates of these variables for the economy behave differently from the variables for firms and households, macro behaviour is clearly distinguished from micro behaviour. This is the origin of formal systematic macroeconomics as we know it.

5.4 The Derivation of the Keynesian Mum Equation, with Consumption and Investment as Substitutes

Keynes (1936) sets out his whole model of aggregate demand for output ($\sum \Upsilon$) in Book 1, Chapter 3, of the *General Theory of Employment, Interest and Money*. He bases this on eight propositions, expanded here for elucidation to 12 in Box 5.2. All the variables are macro aggregates for the economy.

- Proposition 1 states that income (y) is a positive function of employment (N), as given by Eq. (5.5).
- Proposition 2 states that the quantum of consumption (C) will be a function given by the marginal propensity to consume (MPC) out of income (y), as in Eq. (5.6).
- Proposition 3 says that the quantum of investment (I) will be a function given by the marginal propensity to invest (MPI) out of income (y), as in Eq. (5.7).
- Proposition 4 says that the quantum of aggregate demand for output ($\sum \Upsilon d$) will be equal to the quanta of consumption (C) and investment (I), as in Eq. (5.8). This constitutes the basic Keynesian mum equation.
- Keynes then proceeds to make consumption (C) and investment (I) substitutes. This is important for the concept of consumption-led regimes and investment-led regimes, as our conceptual framework uses ahead to give empirically observable drivers of growth. Keynes does this using employment (N), employment (N) and aggregate demand for output ($\sum \Upsilon d$) being the variables he wishes to explain.

5 THE KEYNESIAN MUM EQUATION   105

Box 5.2   Theoretical Propositions for Keynes's Model

$$\text{Prop.1}: y = fn(N) \tag{5.5}$$

$$\text{Prop.2}: C = MPC(Y) \tag{5.6}$$

$$\text{Prop.3}: I = MPI(Y) \tag{5.7}$$

$$\text{Prop.4}: \sum Y_D = fn(mpc)(Y) + fn(MPI)(Y) \tag{5.8}$$

$$\text{Prop.5}: N = fn\left(\sum Y_D\right) \tag{5.9}$$

$$\text{Prop.6}: \therefore N = fn(MPC)(Y) + fn(MPI)(Y) \tag{5.10}$$

$$\text{Prop.7}: \sum Y_{\sup} = Z \tag{5.11}$$

$$\text{Prop.8}: \text{Revenue} = mpc(Y) \tag{5.12}$$

$$\text{Prop.9}: \pi = Z - mpc(Y) \tag{5.13}$$

$$\text{Prop.10}: \text{If } C = a + c(Y) \tag{5.14}$$

$$\text{Then } c' = \frac{dC}{dy} > 0 \tag{5.15}$$

$$\text{But } c'' = \frac{d_2 C}{d_Y 2} < 0 \tag{5.16}$$

$$\text{Prop.11}: \text{if } Z = a + z(y) \tag{5.17}$$

$$\text{Then } z' = \frac{dZ}{dy} \tag{5.18}$$

$$\text{Then } z' = \frac{dZ}{dy} > c' = \frac{dC}{dy} \tag{5.19}$$

Prop. 12: ∴ N will be constrained to reach N_F by ΔMPC, unless ΔMPI can supplement it

Ergo: as a general case, there will be unemployment U

- Proposition 5 then makes employment (N) a positive function of the quantum of aggregate demand for output ($\sum Yd$), as in Eq. (5.9). In current modelling terms, this proposition can be seen as the theory underlying Okun's law, which empirically derives employment (N), whereby employment (N) moves with income (y) or output (Y).
- Propositions 4 and 5 in turn give Proposition 6, which makes employment (N) a function of the quanta of consumption (C) and investment (I), where consumption (C) is determined by the MPC out of income (y) and investment (I) is determined by the MPI out of income (y).
- Keynes (1936) proceeds to show that MPC (out of income y) and MPI (out of income y) are substitutes. He bases this on a psychological law that the MPC is a positive but decreasing function of income (y). Proceeding stepwise, in Proposition 7, Keynes brings in aggregate supply of output ($\sum Y\text{sup}$) with a quantum value equal to Z, as in Eq. (5.11). This quantum value of aggregate supply ($\sum Y\text{sup}$) can be considered the cost of production of aggregate output.
- Proposition 8 makes the revenue earned by selling aggregate output equal to the MPC (out of income y), which is the quantum of consumption (C) spent by consumers, as in Eq. (5.12).
- This makes profits (Π), in Proposition 9, equal to the cost of production, given by the quantum value of aggregate supply of output ($\sum Y\text{sup}$), which is Z minus the revenue earned by selling aggregate output, which is the quantum of consumption (C), given by MPC out of income y. This is given in Eq. (5.13).
- However, in Proposition 10, Keynes now crucially makes MPC out of income (y) a positive but decreasing function of income (y). Mathematically, this makes the first derivative of consumption (C), denoted by c' out of income (y), positive. It makes the second derivative of consumption (C), denoted by c'' out of income (y), negative, as given in Eqs. (5.14), (5.15), and (5.16).
- Proposition 11 then follows crucially. As employment (N) and output (Y) increase, aggregate supply of output ($\sum Y\text{sup}$) will also increase, that is, the value of the cost of output (Z) will increase. Since MPC is a positive but decreasing function of income (y), revenue from consumption (C) will not increase proportionately to the cost of output (Z). Therefore, there will be an increasing gap between the cost of output (Z) and revenue from consumption (C). This is given in Eqs. (5.17), (5.18), and (5.19).

This yields two possibilities for the economy to keep expanding employment (N) to reach full employment (Nf): (a) the MPC can increase, which Keynes considers unlikely; or (b) the MPI can increase to fill the gap between Z and C to reach full employment (Nf), which is what the classical model assumes. But Keynes considers this to be a special case. In general, aggregate supply and aggregate demand will intersect to produce less-than-full employment (Nf). Ergo, Keynes's model makes out consumption (C) and investment (I) to be substitutes. Aggregate demand for output (ΣY) can be consumption-driven by the MPC or investment-driven by the MPS feeding the MPI because aggregate demand for output (ΣY) is determined in the Keynesian model by investment (I) times the Kahn-Keynes multiplier (k), as elaborated above.

The Kahn-Keynes multiplier (k) itself is given by the term $1/1 - \text{MPC}$ or $1/\text{MPS}$, where MPC plus MPS sum to 1. Then, the value of the multiplier (k) is driven up by the MPC but driven down by the MPS. However, if the value of the Kahn-Keynes multiplier (k) is driven up by a high MPC, the MPS falls, which drives down investment (I). This growth path can be defined as consumption-driven. Alternatively, if the value of the Kahn-Keynes multiplier (k) is driven down by a low MPC, the MPS rises, which drives up investment (I). This growth path can be defined as investment-driven. This meets our modelling needs perfectly.

5.5   Completing the Full Keynesian Mum Equation

Propositions 1 to 11 give the basic Keynesian mum equation, derived as Eq. (5.8) in Box 5.2, where aggregate demand for output (ΣYd) is determined by consumption (C) and investment (I). To this, two more variables need to be added: government expenditure (G) and net exports ($X - M$).

5.5.1   Government Expenditure

The variable of government expenditure (G) enters the *General Theory of Employment, Interest and Money* in Chapter 24, where Keynes (1936) reiterates the role of the state in maintaining full employment (Nf). The principal determinant of aggregate demand for output (ΣY) for full employment (Nf) being the MPC, this must be nudged up. For this, the primary policy instrument must be the rate of taxation, making consumption (C) a function of disposable income, given by income (y) minus taxation (T), as in Eq. (5.2) in Box 5.1 above.

Keynes (1936) also considers the role of investment in raising aggregate demand for output (ΣY) to generate full employment (Nf). He doubts that banking policy to lower the interest rate will be sufficient to raise investment to the desired optimum level needed for full employment (Nf). This makes investment (I) a function of income, as elaborated above, as well as the rate of interest, as in Eq. (5.3) in Box 5.1.

For Keynes (1936), what is needed is a comprehensive socialization of investment to obtain full employment (Nf). The state does not need to own the instruments of the means of production for this, but it does have to determine the aggregate amount of resources devoted to augmenting these instruments of the means of production. This clearly implies that private investment (I) needs to be supplemented by government investment (G).

There is thus no need for capital, says Keynes, to be scarce and earn high interest as rent when capital can be augmented as required, thus driving down the interest rate—and incidentally removing the justification for an inequitable distribution of wealth. This is the euthanasia of the rentier. Keynes's (1933) letter to President Roosevelt, cited earlier, to print money for shovel-ready projects then clarifies that government expenditure (G) becomes a function of taxation (T) and the budget deficit (D), as in Eq. (5.4) in Box 5.1.

5.5.2 Net Exports

The variables for net exports, exports minus imports ($X - M$), also come in at the end of the *General Theory of Employment, Interest and Money* in Chapter 24. The context is the international struggle for markets, which Keynes (1936) sees as driven by population pressure and the need to raise domestic employment. International trade is then merely a desperate expedient to maintain employment at home by forcing sales on foreign markets. This makes exports (X) additive to domestic output (Y) and employment (N), as in the Keynesian mum Eq. (5.1) in Box 5.1.

Keynes's (1936) argument continues thus. Restricting purchases, which if successful, will merely shift the problem of unemployment to the neighbour, which is worsted in the struggle. This determines that imports (M) are subtracted from domestic output (Y) and employment (N), as in the Keynesian mum Eq. (5.1) in Box 5.1.

To complete Keynes's argument on international trade, it is this drive to maintain employment at home that leads to beggar-thy-neighbour trade, based on market capture, and accounts for much of the nineteenth century's conflicts. Instead, if nations were to achieve full employment through their domestic policies, international trade could then be based on Ricardian relative advantage.

This completes the Keynesian mum equation, derived from the *General Theory of Employment, Interest and Money*, inherited by students from Samuelson's textbook of 1948. This Keynesian model, derived in this first part of the book, is now used to explain long-run output growth in Pakistan.

REFERENCES

Bowles, S., & Carlin, W. (2020). What students learn in economics 101: Time for a change. *Journal of Economic Literature, 58*(1), 176–214.

Glyn, A., Hughes, A., Lipietz, A., & Singh, A. (1988). *The rise and fall of the golden age*. Working Paper No. 43. UNU-WIDER.

International Labour Organization. (2009). *Global employment trends 2009*. International Labour Office.

International Labour Organization. (2010). *Global employment trends 2010*. International Labour Office.

International Labour Organization. (2011). *Global employment trends 2011: The challenge of a jobs recovery*. International Labour Office.

Keynes, J. M. (1933, December 31). Open letter to President Roosevelt. *The New York Times*. https://www.nytimes.com/1933/12/31/archives/from-keynes-to-roosevelt-our-recovery-plan-assayed-the-british.html

Keynes, J. M. (1936). *The general theory of employment, interest and money*. Macmillan Cambridge University Press, for Royal Economic Society.

Keynes, J. M. (1942). *Théorie générale de l'emploi, de l'intérêt et de la monnaie* (J. de Largentaye, Trans.). Éditions Payot. Original work published 1936.

Klein, L. R. (1947a). *The Keynesian revolution*. Macmillan.

Klein, L. R. (1947b). Theories of effective demand and employment. *Journal of Political Economy, 55*, 108–131.

Klein, L. R. (1955). The empirical foundations of Keynesian economics. In K. K. Kurihara (Ed.), *Post-Keynesian economics* (pp. 277–319). Routledge.

Krugman, P. (2018). Introduction. In J. M. Keynes (Ed.), *The general theory of employment, interest and money*. Springer.

Mahmood, M. (2001). A comparative study of the Asian financial crisis and the Latin American crisis. *ILO Regional Office for Asia-Pacific*.

Mahmood, M. (2009). *Growth and jobs in the global financial crisis*. ILO Policy Integration Department.

Mahmood, M., & Aryah, G. (2001). The labour market and labour policy in a macroeconomic context: Growth, crisis and competitiveness in Thailand. In G. Betcherman & R. Islam (Eds.), *East Asian labour markets and the economic crisis: Impacts, responses and lessons* (pp. 245–292). World Bank and International Labour Office.

Samuelson, P. A. (1948). *Economics: An introductory analysis.* McGraw-Hill.

PART II

Explaining Long-Run GDP Growth for Pakistan

CHAPTER 6

Application of a Keynesian General Equilibrium Model to Analysing Growth of Output Over Time for Pakistan

This essay sets out to examine the pattern of Pakistan's gross domestic product (GDP) growth using a Keynesian general equilibrium model to analyse and explain the trajectory of GDP growth over the long run of the last 50 years. The model gives a very clear answer. Pre-1992, high GDP growth of 6 per cent on trend was driven significantly by investment. Post-1992, lower GDP growth of 4 per cent on trend was driven significantly by consumption.

This dichotomy between investment-driven growth and consumption-driven growth is explored further using the Kahn-Keynes multiplier. We see that high GDP growth pre-1992 is driven by high investment growth, paired with low consumption growth. Low GDP growth post-1992 is driven by low investment growth, paired with high consumption growth. This is a strong vindication of the use of the generic Keynesian general equilibrium model of aggregate demand and its more elaborate adaptations.

6.1 The Pattern of Long-Run GDP Growth in Pakistan

We begin by observing the long-run pattern of Pakistan's GDP growth. Figure 6.1 shows GDP growth for Pakistan—its long-run trend and short-run cyclicality from 1961 to 2017. Long-run GDP growth in Pakistan seems to have fallen in the past three decades. The earlier decades of the

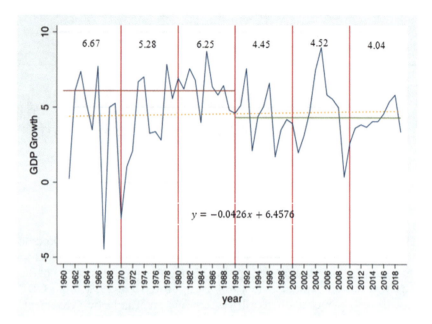

Fig. 6.1 GDP growth in Pakistan

1960s, 1970s and 1980s saw trend GDP growth of over 6 per cent per annum. From about 1990 onwards, however, trend growth is observed to have lowered significantly to just above 4 per cent per annum. This trend for Pakistan also runs contra the comparative trend in other developing countries, whose GDP growth rates have largely improved over time, as the International Monetary Fund (IMF) (2003) shows.

In addition to the concern of long-run trend growth, Fig. 6.1 shows short-run fluctuations, which may well be increasing in frequency, intensity and duration. If so, this cyclicality in short-run GDP growth may well be interacting with the longer-run trend in GDP growth, dragging it down.

Clearly, the pattern of Pakistan's GDP growth in Fig. 6.1 identifies two possible growth trajectories to study: high growth pre-1990s and low growth post-1990s. Our aim is to empirically identify and explain the two growth trajectories. Before we do so, we will review the explanation provided by the development and structural literature in this regard.

The development literature oscillates between the policy objectives of growth, distribution and human development, and the trade-offs between them. The pursuit of one objective by a policy regime has meant the neglect of others, followed by a dialectical reaction in pursuit of another objective by a successive policy regime. Therefore, the development debate has been caught up in this dialectic between policy objectives rather than a more detailed examination of the determinants of growth.

The later structural literature has a more general equilibrium conceptual framework. The key determinants to explain long-run growth of output are macro variables.

6.1.1 The Development Literature Explaining the Pattern of Long-Run GDP Growth

In the development literature, Husain's (2009, 2018) characterization of Pakistan's economic policy regimes can be used here to illustrate the dialectic between policy objectives. The 'Golden Sixties' from 1958 to 1969, under General Ayub Khan, pursued growth of GDP because allegedly there was no point in redistributing the abiding mass of poverty. The growth of output had to precede redistribution. An argument was made to foster functional inequality, directing more income towards the upper-income deciles whose higher savings rate compared to lower-income deciles was needed to increase investment and output growth. If there was a macro model for this policy regime, it was a two-gap model identifying a larger savings gap in the goods market and a smaller foreign exchange gap in the tradeables market, with both needed to enhance investment (Chenery & Strout, 1968; McKinnon, 1964).

GDP growth in the 1960s jumped to an average annual rate of 6 per cent from 3 per cent in the 1950s. The manufacturing sector expanded by 9 per cent. Agriculture grew at 4 per cent with the introduction of Green Revolution technology. Governance improved, with a major expansion in the government's capacity for policy analysis, design and implementation as well as a process of institution building. By 1969, Pakistan's manufacturing growth rate was higher than that of Thailand, Malaysia and Indonesia.

However, the economic policies that were meant to create development through a 'trickledown effect' led to increasing disparity in incomes across regions and provinces, with the creation and concentration of economic and monopoly powers in a few hands, the failure of real wages to increase for lower-income deciles, and a substantial increase in personal inequalities (Ahmed & Amjad, 1984; Amjad, 1982, 2014; Amjad & Mahmood, 1982; Husain, 2009; Zaidi, 2015). Despite the great achievement on the economic side, Mahbub ul Haq, the chief economist of the Planning Commission, raised serious concerns about growing social inequality in 1973.

The overwhelming policy reaction to the mono pursuit of the objective of growth of output and neglect of distribution and poverty led to the 'Socialist Seventies' as characterized by Husain (2009), from 1971 to

1977. Zulfikar Ali Bhutto's populist policies of nationalizing industries, banks and insurance companies, and of land reforms in agriculture, redistributed income significantly, but lowered GDP growth. The East Asian countries that were lagging behind Pakistan in growth in the late 1960s not only overtook it but also became the 'Asian tigers'. The oil price shock of the 1970s as well as droughts, floods and the withdrawal of external assistance did not help the situation either. GDP growth in the 1970s fell to 3.7 per cent per annum from 6 per cent in the 1960s.

The right-wing reaction to the policy objective of redistribution and slumping of growth led in turn to the policy regime characterized by Husain (2009) as the 'Revivalist Eighties', led by General Zia-ul-Haq, from 1977 to 1988. Redistribution policies ended. Religious fundamentalism allied Pakistan with the US-led war against Soviet Afghanistan, with huge and far-reaching economic and social blowback.

GDP grew at 6.6 per cent annually, with agriculture at 4 per cent and the manufacturing sector at 9 per cent. Fiscal deficits, however, widened to 8 per cent of GDP despite a decline in development expenditure. Domestic borrowing to finance these deficits did not weaken growth immediately but had serious repercussions for public finances and macroeconomic stability in the 1990s. Consequently, Pakistan had to approach the IMF for assistance in 1988.

The policy regime succeeding the revivalist 1980s has been characterized by Husain (2009) as the 'Muddling Nineties', from 1988 to 1999, as nine different governments (four interim-appointed, four elected and one following the military coup of October 1999) ruled Pakistan in this period. However, we would like to characterize this policy regime from a more economic point of view as the 'Liberalizing Nineties'.

There was persistence of fiscal deficits above 7 per cent of GDP and external deficits of 4–5 per cent of GDP. This led to the accumulation of large levels of domestic and external debt throughout the decade. Total external debt levels became unsustainable, rising from USD20 billion in 1990 to USD43 billion (47.6 per cent of GDP) in 1998, which implied repeated recourse to the IMF for assistance in meeting external payments. This assistance came with the conditionality of liberalization of the economic regulatory environment, but whose outcomes became difficult to sustain, sometimes having to be reversed temporarily.

The most far-reaching liberalization reforms were introduced in 1991 with the opening up of the capital account (Khan, 2009; Zaidi, 2015). Domestic foreign currency deposits were allowed, but then become unsustainable and had to be frozen. This led to a huge loss in domestic investor confidence. Tariff liberalization was led by a reduction in import tariffs, which led to a surge in imports against weak exports, not improving the already weak current account (Amjad, 2014). There was significant privatization of state-owned enterprises and opening up of newer sectors—such as energy—to the private sector.

Political instability coupled with this policy regime to reduce GDP growth to 4 per cent. While the agriculture sector recorded higher output, the growth of the manufacturing sector was low. The investment ratio fell to 13.9 per cent between 1998 and 1999 as foreign savings, which had formerly bridged the gap between national savings and investment, dried up in May 1998. Development expenditures took a major hit and GDP dropped to 3 per cent from 8 per cent in the first half of the 1990s. Social sector expenditures were squeezed to accommodate higher debt servicing and defence expenditures. The incidence of poverty nearly doubled from 18 to 34 per cent and the unemployment rate rose as well. Pakistan's social indicators lagged behind those of other countries in the region. The human development index of the United Nations Development Programme ranked Pakistan in one of its lowest development categories.

Husain (2009, 2018) characterizes the succeeding policy regime from 1999 to 2018 as the 'Reforming Hundreds'. We would like to qualify this as the 'Social Reforming Hundreds'. The reaction to rising poverty and weak social indicators has led to the prioritization of social policy over this last policy regime. The political regimes themselves have been mixed, with General Pervez Musharraf's regime from 1999 to 2007 and then civilian regimes from 2008 to 2019. The growth of GDP has been more volatile over this period: it began very low from 1999 to 2001 at 3 per cent per annum, peaked at 7 per cent during 2002–2007, and was then lowered by the global financial crisis of 2008–2013 to 2.5 per cent, with some recovery over 2014–2019 to 4 per cent.

The prioritization of social policies and welfare programs has resulted in a major reduction in the extreme poverty headcount from 31 per cent in 2000 to 4 per cent by 2018 (Mahmood & Tanvir, 2018). This has been a remarkable social outcome, unparalleled in the region. However, macroeconomic instability in the fundamentals of the economy has continued to dog this period, especially from the onset of the global financial crisis in 2008 (Amjad et al., 2011; Haque, 2011; Husain, 2009). Current account deficits have mounted. The exchange rate has depreciated as a consequence and budget deficits have mounted in turn. This has led to increasing recourse to the IMF's Extended Fund Facilities and Stand-By Arrangements. GDP growth has therefore fallen.

Our argument in analysing this development literature is that while each of these variables identified in different policy regimes as determining

GDP growth may be necessary, they are not sufficient by themselves to explain the lowered long-run trend. This is termed partial equilibrium analysis, based on examining one particular market. What is better is to examine all these variables put together in a conceptual framework called general equilibrium analysis, which looks at all the major markets—for goods, money, labour, tradeables, and global capital flows. The structural literature moves towards such a general equilibrium analysis slightly better.

6.1.2 The Structural Literature Explaining the Pattern of Long-Run GDP Growth

The structural literature on Pakistan's growth moves from partial equilibrium analysis based on one market to examining several markets. However, we find that there remain some gaps in moving towards general equilibrium analysis in all key markets.

For Pakistan, the review of the structural literature shows a large explanatory bias towards exogenous demand variables and monetary variables rather than domestic demand variables to explain long-run growth (Khan & Jawed, 2019; Mahmood & Arby, 2012; Shahbaz et al., 2008). The decomposition of domestic demand variables into consumption and investment is consistently missing in the literature except in studies by Choudhry and Pasha (2013) and Choudhry et al. (2017), but which then miss government expenditure.

The structural model has long antecedents in identifying constraining gaps on growth in Pakistan. Studies begin with simple two-gap models, with savings being shy of investment and foreign exchange gaps to import needed capital goods. These argue for foreign aid to gradually fill the smaller foreign exchange gap first and then the larger savings gap. More recent studies incorporate a third gap in the government's budget—running deficits between expenditures and revenues (Iqbal & Rehman, 1995; Iqbal et al., 2000).

These studies still miss key structural variables and do not provide a very comprehensive explanation for output growth. There is a paramount need therefore to examine the macro determinants of Pakistan's GDP growth in the longer run, over both the highs and lows, to see what has worked to raise it earlier and lower it more recently. Moreover, the frequency of Pakistan's recourse to IMF bailouts (23 and counting) has pushed the recent debate towards examining shorter-run cyclicality in GDP, putting on the back burner the earlier debate about the longer-run structural determinants of GDP growth.

The fundamental concern posed by observing the long-run trend in GDP growth and reviewing the literature is to determine what explains the discrete and significant drop in long-run GDP growth post-1990s. This essay seeks to explain the concern through the structural determinants of growth in a general equilibrium analysis. This proceeds sequentially by testing the three fundamental propositions concerning GDP growth.

6.2 A General Theoretical Framework to Analyse GDP Growth in Pakistan

We recall from the theoretical first part of the book, the Keynesian mum equation, as given in Box 6.1, where output (Y) is determined by consumption (C), investment (I), government expenditure (G) and exports (X) minus imports (M).

Box 6.1 The Keynesian Mum Equation Revisited

$$Y = C + I + G + X - M \qquad (6.1)$$

Where

$$C = \mathrm{mpc}(Y) \qquad (6.2)$$

And $I = \mathrm{mpi}(Y) \qquad (6.3)$

The Kahn-Keynes multiplier:

$$Y = I * k \qquad (6.4)$$

Where $k = \dfrac{1}{1-\mathrm{mpc}} \qquad (6.5)$

Giving

$$Y = I * \left(\dfrac{1}{1-\mathrm{mpc}}\right) \qquad (6.6)$$

Putting the Keynesian mum equation into growth terms gives

$$\dfrac{\Delta Y}{Y} = \dfrac{\Delta C}{C} + \dfrac{\Delta I}{I} + \dfrac{\Delta G}{G} + \dfrac{\Delta X}{X} - \dfrac{\Delta M}{M} \qquad (6.7)$$

6.2.1 Assessing the Impact of the Quantum of the Macro Aggregates on Output

The first relationship to be examined is given by the Keynesian mum Eq. (6.1) in Box 6.1. On the right-hand side of the equation are the quanta of private consumption (C), private investment (I), government expenditure (G), exports (X) and imports (M), which determine on the left-hand side, the quantum of output (Y). The more complex relationships lie on the right-hand side of the equation between the determining variables themselves. It is these interactions between the determining variables that give the final quantum on the right-hand side, determining on the left-hand side of the equation the quantum of output.

6.2.2 Examining the Relationship Between the Long-Run Structural Determinants Themselves: Consumption and Investment

The second relationship to be examined is between the right-hand-side determinants of private consumption (C) and private investment (I) in Eq. (6.1) in Box 6.1. These are the two structural determinants of output (Y) in that the literature considers them to be slow movers over time, relatively less policy-amenable in the short run, and therefore determinants of long-run output and its growth.

Recalling from the theoretical first part of the book, Keynes (1936) posits consumption (C) and investment (I) to be substitutes. This is done by making consumption (C) a function of the marginal propensity to consume (MPC) out of output (Y), as in Eq. (6.2), where output (Y) can be read as equal to income (y). Investment (I) is made a function of the marginal propensity to invest (MPI) out of output (Y), as in Eq. (6.3). Thus, consumption (C) and investment (I) compete for the same output (Y). This trade-off between consumption (C) and investment (I) is given through the quantitative relationship of the Kahn-Keynes multiplier, as discussed in the theoretical part of the book.

Keynes (1936) adds another macro relationship to explain output (Y) and its growth over time: ΔY. This is through consumption (C) and investment (I). Consumption (C) is used to make a specific determination of the Kahn-Keynes multiplier (k) such that investment (I) times the multiplier (k) gives output (Y), as in Eq. (6.4) in Box 6.1.

The Kahn-Keynes model uses the MPC to determine k such that the multiplier (k) is equal to 1 over 1 minus the MPC, as in Eq. (6.5). This makes output (Y), on the left-hand side of Eq. (6.6), determined by investment (I) times 1 over 1 minus the MPC.

Investment (I) determines output (Y) but is aided (multiplied) by the share of incremental income that is consumed, which is the MPC. For example, if all the output is saved rather than being consumed, the multiplier becomes just 1, implying that $1 of investment ($I$) will generate only $1 of output ($Y$). If half of output ($Y$) is consumed, giving an MPC of 0.5, the multiplier rises to 2, now implying that $1 of investment ($I$) will generate output ($Y$) of $2.

The Kahn-Keynes multiplier model thereby poses an interesting trade-off between consumption-driven growth and investment-driven growth, where investment (I) determines output (Y) but is constrained by consumption (C). Higher investment (I) will lead to higher output (Y) but this higher output (Y) will be constrained by lower consumption (C) through a lower multiplier (k). Consumption (C) and investment (I) are therefore trade-offs.

These two long-run structural determinants of output (Y), consumption (C) and investment (I) give three possible growth paths. Growth of output (ΔY) can be investment-led or consumption-led or balanced between these two drivers, consumption (C) and investment (I).

6.3 Theoretical Framework for This Essay

This essay focuses on explaining the observed drop in Pakistan's output growth between two periods: pre-1990 and post-1990. It does this by examining the impact on output (Y) of the macro aggregate determinants of output growth. Thus, we focus on examining the two relationships defined above by Eqs. (6.1), (6.2), (6.3), (6.4), (6.5), and (6.6).

The first relationship examined will assess the impact of the quantum of the macro aggregates on output (Y). On the right-hand side of Eq. (6.1), the quanta of private consumption (C), private investment (I), government expenditure (G), exports (X), and imports (M) will determine on the left-hand side of the equation the quantum of output (Y).

While Eq. (6.1) expresses the economic notion in terms of output and its macro aggregates at one point in time ($t0$), we want to distinguish between changes in output (ΔY) to compare it between two periods, $t0$ and $t1$. Therefore, we need to establish output growth, given by $\Delta Y/Y$, as determined by growth in the macro aggregates of consumption ($\Delta C/C$), investment ($\Delta I/I$), government expenditure ($\Delta G/G$), and exports ($\Delta X/X$) minus imports ($\Delta M/M$), as in Eq. (6.7) in Box 6.1. We can then examine the change in which the quantum of determinants on the right-hand side of Eq. (6.7) explains the higher output growth pre-1990 and lower output growth post-1990, on the left-hand side.

We also examine the relationship between the long-run structural determinants themselves: consumption (C) and investment (I) and their complex impact on output (Y). Thus, the second relationship is between the right-hand side of the equation's determinants of private consumption (C) and private investment (I) and their complex and joint determination of output (Y).

Equations (6.4), (6.5) and (6.6) in Box 6.1 develop this complex and joint determination by investment (I) and consumption (C) of output (Y). Equation (6.6) says that output (Y) on the left-hand side will be determined jointly through a complex interaction on the right-hand side between the quantum of investment (I) and the share of consumption (C) out of output (Y).

In sum, in this essay, our central problem is to explain the drop in output growth in Pakistan from 6 per cent per annum in the 1960s, 1970s and 1980s to 4 per cent from the 1990s onwards. To explain this drop in growth of output, this set of Eqs. (6.1), (6.2), (6.3), (6.4), (6.5), (6.6), and (6.7) can be run separately for each of the two periods, pre-1990s and post-1990s, showing the change in output over that period on the left-hand side of the equations, as determined by the change in the quantum of macro aggregates on the right-hand side, as in Eq. (6.7).

This theoretical framework adopted gives a set of propositions to be tested empirically.

6.4　Three Fundamental Propositions About GDP Growth in Pakistan

The first proposition is aimed at empirically identifying the year after which GDP growth in Pakistan can be observed to have lowered on trend. Therefore, the first proposition to test is:

Proposition 1: There has been a discrete reduction in GDP growth over the period 1973–2017.

Having empirically tested that there is a discrete and significant reduction in GDP growth, the next step will be to identify the timing of the discrete reduction. We refer to the discrete reduction in GDP growth at a particular time as a structural trend break in GDP growth. We then need to examine which of the structural determinants of growth explains the drop in GDP growth.

The adapted Keynesian general equilibrium model explains the change in GDP growth (on the left-hand side of the equation) through five sets of determinants (on the right-hand side). These are consumption (C), investment (I), government expenditure (G), exports (X), imports (M) and global capital flows (KA). Global capital flows (KA) are given by the current account (CA) being equal to the capital account (KA).

Particularly, we would like to test the proposition that high investment growth explains high GDP growth in the first phase of GDP growth, while a drop in investment growth explains the drop in GDP growth in the second phase. We test the following propositions:

Proposition 2a: There has been a significant drop in investment growth over the period 1973–2017.

Proposition 2b: Investment growth significantly explains high GDP growth in the first phase and a drop in investment growth explains the drop in GDP growth in the second phase.

Our Keynesian theoretical framework further drives GDP growth through two channels. One channel is through the quantum of investment, but the impact of investment on GDP growth is determined through a second channel. The extent of the impact of investment on GDP growth is seen to be determined by the multiplier specified through the Kahn-Keynes model. This multiplier is based on consumption. A rise in the share of consumption in total GDP raises the multiplier and thus the extent of the impact of investment on GDP growth. We now have two major determinants of GDP growth. The quantum of investment determines GDP growth, but not unaided—the share of consumption determines the extent of the impact of the quantum of investment on GDP growth.

Our theoretical framework argues that consumption and investment must not be taken as simple complements in an apparent Keynesian identity because a rise in the share of consumption, while raising the multiplier, simultaneously lowers the share of savings. Savings are a major determinant of investment, potentially lowering the quantum of investment. This gives an interesting trade-off between the two major drivers of growth, consumption and investment, making it conceivable that GDP growth could be led episodically, with some phases led more by consumption growth and other phases led more by investment growth.

Proposition 3: Growth in output will be better explained episodically, with some cycles being more investment-led, others more consumption-led and still others following more balanced growth paths.

Proposition 3a: High GDP growth in phase 1 will not be equally explained by high investment growth and high consumption growth. If high GDP growth in phase 1 is explained well by high investment growth, then the MPC and the consumption share in GDP and its growth in this phase will be low.

Proposition 3b: Low GDP growth in phase 2 will then equally not be explained by both low investment growth and low consumption growth. If low GDP growth in phase 2 is explained by low investment growth, then the MPC and the consumption share in GDP and its growth in this phase will be high.

These sets of propositions will help us examine whether (a) the first phase of growth is investment-led, with investment contributing significantly more to GDP growth, and (b) the second phase of growth is consumption-led, with the MPC and consumption share in GDP and its growth contributing significantly more to GDP growth.

6.5 Data

The time-series data for the macroeconomic aggregates for Pakistan over 1960–2017 has been obtained from the Pakistan Bureau of Statistics and State Bank of Pakistan (SBP).

While it would have been useful to analyse the entire time series available for 1960–2017, the data for pre-1971/1972 includes two wings of the country, West Pakistan and East Pakistan, whereas the data from 1972/1973 onwards includes just what was West Pakistan. It may have been possible to separate out the West Pakistan data pre-1971/1972 to make it consistent and comparable to the post-1971/1972 data, but we would still be comparing a structurally very different economy for West Pakistan pre-1971/1972 (integrated with East Pakistan) with the West Pakistan economy post-1971/1972 (no longer connected to East Pakistan/Bangladesh). Accordingly, we begin our analysis from 1972/1973 and consider the time series up to 2017.

6 APPLICATION OF A KEYNESIAN GENERAL EQUILIBRIUM MODEL... 125

We have also used the time series provided by the Pakistan Bureau of Statistics and made consistent by the Pakistan government's finance ministry.[1] This time series coincides with the series adopted by the IMF's World Economic Indicators. The entire data series has been put into real terms, as indexed by the SBP.

6.6 Is There an Observable, Discrete and Significant Drop in GDP Growth?

To test Proposition 1, we examine the mean shift in the series of GDP growth over the period 1973–2017. A structural break analysis based on linear regressions (Andrews, 1993; Chow, 1960) and a break test (Bai & Perron, 1998, 2003) are applied to detect discrete mean shifts in GDP growth. The series of tests under Bai and Perron's technique all identify a single, most significant, regime-specific mean shift in GDP growth in the year 1992. The linear regression results exhibited in Fig. 6.2 show that average GDP growth dropped from 5.89 per cent between 1973 and 1992 to 4.04 per cent post-1992.

This structural break analysis supports our proposition of a discrete drop in GDP growth. The break result is illustrated in Fig. 6.3, clearly showing the discrete drop in average GDP growth in the year 1992. It shows that average GDP growth drops from a higher value of 5.89 per cent in the period 1973 to 1992, to a lower value of 4.04 per cent

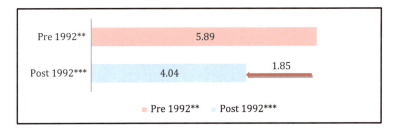

Fig. 6.2 Dummy regression for testing a known break date. (Note: The coefficient shows that after 1992, on average, GDP growth drops by 1.85 per cent. Standard errors given in parentheses. ***$p < 0.01$; **$p < 0.05$; *$p < 0.1$. Dummy variable Dummy1992t = 1 for $t > 1992$, DUt = 0 otherwise)

---

[1] We are grateful to Dr. Kalim Hyder at the SBP for providing us with the consistent time series of Pakistan's macro indicators.

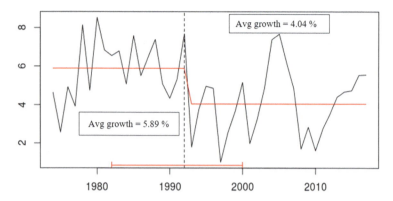

Fig. 6.3 Structural break in real GDP growth series for 1973 to 2017. (Note: The tests confirm that the year 1992 has a significant structural break in the GDP growth series. All the coefficients are significant at the 0.01 level)

post-1992. The discrete drop is well within the 95 per cent confidence interval as shown by the interval line around the break date.

The application of these three procedures, Bai and Perron (1998, 2003), Andrews (1993) and Chow (1960), and the dummy regression analysis consistently choose the year 1992 as a break date in GDP growth. They show that after 1992, GDP growth drops significantly by 1.84 per cent. Therefore, the first set of results in this section significantly support our first proposition. We can conclude that there has been a discrete drop in GDP growth in the year 1992 and that pre-1992 can be considered a high-growth phase and post-1992 a low-growth phase.

6.7 Which of the Keynesian Macro Aggregates Explain This Drop in GDP Growth?

We now seek to explain the drop in GDP growth using the macro aggregates from our theoretical framework of consumption, investment, government expenditure and net exports. The series for the macro aggregates is observed over the period 1973–2017 as our GDP growth series. In our theoretical framework, GDP growth, on the left-hand side of the equation, is explained by the right-hand side variables of investment growth, consumption growth, government expenditure growth, export growth and import growth. Based on Propositions 2a and 2b, we expect higher investment growth to explain higher GDP growth in the first phase. A

6 APPLICATION OF A KEYNESIAN GENERAL EQUILIBRIUM MODEL… 127

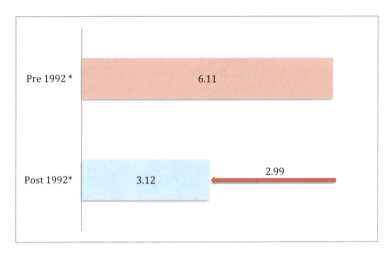

Fig. 6.4 Drop in investment growth. (Note: The figure shows the dummy regression for testing a known break date in investment growth. For the investment growth regression, the coefficient of the break dummy variable θ takes the value −2.99 per cent and is significant at the level of 0.01. The coefficient shows that after 1992, on average, investment growth drops by 2.99 per cent. Standard errors given in parentheses. ***$p < 0.01$; **$p < 0.05$; *$p < 0.1$. Dummy variable Dummy1992t = 1 for $t > 1992$, DUt = 0 otherwise)

statistically significant drop in investment growth should explain the drop in GDP growth in the second phase.

Figure 6.4 illustrates the results based on the Wald test and Chow tests at a known break date. Of all the explanatory variables (investment growth, consumption growth, government expenditure growth, exports growth and imports growth), only the break in the investment variable coincides with the break in GDP growth. Figure 6.4 shows that investment growth drops significantly from 6.11 per cent pre-1992 to 3.12 per cent post-1992.

Summarizing, the break in investment growth coincides with the break in GDP growth. Our findings above suggest that, on average, we observe GDP growth to drop by 1.84 per cent after 1992. We observe a similar trend for investment growth, which drops on average by 3.11 per cent after 1992. Thus, we can say that the better explanatory variable, coinciding with the downward trend in GDP growth in Pakistan, is investment growth in Pakistan.

To further show that investment growth explains GDP growth, as in Proposition 2b, we can estimate the correlation between the two series across the two phases, pre-1992 and post-1992. We expect higher investment growth to explain higher GDP growth in the first phase, pre-1992, and a statistically significant drop in investment growth to explain the drop in GDP growth in the second phase, post-1992.

The results for running the empirical growth model given in Box 6.2 for the two phases are illustrated in Fig. 6.5. This is not a simple test of the correlation of growth in each macro aggregate with GDP growth in each phase. That is of course expected but would be unremarkable. The real test is for a significant drop in the mean growth of the macro aggregate, with the drop in mean growth of GDP. Only the investment variable passes this more stringent test.

Box 6.2 Empirical Estimation Model for Growth

We recall from the theoretical part of this essay, the Keynesian mum equation put into growth terms in Eq. (6.7). We denote for brevity, growth as g, which gives GDP growth g_t^Y as a function of growth in macro aggregates. The macro aggregates are consumption growth (g_t^C), investment growth (g_t^I), government growth (g_t^G), exports growth (g_t^X), and imports growth (g_t^M).

$$g_t^Y = f\left(g_t^C, g_t^I, g_t^G, g_t^X, g_t^M\right) \qquad (6.8)$$

The functional form is estimated using the double log form as the following:

$$\log y_t = \alpha_0 + \alpha_1 \text{logreal} C_t + \alpha_2 \text{logreal} I_t + \alpha_3 \text{logreal} G_t \\ + \alpha_4 \text{logreal} X_t + \alpha_5 \text{logreal} M_t + \epsilon_t \qquad (6.9)$$

where $\log y_t$ represents the log of real GDP, $\text{logreal} C_t$ represents the log of real consumption, $\text{logreal} I_t$ represents the log of real investment, $\text{logreal} G_t$ represents the log of real government, $\text{logreal} X_t$ represents the log of real exports and $\text{logreal} M_t$ represents the log of real imports. The double log form coefficients for Eq. (6.9) represent the same effect as if the equation was run as a growth equation. For example, α1 shows the effect of consumption growth on GDP growth. We run this equation independently for pre-1992 and post-1992. The coefficients of the model are then tested for equality across the two periods.

6 APPLICATION OF A KEYNESIAN GENERAL EQUILIBRIUM MODEL... 129

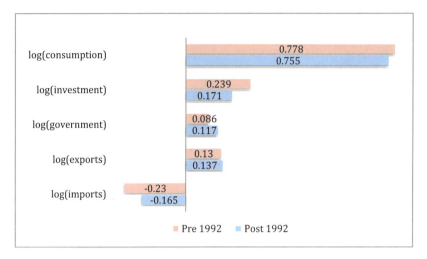

Fig. 6.5 Correlating GDP growth to growth in the macro aggregates. (Note: All the coefficients are significant at the 0.01 level. However, the only significant drop in growth for the explanatory variables is for investment. The Durbin-Watson value provides no evidence of autocorrelation. All the variables in the model are integrated to order one, hence the variables are cointegrated and the OLS regression yields consistent results. The Johanson multivariate cointegration shows we cannot reject the hypothesis of a cointegrating rank at a 5 per cent confidence interval. Standard errors given in parentheses. ***$p < 0.01$; **$p < 0.05$; *$p < 0.1$)

The investment growth variable coefficient shows that a 1 per cent increase in investment growth is associated with a 0.24 per cent increase in GDP growth pre-1992. The coefficient of investment growth drops post-1992 and is associated with a 0.17 per cent increase in GDP growth. Both coefficients are significant at a 1 per cent level and positive in both phases. The investment growth coefficient has a higher value in the first phase (pre-1992) and a lower value in the second phase (post-1992). The drop in investment growth coefficient is highly significant between the two phases.

Therefore, there is strong empirical support for Propositions 2a and 2b showing that:

- There has been a significant drop in investment growth over the period 1973–2017.
- Investment growth significantly explains high GDP growth in the first phase and a drop in investment growth explains the drop in GDP growth in the second phase.

6.8 Are the Phases of Growth Investment-Led or Consumption-Led?

So far, we have posed an explanation to our central problem that there has been a drop in long-run GDP growth. We have identified investment growth as the most significant explanatory variable to explain the drop in GDP growth post-1992. Recalling our theoretical framework takes the economic argument for the determination of GDP growth further beyond just investment growth. It pairs investment growth with the share of consumption, specifically the MPC. This pairing is added by Proposition 3 and further nuanced because the proposition expects that long-run GDP growth is better explained through the quantum of investment growth, paired with the MPC. Further, this Keynesian multiplier can be expected to work inversely with the quantum of investment growth.

The MPC is relatively lower when the quantum of investment growth is high and relatively higher when the quantum of investment growth drops. Therefore, Proposition 3 expects that high GDP growth in the first phase will be explained by high investment growth, paired with a relatively lower MPC on average. The drop in GDP growth in the second phase will be explained by a drop in the quantum of investment growth, paired with a relatively higher MPC on average.

To further clarify, we are now positing that GDP growth is determined through two major channels: an investment channel and a consumption channel. The investment channel has been strongly corroborated empirically in the section above. We now wish to test Proposition 3 on the consumption channel.

Box 6.3 gives the econometric methodology for estimating the MPC. Real consumption is run as a function of real GDP, as in Eq. (6.10). The coefficient of GDP in the regression gives the MPC. This regression is run separately for the two periods: high GDP growth pre-1992 and low GDP growth post-1992. This will give us two MPCs: one for the high GDP growth phase pre-1992 and one for the low GDP growth phase post-1992.

Figure 6.6 shows the estimated results for the MPC given by Eq. (6.10). The MPC in the high GDP growth phase pre-1992 takes a value of 68.5 per cent and is highly significant. In the low-growth phase post-1992, the MPC takes a higher value of 76.4 per cent and is again highly significant. The estimated values for the MPC in the two phases show that Proposition 3 holds: that the MPC value in the high GDP

Box 6.3 MPC and the Determination of GDP
GDP growth is related to the quantum of investment growth and the MPC from the theoretical part of this chapter and as set out in Box 6.1. We have already established the significance of the quantum of investment growth in explaining GDP growth above. However, in Box 6.1, Eq. (6.6), we paired the quantum of investment growth with consumption by introducing the multiplier term of the MPC. Therefore, our test for Proposition 3 must now be based on estimating the MPC across two phases of GDP growth: pre-1992 with its high GDP growth and post-1992 with its drop in GDP growth.

Estimating the MPC
The MPC is estimated econometrically by making real consumption, on the left-hand side of the equation, a function of real GDP on the right-hand side, as in Eq. (6.10). Estimating the MPC requires running a regression of real consumption on real GDP. The regression is run independently for two periods: pre-1992 and post-1992. The coefficient of real GDP in each regression gives us the average value for the MPC for each period.

$$\text{real}C_t = \alpha_{i0} + \gamma_{i1}\,\text{realGDP}_t + \epsilon_{it} \tag{6.10}$$

Where i represents two periods (pre-1992 and post-1992), realC represents real consumption and realGDP represents real GDP. Since we estimate the equation for two periods, we will have two estimated values for MPC, represented by $\gamma_{\text{pre}1992,1}$ and $\gamma_{\text{post}1992,1}$. Based on our results above, pre-1992 is considered a high GDP growth phase and post-1992 is considered a low GDP growth phase.

Accordingly, to support Propositions 3a and 3b, we expect the following conditions to hold true:

- The estimated MPC value for pre-1992 (high GDP growth phase) should be lower than the estimated MPC value for post-1992 (low growth GDP phase). That is, $\gamma_{\text{pre}1992,1} < \gamma_{\text{post}1992,1}$.
- In addition to Proposition 3a, the estimated MPC value pre-1992 should be significantly different from the estimated MPC value post-1992. That is, $\gamma_{\text{pre}1992,1} \neq \gamma_{\text{post}1992,1}$.

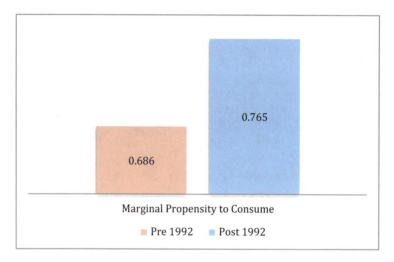

Fig. 6.6 Estimates of the MPC

growth phase is lower than the MPC value in the low GDP growth phase. This result goes on to support Hypotheses 3a and 3b.

To test proposition 3b, we perform a Chi square test to confirm that the two values are significantly different across the two phases of GDP growth: pre-1992 (MPC = 0.68) and post-1992 (MPC = 0.76). The Chi square test statistic is significant and shows that the two coefficients, representing MPC values, are significantly different. This result supports condition 3b.

We can conclude that Pakistan's high GDP growth in the first phase, pre-1992, is explained by high investment growth and that the MPC in this phase is low. This makes this high GDP growth phase investment-led. Pakistan's low GDP growth in the second phase, post-1992, is explained by low investment growth. The MPC in this phase is higher, making this phase consumption-led.

6.9 Conclusions

This essay aims to establish the determinants of Pakistan's long-run GDP growth. The problem of doing so is a perennial one for all economies to be able to choose their policy levers and gauge their impact more precisely. The problem becomes more acute and even existential for Pakistan because of an observable long-run decline in GDP growth rates. The 1960s, 1970s and 1980s appear to have had higher growth rates on trend, nearer 6 per cent per annum, compared to the 1990s onwards, nearer 4 per cent per annum. Not least, the past three years appear to have sunk GDP growth even lower than this 4 per cent trend.

Further, Pakistan's GDP growth appears to be subject to periodic cycles of instability characterized by budget deficits, pressuring inflation and requiring some form of inflows, also raising debt. This in turn pressures current account deficits and is not helped by persistent trade deficits. The twin deficits have required periodic recourse to multilateral support to tide over the deficits. Pakistan has entered 23 agreements of IMF support to date.

Policy debate and multilateral and donor advice, we find, focus more on the shorter-run cyclical concerns and policy variables. These are no doubt important but they do not address longer-run structural factors such as investment. Neither does the publicly available literature on Pakistan pursue such a characterization of Pakistan's long-run GDP growth or estimate it empirically. Our analysis appears to be a first in the growth literature on Pakistan.

This essay has sought to examine the pattern of Pakistan's GDP growth using a Keynesian general equilibrium model to analyse and explain the trajectory of GDP growth over the long run of the last 50 years. The model gives a very clear answer. Pre-1992, high GDP growth of 6 per cent on trend is driven significantly by investment. Post-1992, lower GDP growth of 4 per cent on trend is driven significantly by consumption.

This dichotomy between investment-driven growth and consumption-driven growth is explored further using the Kahn-Keynes multiplier, with high GDP growth pre-1992 being driven by high investment growth, paired with low consumption growth, and low GDP growth post-1992 being driven by low investment growth, paired with high consumption growth. This is a strong vindication of the use of the generic Keynesian general equilibrium model of aggregate demand and its more elaborate adaptations.

References

Ahmed, V., & Amjad, R. (1984). *The management of Pakistan's economy 1947–82*. Oxford University Press.

Amjad, R. (1982). *Private industrial investment in Pakistan 1960–70*. Cambridge University Press.

Amjad, R. (2014). Pakistan's growth spurts and reversals: A historical perspective. *Lahore Journal of Economics, 19*, 91–104.

Amjad, R., Din, M., & Qayyum, A. (2011). Pakistan: Breaking out of stagflation into sustained growth. *Lahore Journal of Economics, 16*, 13–30.

Amjad, R., & Mahmood, K. (1982). *Industrial relations and the political process in Pakistan 1947–1977*. International Institute for Labour Studies.

Andrews, D. W. (1993). Tests for parameter instability and structural change with unknown change point. *Econometrica, 61*(4), 821–856.

Bai, J., & Perron, P. (1998). Estimating and testing linear models with multiple structural changes. *Econometrica, 66*(1), 47–78.

Bai, J., & Perron, P. (2003). Computation and analysis of multiple structural change models. *Journal of Applied Econometrics, 18*(1), 1–22.

Chenery, H. B., & Strout, A. M. (1968). Foreign assistance and economic development: Reply. *American Economic Review, 58*(4), 912–916.

Choudhry, M. A., Khan, S., & Pasha, F. (2017). *Comparison of various business cycle models for Pakistan*. Working Paper No 89. State Bank of Pakistan.

Choudhry, M. A., & Pasha, F. (2013). *The RBC view of Pakistan: A declaration of stylized facts and essential models*. Working Paper No. 56. State Bank of Pakistan.

Chow, G. C. (1960). Tests of equality between sets of coefficients in two linear regressions. *Econometrica, 28*(3), 591–605.

Haque, I. (2011). The capital account and Pakistani rupee convertibility: Macroeconomic policy challenges. *Lahore Journal of Economics, 16*, 95–121.

Husain, I. (2009). The role of politics in Pakistan's economy. *Journal of International Affairs, 63*(1), 1–18.

Husain, I. (2018). *Governing the ungovernable: Institutional reforms for democratic governance*. Oxford University Press.

International Monetary Fund. Independent Evaluation Office. (2003). *Chapter 9: Pakistan*. Evaluation of prolonged use of IMF resources, International Monetary Fund.

Iqbal, Z., James, J., & Pyatt, G. (2000). Three-gap analysis of structural adjustment in Pakistan. *Journal of Policy Modeling, 22*(1), 117–138.

Iqbal, Z., & Rehman, Q. N. (1995). Constraints to the economic growth of Pakistan: A three-gap approach [with comments]. *Pakistan Development Review, 34*(4), 1119–1133.

Keynes, J. M. (1936). *The general theory of employment, interest and money*. Macmillan Cambridge University Press, for Royal Economic Society.

Khan, M. Z. (2009). Liberalization and economic crisis in Pakistan. In *Rising to the challenge in Asia: A study of financial markets* (Vol. 9). Asian Development Bank.

Khan, U. E., & Jawed, S. M. (2019). Dynamics of business cycle and long-term economic growth of Pakistan. *Theoretical and Applied Economics, 26*(2), 173–184.

Mahmood, M., & Tanvir, A. (2018, March 28–29). *Macroeconomic determinants of poverty in Pakistan: 1963–2013*. Paper presented at the Fourteenth International Conference on the Management of the Pakistan Economy.

Mahmood, T., & Arby, M. F. (2012). Business cycles in Pakistan. *International Journal of Business and Social Science, 3*(4), 271–277.

McKinnon, R. I. (1964). Foreign exchange constraints in economic development and efficient aid allocation. *The Economic Journal, 74*(294), 388–409.

Shahbaz, M., Ahmad, K., & Chaudhary, A. R. (2008). Economic growth and its determinants in Pakistan. *Pakistan Development Review, 47*(4), 471–486.

Zaidi, S. A. (2015). *Issues in Pakistan's economy: A political economy perspective*. Oxford University Press.

CHAPTER 7

Analysing Pakistan's Investment Growth Over Time

7.1 The Narrative for the Growth of GDP and Investment

The fifth essay found that a Keynesian aggregate demand model adapted to estimate growth over time explained Pakistan's gross domestic product (GDP) growth trajectory well. The plurality of causal variables on the right-hand side of the equation was the model's advantage in determining output growth on the left-hand side of the equation. Further, the nuance of the model through the Kahn-Keynes multiplier (k) posited investment and consumption as trade-offs rather than additives.

Applying this adapted Keynesian model to Pakistan's GDP growth trajectory identified two primary determinants of growth. Pre-1992, high GDP growth of 6 per cent per annum was shown by the model to be led by high investment growth paired with low consumption growth. Post-1992, the model showed lower GDP growth of 4 per cent per annum, led by high consumption growth and low investment growth. Further, the 2 per cent drop in GDP growth was associated with a 3 per cent per annum drop in investment growth post-1992.

Pursuing causality, Essay 6 explains the drop in investment in terms of its determinants. Mathematically, this requires manipulating the Keynesian mum equation to put investment on the left-hand-side variable to be explained and deriving the resulting causal determinants of investment on the right-hand side. Investment growth is then posited to be a function of supply-side and demand-side determinants.

This implies a model using two equations.

For the supply side, mathematical derivations yield investment on the left-hand side of the equation, causally determined on the right-hand side by the supply variables of domestic investment, net capital inflows and the budget deficit. Again, this equation is set out in growth terms. It is a good test of whether savings and inflows are additive, as observed in many developing countries, or whether they are substitutes, as Griffin and Enos (1970) find.

For the demand side, the mathematical derivation posits that aggregate investment on the left-hand side of the equation is determined on the right-hand side by the budget deficit. For further refinement, aggregate investment is decomposed into private and public investment. So, aggregate investment on the left-hand side of the equation is posited to be determined on the right-hand side by private investment and public investment. This further splits the demand-side equation into two: the demand for private investment and the demand for public investment.

Demand for private investment on the left-hand side of the equation is then explained by the demand variable of public investment. This makes for a good test of the theorem of Ricardian equivalence—that aggregate investment relies on private rather than public investment, and further that private investment in turn is crowded out by public investment. Alternatively, the Keynesian model makes aggregate investment reliant on both private and public investment as complements and additives. Further, private investment is not crowded out by public investment and may even be crowded in.

The results of running the supply equations for Pakistan show that growth in aggregate investment pre-1992 was high, based on the high growth of inflows, and that growth in aggregate investment post-1992 slumped because of a decline in the growth of inflows.

The results of running the demand equations for Pakistan are more significant and compelling. They show that (a) growth in aggregate investment pre-1992 was high, based on the high growth of public investment; (b) growth in aggregate investment post-1992 slumped because of a decline in the growth of public investment; (c) growth in private investment remained fairly constant over both periods, pre-1992 and post-1992; and (d) private investment was equally unaffected by the high growth of public investment pre-1992 and the low growth of public investment post-1992.

These results therefore support the Keynesian model of public investment boosting aggregate investment. They do not support Ricardian equivalence, which states that private investment is crowded out by public investment.

7.2 The Pattern of Long-Run Investment Growth in Pakistan

We begin by observing the long-run pattern of Pakistan's investment growth. Figure 7.1 shows investment growth, its long-run trend and the short-run cyclicality from 1973 to 2019. Long-run investment growth appears to have decreased in the previous three decades. The earlier decades of the 1970s and 1980s saw a trend in investment growth of over 6 per cent per annum. However, from about 1990 onwards, the trend in investment growth decreased significantly to around 3 per cent per annum. This trend also ran contrary to the comparative trend in other developing

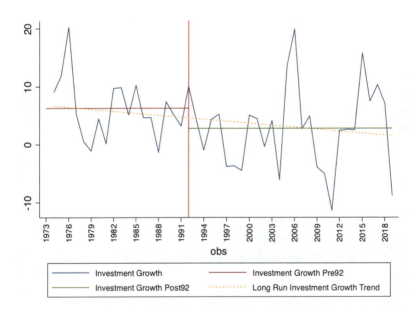

Fig. 7.1 Investment growth

countries where investment growth rates have generally improved over time. Essay 5 empirically showed that, on average, Pakistan's investment growth dropped by approximately 3 per cent post-1992, clearly identifying two trajectories for investment growth in Pakistan: (a) a high-growth trajectory of 6.3 per cent for the pre-1992 period and (b) a low-growth trajectory of 3.2 per cent for the post-1992 period.

The pattern of long-run investment growth appears to be similar to Pakistan's long-run GDP growth in terms of long-run trends and short-run fluctuations. The short-run fluctuations in investment growth seem to increase in frequency, intensity and duration. If so, this cyclicality in short-run investment growth may well be interacting with the longer-run trend in investment growth, dragging it down.

We saw in Essay 5 that the drop in investment growth explained the drop in GDP growth. In this essay, our interest is to examine the key macro determinant explaining the average drop in investment growth. We aim to explain this in terms of the supply-side and demand-side determinants of investment, explained by our theoretical model and the literature.

7.3 Literature Reviewing the Supply-Side and Demand-Side Determinants of Investment

Broadly, the literature categorizes investment in terms of supply-side and demand-side determinants. For supply-side determinants, aggregate investment is run as a function of savings and capital inflows. The literature examining the relationship between savings, capital inflows and investment points to two possibilities:

- Savings and inflows are complements for developing countries such as Pakistan (Oladipo, 2010; Idrees et al., 2020; Elakkad & Hussein, 2021).
- The Griffin-Enos model raises the alternative possibility that inflows may reduce savings (Hasan, 2002; Djankov et al., 2006).

Similarly, for demand-side determinants, aggregate investment is run as a function of public investment and private investment. The literature posits the relationship between public investment, private investment and aggregate investment as two competing models:

- A Ricardian model posits that public investment crowds out private investment and therefore weakens aggregate investment (Gupta, 1992; Blanchard, 1991).
- Alternatively, a Keynesian model posits that public investment can crowd in private investment and therefore raise aggregate investment (Cwik & Wieland, 2011; Clift, 2019).

7.3.1 The Supply-Side Literature

The supply-side determinants of investment are savings and capital inflows. Savings and investment are connected in the fundamental macroeconomic accounting relationship, which treats inflows from outside and savings from within as complements. External inflows increase the total amount of savings available to an economy without in any way substituting for domestic savings. In addition, inflows are positively correlated with domestic production and output in an economy (Oladipo, 2010). Inflows and domestic savings are considered complements. Therefore, foreign aid and grants, which are external inflows, raise GDP growth by raising aggregate savings and investments available to the economy (Fasanya & Onakoya, 2012; Chenery & Strout, 1966; Easterly, 2003).

Inflows themselves are functions of political stability and a good policy environment (Burnside & Dollar, 2000). Foreign direct investment has been an external source of finance for the ASEAN economies, although it has remained a minor source for South Asian economies such as Pakistan (Oladipo, 2010; Idrees et al., 2020; Elakkad & Hussein, 2021).

The Griffin-Enos model raises the alternative possibility that inflows may reduce savings. External capital inflows substitute for domestic savings, distorting the composition of investment and possibly lowering the growth of output. Earlier research by Griffin (1978), Griffin and Enos (1970) and others suggests that capital inflows or loans can sometimes hamper economic growth rather than accelerate it. They specifically contend that foreign aid and capital inflows cause domestic saving rates to decline. Instead of being invested, foreign cash inflows can be used for consumption and wasteful spending.

Foreign assistance inflows have the potential, through a variety of mechanisms, to decrease domestic savings in developing nations. First, foreign aid can replace domestic savings, reducing the need for internal funds for investment. Second, increasing available aggregate resources can push governments and people to consume more now, taking money out of savings. Third, aid inflows can also encourage the distribution of resources towards initiatives with protracted gestation periods or low productivity, which might not effectively support sustained economic growth. Distortion of incentives for domestic savings can also delay needed tax reforms. Reinhart and Talvi (1998), Edwards (1995) and Fry (1994) have come to support such a negative association between foreign and domestic savings.

For Pakistan, the literature finds inflows and savings to be complements (Idrees et al., 2020). Foreign aid plays a critical role in providing the inflows to fill a large savings gap needed to raise investment (Chenery & Strout, 1966) despite raising the country's debt (Khan & Rahim, 1993).

7.3.2 The Demand-Side Literature

The demand-side factors that determine aggregate investment are public investment and private investment, which are proposed by two different economic models. The Ricardian model (Seater, 1993; Ricciuti, 2003) implies that public investment will crowd out private investment and therefore weaken aggregate investment (Gupta, 1992; Blanchard, 1991). The classical Ricardian argument is based on private expectations of public investment having to eventually rely on increased taxation to finance it, inducing a drop in private investment. Public sector enterprises are also perceived to be inefficient, siphoning off public investment that is better spent on public infrastructure needed by the private sector. This disincentivizes private investment.

Alternatively, a second theory of investment demand based on the Keynesian model (Musgrave, 1987) implies that public investment can crowd in private investment, thereby raising aggregate investment (Cwik & Wieland, 2011; Clift, 2019). Public investment can attract private investment by investing in infrastructure projects. This raises productivity, investor confidence and private investment. Thus, public investment acts as an accelerator for economic growth (Cwik & Wieland, 2011).

Public investment is therefore a long-term and short-term complement to private investment (Erden & Holcombe, 2006). Developing country experience from Singapore, Brazil, Rwanda, India, and Vietnam shows that public investments in infrastructure lower private sector expenses and increase the productivity of private capital.

With these two alternative theories of investment demand, Ricardian and Keynesian, the empirical results can be mixed. In India, public investment before the 1980s crowded out private investment. However, some crowding in was observed after 1980 (Bahal et al., 2018; Gupta, 1992). In Greece, public and private investment had a positive relationship pre-1981 and a negative relationship post-1981 (Apergis, 2000).

Reviewing Pakistan's long-run growth, Amjad (2014) finds state support for investment. Looney (1997) finds that public investment in infrastructure resulted in an increase in private sector investment, supporting the theory of crowding in. However, in sectors other than infrastructure, Rashid (2006) holds that the public sector contended with the private sector, resulting in the crowding out of private investment. Khan and Gill (2009) make an interesting link between state borrowing and private investment, which shows crowding in rather than crowding out. The reason for this is the high dependence on public debt, disproportionate financial liquidity and high government spending (Naqvi, 2002).

We aim to examine both the supply-side and demand-side determinants of investment to explain the drop in investment growth.

7.4 Theoretical Framework

Our theoretical framework in Essay 5 argued that the two major determinants of output growth, investment and consumption, would have a trade-off. The theoretical argument was based on the Keynesian determination of output growth by investment and its multiplier given by the marginal propensity to consume (MPC). However, the two drivers of output growth were expected to oppose each other—the trade-off was expected to be based on the role of savings. Investment would be driven up by savings, whereas consumption would be driven down.

Essay 5 found statistically significant empirical support for the trade-off, with high GDP growth pre-1992 driven by high investment, and lower GDP growth post-1992 in turn driven by lowered investment but a raised MPC. Mathematically, the trade-off between investment and consumption was apparent, so only investment needed to be examined. In addition, we chose to examine investment because Essay 1 established it as the primary driver of GDP growth, that is, it drove GDP growth up pre-1992 but drove it down post-1992.

7.4.1 Supply-Side Determinants of Investment

To capture the supply-side determinants of investment, we take our mum macro Eq. (7.1) in Box 7.1, where output (Y) on the left-hand side is determined on the right-hand side by consumption (C), investment (I), government expenditure (G) and net exports (NX). Net exports (NX) give the current account (CA), where the current account (CA) is open but the capital account (KA) is closed. Goods are traded globally between Pakistan and the rest of the world (NX), but there are no claims to assets by the rest of the world investing in Pakistan or Pakistan investing in the rest of the world.

The current account (CA) is equal to the capital account (KA). The capital account (KA) is given by net outflows (CF). Using the textbook derivation, following, for example, Romer and Romer (2007) and Mankiw (2008), we open the capital account (KA) thus, with net outflows (CF). Output (n), on the left-hand side, is determined on the right-hand side by consumption (C), investment (I), government expenditure (G) and net outflows (CF), where net outflows (CF) are given by capital outflows (CO) minus capital inflows (CI).

Expanding the mum Eq. (7.2) with the full term for net outflows (CF), as shown in Eq. (7.3), gives output on the left-hand side, determined on

---

Box 7.1 Supply-Side Determinants of Investment

$$Y = C + I + G + NX \tag{7.1}$$
$$Y = C + I + G + CF \tag{7.2}$$
$$CF = CO - CI \tag{7.3}$$
$$Y = C + I + G + CO - CI \tag{7.4}$$
$$Y = C + S + T \tag{7.5}$$
$$C + S + T = C + I + G + CO - CI \tag{7.6}$$
$$S + T = I + G + CO - CI \tag{7.7}$$
$$I = S + (T - G) - CO + CI \tag{7.8}$$
$$D = T - G \tag{7.9}$$
$$I = S - CO + CI + (D) \tag{7.10}$$
$$I = Sd - CO + CI + (D) \tag{7.11}$$

the right-hand side by consumption (C), investment (I), government expenditure (G), plus capital outflows (CO) minus capital inflows (CI), as in Eq. (7.4). This is one way to carve out output (Y).

However, there is another way to carve out output—through the identity that all output (Y) must be either consumed (C), saved (S) or taxed (T), which is given in Eq. (7.5). We then equate the two ways of carving out output (Y) by putting Eq. (7.5) on the left-hand side of Eq. (7.4). This gives us a somewhat messy Eq. (7.6), where, on the left-hand side, consumption (C) plus savings (S) plus taxes (T) are equal on the right-hand side to our now usual suspects, consumption (C), investment (I), government expenditure (G) and capital outflows (CO) minus capital inflows (CI).

Equation (7.6) is simplified because consumption (C), which is on both sides of the equation, can be cancelled out. This leaves Eq. (7.7), where on the left-hand side, savings (S) plus taxes (T) are equal to investment (I), government expenditure (G) and capital outflows (CO) minus capital inflows (CI). We solve for the determinants of investment (I) by keeping investment (I) on one side of the equation (say, on the right) and moving all the other right-hand-side terms to the left, requiring their signs to flip. Thus, government expenditure (G) and capital outflows (CO) became negative, while capital inflows (CI) became positive.

In Eq. (7.8), we have investment on one side of the equation (say, the left-hand side), being determined on the right-hand side by savings (S) plus taxes (T) minus government expenditure (G) minus capital outflows (CO) plus capital inflows (CI). The left-hand side of Eq. (7.8) plus taxes (T) minus government expenditure (G) is equal to the deficit (D), which is given by taxes minus government expenditure ($T - G$) in Eq. (7.9). The final Eq. (7.10) neatens out to investment (I) on the left-hand side being determined on the right-hand side by savings (S) minus capital outflows (CO) plus capital inflows (CI) plus the deficit (D).

Equation (7.10) is now a good test of the supply-side determinants of investment (I). Investment (I) is expected to be a positive function of savings, a negative function of capital outflows, a positive function of capital inflows and a positive function of the deficit. Correctly stated, Eq. (7.10) is written as Eq. (7.11), where investment (I) is a positive function of domestic savings (Sd), a negative function of capital outflows (CO), a positive function of capital inflows (CI) and a positive function of the deficit (D). Note that the deficit (D) is a negative term denoting excess government expenditure (G) over taxation (T), given by the term ($T - G$). However, the size of the negative term (D) is expected to be positively correlated to investment (I).

7.4.2 Demand-Side Determinants of Investment

The Ricardian versus Keynesian debate captures the demand-side determinants very well. The Ricardian argument (Seater, 1993; Ricciuti, 2003) is that government expenditure (G), unfinanced by revenues (T), giving budgetary deficits (D), will lower investment (I) and consumption (C) because investors and consumers will anticipate a future rise in taxation to cover the current budgetary deficit.

The alternative Keynesian argument (Musgrave, 1987; Feldstein, 2009) is that given excess capacity, a budget deficit (D), can be used to raise investment (I) and consumption (C) through the accelerator. That elevated government expenditure will enhance employment, incomes, consumption, and aggregate demand and therefore private investment. This gives a general expression to begin with, that investment (I) will be a function of the budget deficit (D), as in Eq. (7.12) in Box 7.2. The function will be negative (the Ricardian argument), as in Eq. (7.13a), or positive (the Keynesian argument), as in Eq. (7.13b).

Box 7.2 Demand-Side Determinants of Investment

$$I = (G-T) = D \tag{7.12}$$

or

$$I = -fn(G-T) = -fn(D) \tag{7.13a}$$

$$I = +fn(G-T) = +fn(D) \tag{7.13b}$$

$$I = \mathrm{Ig} + \mathrm{Ip} \tag{7.14}$$

$$\mathrm{Ip} = -fn(G-T) = -fn(D) \tag{7.15a}$$

$$\mathrm{Ip} = +fn(G-T) = +fn(D) \tag{7.15b}$$

$$\mathrm{Ip} = -fn(\mathrm{Ig}) \tag{7.16a}$$

$$\mathrm{Ip} = +fn(\mathrm{Ig}) \tag{7.16b}$$

A negative correlation implies that an increase in the deficit (D) will drive out/down investment (I), as in Eq. (7.13a). This is the crowding-out hypothesis according to the Ricardian model. A positive correlation implies that an increase in deficit (D) will crowd in investment (I), as in Eq. (7.13b). This is the crowding-in hypothesis according to the Keynesian model.

Aggregate investment (I) can itself be split into government investment (Ig) and private investment (Ip), as in Eq. (7.14). Then, a good test of the Ricardian crowding-out hypothesis is whether private investment (Ip) is a negative function of the government's budget deficit (D), as in Eq. (7.15a). By contrast, a good test of the alternative Keynesian crowding-in hypothesis is whether private investment (Ip) is a positive function of the government's budget deficit (D), as in Eq. (7.15b).

A further test of the Ricardian crowding-out hypothesis is whether private investment (Ip) is a negative function of public investment (Ig), as in Eq. (7.16a). Conversely, an equivalent test of the Keynesian crowding-in hypothesis is whether private investment (Ip) is a positive function of public investment (Ig) as in Eq. (7.16b).

7.5 Data Description

The State Bank of Pakistan (SBP) has provided this essay's macro aggregate series, which comes under national income accounts. They are in real terms as indexed for inflation by the SBP. The macro aggregate series was observed over the period 1973–2019. All our macro aggregates were estimated as observed data values by the SBP, taken from the Pakistan Bureau of Statistics. One macro aggregate, savings, was not an observed value but was estimated through national income accounts by the SBP. The estimation of the variable savings was as a residual from the national income accounts identity (Box 7.3).

7.6 Supply-Side Determinants Explaining the Drop in Investment Growth

We begin our empirical analysis by explaining the drop in investment growth in terms of its supply-side determinants, savings and capital inflows. There are four possible propositions to test, based on our theoretical framework. Each proposition is tested separately for each supply-side determinant, that is, capital inflows and savings.

Box 7.3 Estimating Savings
Starting with the national income accounts identity:

$$Sp = G + Ip + Ig + X - M - T \tag{7.17}$$

Sp is private savings, G is government expenditure, Ip is private investment, Ig is government investment, X is exports, M is imports, and T is taxes.

From Eq. (7.14) in Box 7.2 for the theoretical model, we know that:

$$I = Ip + Ig \tag{7.18}$$

Substituting total investment (I) for private investment (Ip) and government investment (Ig) and rearranging the terms of Eq. (7.12) gives:

$$Sp = (G - T) + I + (X - M) \tag{7.19}$$

$$Sp - I = (G - T) + (X - M) \tag{7.20}$$

$(G - T)$ represents the budget balance and $(X - M)$ represents the current account balance.

$$Sp - I = \text{budget balance} + \text{current account balance} \tag{7.21}$$

From the macroeconomic identity, we know that the gap between private savings (Sp) and investments (I) is inflows (i):

$$Sp - I = -i \tag{7.22}$$

or

$$I = Sp + i$$

Therefore,

$$i = \text{CA balance} + \text{budget balance} \tag{7.23}$$

(continued)

Box 7.3 (continued)

This is the neoclassical equation where the budget balance and current account balance add up to inflows. The inflows will be negative if the current account balance plus the budget balance is positive. Conversely, the inflows will be positive if the current account balance plus the budget balance is negative.

The SBP was able to estimate inflows (i) from its two balances in Eq. (7.23).

From Eq. (7.22),

$$\text{Sp} = I - i \tag{7.24a}$$

The SBP estimated (I) and (i) to obtain (Sp) in Eq. (7.24a).

We cannot test the shares in output for the variables in (7.24a) because they are true, by definition, in the identity (8). However, it is legitimate to test growth for the variables in (7.24a).

A second issue arises in whether we can test the Griffin-Enos hypothesis (Griffin & Enos, 1970), that is, the relationship between savings and inflows, using Eq. (7.24a). According to this hypothesis, foreign capital inflows substitute for domestic savings, distorting the composition of investment and possibly lowering the growth of output.

Expressing Eq. (7.24a) in terms of growth:

$$\Delta \text{Sp} = \Delta I - \Delta i \tag{7.24b}$$

If $\Delta I = 0$

$$\text{Then, } \Delta \text{Sp} = 0 - \Delta i \tag{7.24c}$$

Or $\Delta \text{Sp} = -\Delta i$

Only if $\Delta I = 0$ will Eq. (7.24c) result in a definitional inverse relationship. However, if $\Delta I >$ or < 0, Eq. (7.24b) will hold and Eq. (7.24c) will not, and ΔSp will not be definitionally inverse to Δi. Thus, the Griffin-Enos hypothesis can be empirically tested. Deriving savings as a residual has not constrained us from examining its behavioural relationship with investment and other macro aggregates.

- Proposition (1a): The structural break in the investment growth in 1992 significantly coincides with the structural break in supply-side growth variables.
- Proposition (1b): The supply-side growth variables drop significantly post-break date 1992, matching the direction of change of the investment growth variable.
- Proposition (2): The shares of the supply-side variables in output have a significant declining trend post-1992.
- Proposition (3): The drop in investment growth post-1992 is significantly associated with the drop in the growth of supply-side variables.
- Proposition (4a): Savings and inflows are significantly, positively correlated and are complements.
- Proposition (4b): Savings and inflows are significantly, negatively correlated and are substitutes.

The propositions proceed with sequential and intuitive logic.

We established in Essay 5 that there was indeed a statistically significant drop of 3.11 per cent in Pakistan's investment growth. The aim is to identify the explanatory variable that is statistically well correlated with investment growth. Proposition (1) tests for the supply-side variables coinciding with the break date in investment growth.

Further, Proposition (2) extends the analysis to examine the supply-side determinants as shares in output. We see not only a drop in investment growth but also statistically show a declining trend in the share of investment in output. Proposition (2) tests the trend coefficient in each share—savings share and inflows share—to be statistically different in the pre-1992 and post-1992 periods and whether the post-1992 trend coefficient has a statistically higher negative value than the pre-1992 coefficient value.

We then proceed to Proposition (3) using a functional form specifying that investment growth on the left side of the equation is well explained by growth in savings and inflows on the right side.

Finally, Proposition (4) examines the relationship between the supply-side variables themselves, testing to check the complementarity and substitutability between savings and inflows.

The results from our empirical exercise from the supply side thus provide us with two possible explanations—one for the drop in investment growth and another for the relationship between savings and inflows.

7.7 Testing the Supply-Side Propositions

7.7.1 Structural Break Analysis of Supply-Side Growth Variables

Proposition (1a) expects that savings or inflows or both (supply-side determinants of investments) will follow the pattern of the drop in investment growth. Proposition (1b) goes on further to specify that if Proposition (1a) is to hold true, then the growth in supply-side variables drops significantly post-1992, matching the direction of change in the investment growth variable.

We examine the mean shift in the series of savings growth and inflows growth over the period 1973–2019 to test Propositions (1a) and (1b). The structural break analysis explained in Box 7.4 is applied to detect discrete mean shifts in the series of savings and inflow growth. Of the two supply-side determinants, the structural break tests identify the single most significant regime-specific mean shift only in savings growth in 1992.

Box 7.4 Test for a Structural Break in the Growth of Savings and Inflows

One statistical test is based on a classical Chow test to check the shift in the series at a known break date. A second econometric test is based on a dummy regression analysis to test for the significance of the year 1992 as a break dummy in the growth series.

A structural break test at a known break date for all explanatory supply-side variables

To test our explanatory variables series for the single mean shift at a known break date, we use the structural break model specified to test for the break at a known break date. This gives us a specific test for Proposition (1a):

$$y_{it} = \beta_{ij} + \epsilon_t \text{ where } \beta_{i1} \neq \beta_{i2} \qquad (7.25a)$$

y_{it} represents growth in variable (i) in period (t). β_{ij} is the mean shift parameter for the growth rate of variable (i). This model allows the coefficient β_{ij} to change after the break. If TB is the break date, the model is:

(continued)

Box 7.4 (continued)

$$y_{it} = \begin{cases} \beta_{i1} + \epsilon_t \text{ if } t \leq TB \\ \beta_{i2} + \epsilon_t \text{ if } t > TB \end{cases} \quad (7.25b)$$

For this model, we test the null hypothesis that the mean shift parameter does not vary over the subsamples defined by the specified known break date. The known break date (TB) is taken as the year 1992 and identified as the break date in the investment growth series. Our next step is to test the mean shift in our explanatory supply-side growth series, savings and inflows, at the known break date year 1992.

Chow's test for a known break date for supply-side explanatory variables

The Wald test for the known break date, using Chow's procedure, is performed to determine a break in the growth of the explanatory variables. The explanatory variables are savings growth and inflows growth.

Dummy regression for testing a known break date in investment growth

The dummy regression to test for the intercept break is specified for the growth of supply-side explanatory variables. We run the regression for the savings growth and inflows growth variables. The dummy regression is:

$$g_t = \beta + \theta \text{DU}_t + u_t, \quad (7.25c)$$

g_t represents the growth of supply-side variables and DUt is the break dummy variable. The break dummy variable takes the following values: DUt = 1 if t > 1992 and DUt = 0 otherwise. The dummy regression, Proposition (1b), allows us to check whether savings and inflow growth, on average, exhibit a downward or upward trend.

The structural break analysis allows us to test for Propositions (1a) and (1b) to see whether a break exists in our supply-side variables in the year 1992 and if the growth in any of these supply-side variables drops after 1992.

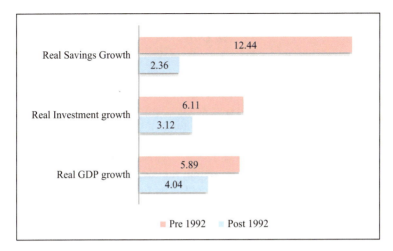

Fig. 7.2 Structural break dummy regression for growth in GDP, investment and savings. (Note: The coefficient of the break dummy variable, the savings growth variable, takes the value −10.07 and is significant at the 0.1 level. The coefficient shows that after 1992, on average, savings growth dropped by 10 per cent to 2.36. The coefficient of the break dummy variable, the investment growth variable, takes the value −2.99 and is significant at the 0.1 level. The coefficient shows that after 1992, on average, investment growth dropped by 2.99 per cent to 3.12. The coefficient of the break dummy variable, the real GDP variable, takes the value −1.85 and is significant at the 0.01 level. GDP growth fell by 1.85 per cent post-1992 to 4.04. Standard errors given in parentheses. ***$p < 0.01$; **$p < 0.05$; *$p < 0.1$. Dummy variable post-1992 = 1 for years 1993 to 2019, post-1992 = 0 for 1973 to 1992)

In addition, the linear regression results in Fig. 7.2 show that average savings growth drops from 12.4 per cent between 1973 and 1992 to 2.4 per cent post-1992. Therefore, the statistical analysis supports Propositions (1a) and (1b): that there was a significant drop in the saving growth series and that the break in the savings growth series coincided with the break in investment growth

We proceed to test Proposition (2), which examines the trend in investment, savings and inflows as percentage shares in GDP. The trends are analysed pre-1992 and post-1992.

7.7.2 Trend Analysis for the Shares of Supply-Side Variables in Output

Figure 7.3 plots investment and savings as shares of GDP for the years 1973–2019. There is a complex relationship between the share of investment in GDP and the share of savings in GDP. The share of investment declines over time with a visibly faster pace post-1992. The share of savings in GDP rises to a peak in 1992 and then declines. This implies that when the investment share was high in pre-1992, the savings share was low but increasing, creating a large gap between savings and investment. Post-1992, as the investment share fell, the savings share did as well, but there was a smaller gap with investment. The relationship is thus indeed a complex one.

To capture this relationship between the investment and savings share, they are best run separately in the form of trend regressions. Moreover, we observe a large gap between the investment and savings shares pre-1992 (Fig. 7.3). This gap is the share of inflows. Therefore, we run the savings and inflow shares in the form of trend regressions.

The trend regressions based on the empirical methodology explained in Box 7.5 are shown in Figs. 7.4, 7.5, and 7.6), which shows that of the shares of the supply-side variables in output, the share of inflows has a significant declining trend post-1992. In addition, the trend in the share of inflows matches the declining trend in the share of investment in output

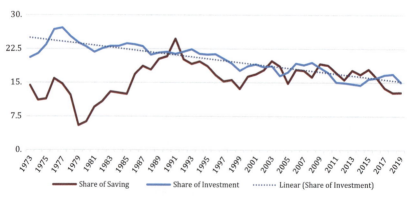

Fig. 7.3 Investment and savings shares as percentages of GDP

Box 7.5 Trend Analysis for the Shares of Supply-Side Variables in Output

To test Proposition (2), we perform a trend analysis for our supply-side variables: savings shares and inflow shares. First, the trend analysis is based on examining the trends of the investment share and the shares of supply-side variables as a time-series plot. Second, it is based on estimating the functional form of the investment share and shares of supply-side variables in output using trend regressions.

Using trend regressions to examine the shares of supply-side variables in the output

A regression equation of the following form is run on the investment variable and supply-side variables. The coefficients of the following equation provide us with the functional forms for the investment share variable and the shares of the supply-side variables in output.

$$\text{share}_{kt} = \alpha_0 + \alpha_1 \text{trend}_{kt} + \alpha_2 \text{trend}^2_{kt} + e_{kt} \quad (\text{Proposition 2})$$

share$_{kt}$ represents the share of the kth variable in period (t). $\alpha 1$ is the coefficient representing the linear trend and $\alpha 2$ represents the quadratic trend.

Our analysis of shares is limited to studying them as time plots or analysing them in trend regressions to see if a particular share variable has an increasing or declining trend. However, our primary purpose is to identify the determinant that explains the declining trend in the investment share in output post-1992. Running a regression with the investment share as a function of the savings share and inflows share is not econometrically correct because the three variables are governed by an additive macroeconomic accounting relationship. Recalling our theoretical equation:

Investment share = savings share + inflows share

However, it would be econometrically correct if we were to run the above equation in the form of growth rates.

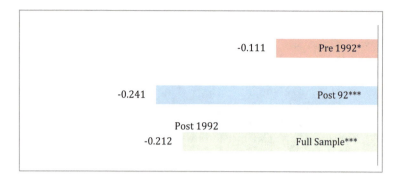

Fig. 7.4 Trend regression of share of investment as percentage of GDP. (Note: The coefficient of −0.111 pre-1992 shows a declining linear trend at the 0.1 significance level. For the overall sample, the −0.212 coefficient of the trend variable shows a declining linear trend at the 0.01 significance level. Standard errors given in parentheses. ***$p < 0.01$; **$p < 0.05$; *$p < 0.1$)

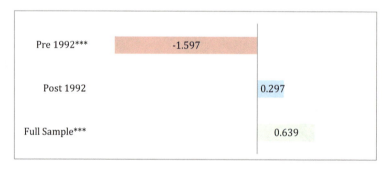

Fig. 7.5 Trend regression of share of savings as percentage of GDP. (Note: For pre-1992, the coefficient −1.597 of the share of savings function shows a declining trend. However, for post-1992, the trend coefficient is insignificant. For the overall sample, the significant coefficient 0.639 for the time trend variable shows an increasing trend over time. Standard errors given in parentheses. ***$p < 0.01$; **$p < 0.05$; *$p < 0.1$)

post-1992. The savings result is insignificant post-1992. However, the results appear to be mixed, and further investigation of the supply-side variables is merited. In the next test, we present the results for the supply-side variables—savings and inflows run jointly.

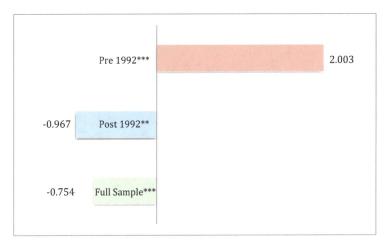

Fig. 7.6 Trend regression of share of inflows as percentage of GDP. (Note: Pre-1992, the coefficient of 2.003, and post-1992, the coefficient of −0.967 are significant at the 0.01 level. The coefficient of the trend variable for the full sample, −0.754, is significant at the 0.01 level and shows a significant decline over time. Standard errors given in parentheses. ***$p < 0.01$; **$p < 0.05$; *$p < 0.1$)

7.7.3 Analysis of the Investment Growth Variable in Relation to both Supply-Side Growth Variables Run Jointly

To test Proposition (3), we run investment growth as a function of savings growth and inflows growth in a multiple linear regression model (Box 7.6). The left-hand-side variable is investment growth and the right-hand-side variables are savings growth and inflows growth. Figure 7.7 shows that investment growth is significantly correlated with only inflows growth. Pre-1992, investment growth is significantly correlated with inflows growth but not significantly correlated with savings growth. Post-1992, investment growth is significantly correlated with inflows growth, although the magnitude of the coefficient drops significantly, while post-1992, investment growth continues to be not well-correlated with savings growth. Therefore, growth in the investment function is well correlated with growth in inflows.

> **Box 7.6 Analysis of the Investment Growth Variable in Relation to Supply-Side Growth Variables**
>
> Proposition (3) is explained based on a linear regression model specified to explain the drop in investment growth. The model of the investment growth variable (g_t^I) as a function of savings growth (g_t^S) and inflows growth (g_t^i) is written as:
>
> $$g_t^I = f\left(g_t^S, g_t^i\right) (\text{Proposition 3})$$
>
> We run the specification for investment growth as a combined function of savings growth and inflows growth in a multiple linear regression framework. The specifications are run independently for the pre-1992 and post-1992 periods. The coefficients of the model are then tested for equality across the two periods, pre-1992 and post-1992.
>
> $$g_t^I = \delta_0 + \delta_1 g_t^S + \delta_2 g_t^i + \epsilon_t \,(\text{Proposition 3})$$
>
> g_t^I represents investment growth, g_t^S represents savings growth and g_t^i represents inflows growth.
>
> This essay aims to explain the drop in investment growth and test the break in investment growth coinciding with the break in the supply-side growth variables. Thus, we want our supply-side growth variables to significantly explain the drop in the investment growth variable. Therefore, while testing Proposition (3) using the specifications above, we expect the following proposition to hold:
>
> > The savings growth and/or inflows growth coefficient should be positive and significant for both pre-1992 and post-1992, but with a higher coefficient pre-1992 than post-1992.

7.7.4 Relationship Between the Supply-Side Determinants, Savings and Inflows

Our last set of empirical results for the supply-side variables was based on the two testable propositions, (4a) and (4b). These tested the relationship between the supply-side determinants themselves, savings and inflows

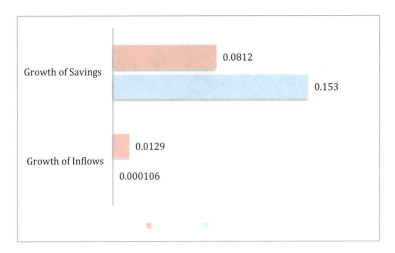

Fig. 7.7 Regression result for growth of investment, savings and inflows. (Note: The investment growth coefficients of 0.0129 pre-1992 and 0.000106 post-1992 are significant and correlated with inflows growth at the 0.1 and 0.01 significance levels, respectively. Investment growth is not correlated with savings growth. Standard errors given in parentheses. ***$p < 0.01$; **$p < 0.05$; *$p < 0.1$)

(Box 7.7). Figure 7.8 shows the results of the regression where the left-hand-side variable is savings growth and the right-hand-side variable is inflows growth. Pre-1992, the significant and negative coefficient of −0.079 goes in favour of the Griffin-Enos hypothesis—that savings and inflows are indeed substitutes. For post-1992, however, the negative correlation coefficient becomes negligible—it is significant. Our findings suggest that inflows were a substitute for savings, more in the pre-1992 period but hardly so in the post-1992 period.

So far, this section's analysis has given us evidence to answer a central question—that of the supply-side determinants of investment, which explain the drop in investment growth. We can say that the drop in investment growth in Pakistan post-1992 was significantly associated with the drop in the growth of inflows in Pakistan post-1992. However, the relationship appears weak.

Box 7.7 The Relationship Between the Supply-Side Determinants, Savings and Inflows
To test the relationship between savings and inflows

To test the two possibilities, Propositions (4a) and (4b), we specify the relationship between savings and inflows as:

$$g_t^s = \alpha_0 + \alpha_1 g_t^i + \epsilon_t \text{ (Proposition 4)}$$

g_t^s represents the growth in savings and g_t^i represents the growth in inflows.

The model is run separately for the pre-1992 and post-1992 periods. The coefficients of the model are then tested for equality across these two periods. The nature of the relationship between savings and inflows depends on the sign of the coefficient (α_1). If α_1 is significant and positive, the relationship favours the first argument—that savings and inflows are complements. On the contrary, a significant and negative α_1 favours the alternative possibility—that savings and inflows are substitutes.

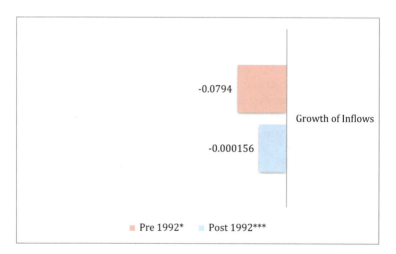

Fig. 7.8 Regression showing relationship between growth of savings and inflows. (Note: For pre-1992, the coefficient of −0.079 is significant at the 0.1 level, which goes in favour of the Griffin-Enos hypothesis. For post-1992, the coefficient of −0.000156 is significant at the 0.01 level. Standard errors given in parentheses. ***$p < 0.01$; **$p < 0.05$; *$p < 0.1$)

7.8 Demand-Side Determinants Explaining the Drop in Investment Growth

We now explain the behaviour and decline in investment growth post-1992 using the demand-side determinants. Recalling our literature and theoretical framework, the demand-side determinants of investment are public and private investment. Explaining the determinants of Pakistan's long-run investment growth using demand-side variables and the theoretical framework adopted gives us the following testable proposition:

- Proposition (5a): The structural break in investment growth coincides significantly with the structural break in the demand-side growth variables of public and private investment.

Assuming proposition (5a) holds, we have:

- Proposition (5b): The demand-side growth variables of public and private investment have significantly lower growth post-break date, matching the direction of change of the investment growth variable.
- Proposition (6): The shares of the demand-side variables of public and private investment in output have a significant declining trend post-1992.
- Proposition (7): The drop in investment growth post-1992 is significantly associated with the drop in growth of the demand-side variables of public and private investment.
- Proposition (8a): Public and private investment are significantly positively correlated, which results in crowding in.
- Proposition (8b): Public and private investment are significantly negatively correlated, which results in crowding out.

The propositions proceed in a sequential and intuitively logical way.

Having established that there was indeed a statistically significant drop in Pakistan's investment growth, we aim to identify the explanatory variable that is statistically well correlated with investment growth. Proposition (5) tests for the better demand-side variable coinciding with the break date in investment growth.

Proposition (6) tests for a declining trend in the shares of public investment and private investment in output. The proposition tests for the trend coefficient in each share, public and private investment, to be statistically different in two periods, pre-1992 and post-1992, and to see if the post-1992 trend coefficient is statistically more negative than the pre-1992 coefficient value.

We then proceed to Proposition (7), which specifies that investment growth is well explained by growth in public and private investment. Finally, Proposition (8) establishes the relationship between the demand-side variables of public and private investment themselves. It tests whether the relationship between the two variables will result in crowding in or crowding out.

The results from our empirical exercise from the demand side will thus provide us with two possible explanations—one for the drop in investment growth and another for the relationship between public and private investment.

7.9 Testing the Demand-Side Propositions

7.9.1 *Structural Break Analysis of Demand-Side Growth Variables*

Proposition (5a) expects that the demand-side determinants of investment (either public and private investment growth or both) will follow the pattern of the drop in investment growth post-1992. Proposition (5b) goes further to specify that if Proposition (5a) holds true, then the growth in demand-side variables will drop significantly post-1992, matching the direction of change in the investment growth variable. Therefore, we test Proposition (5) using a structural break analysis and a two-sample t test analysis (Box 7.8).

The Wald test for a known break date using Chow's procedure is performed to determine a break in the growth of the explanatory demand-side variables. Table 7.1 shows the findings for the Wald test at a known break date. Of the explanatory demand-side variables, only the public investment growth variable rejects the null posit of having no structural break. The Wald statistic takes a value of 4.72 and is significant at a 10 per cent level. This shows that public investment growth had a significant break in 1993. We conclude that under Chow's procedure, the public investment growth series shows a significant structural break in 1993. This structural break analysis supports Proposition (5a), which states that there is a significant break in the public investment growth series and that the break in the public investment growth series coincides with the break in investment growth.

Box 7.8 A Structural Break Test at a Known Break Date for All Explanatory Demand-Side Variables

To test our explanatory demand-side series for the single mean shift at a known break date, we repeat the structural break model specified to test for the break at a known break date:

$$y_{it} = \beta_{ij} + \epsilon_t \text{ where } \beta_{i1} \neq \beta_{i2} \text{ (Proposition 5a)}$$

y_{it} represents the growth in variable (i) in period (t). βij is the mean shift parameter for the growth rate of variable (i). This model allows the coefficient (β_{ij}) to change after the break. If TB is the break date, then the model is:

$$y_{it} = \begin{cases} \beta_{i1} + \epsilon_t \text{ if } t \leq \text{TB} \\ \beta_{i2} + \epsilon_t \text{ if } t > \text{TB} \end{cases} \text{(Proposition 5a)}$$

For this model, we test the null hypothesis, which means that the shift parameters do not vary over the subsamples defined by the specified known break date. The known break date (TB) is taken as the year 1992, as identified in the investment growth series. Our next step is to test the mean shift in our explanatory demand-side growth series, public investment and private investment, at the known break date year 1992.

Chow's test for a known break date for demand-side explanatory variables

The Wald test for the known break date, using Chow's procedure, is performed to determine a break in the growth of the explanatory variables, public and private investment growth.

Two-sample t tests for the equality of means

This t test is designed to compare the means of the same variable between two groups, pre-1992 and post-1992. We calculate the average growth rates for the pre-1992 and post-1992 periods for each of our demand-side growth variables, public investment growth and private investment growth. Our sample ranges from 1973 to 2019. We then test the difference in the average growth rates using the t test, which allows us to test the following propositions:

(continued)

Box 7.8 (continued)

$$\text{Ha}: \mu i1 \ne \mu i2 \quad \text{(Proposition 5b i)}$$

$$\text{Ha}: \mu i1 < \mu i2 \quad \text{(Proposition 5b ii)}$$

$$\text{Ha}: \mu i1 > \mu i2 \quad \text{(Proposition 5b iii)}$$

$\mu i1$ is the average growth rate of the ith variable pre-1992, and $\mu i2$ is the average growth rate of the ith variable post-1992.

To support Proposition (5b), that the average growth rate of the demand-side variables dropped post-1992, we are particularly interested in the result of Proposition (5b iii), which tests for the alternative hypothesis that the average growth rate pre-1992 was significantly greater than the average growth rate post-1992.

This section's structural break analysis allows us to test for Propositions (5a) and (5b): whether a break exists in our demand-side variables in 1992 and if the average growth in any of these demand-side variables was significantly higher pre-1992 and lower after 1992.

Table 7.1 Structural break test for real public investment growth

Results: Test for known structural break

Variable description	Break in year 1992 ± 1	Tests and probability		
		Test	Statistics	p value
Real public investment growth	1993	$\chi^2(1)$	4.72*	0.091

Standard errors given in parentheses

Note: The Wald statistic takes the value of 4.72 and is significant at the 10 per cent level. This shows that public investment growth has a significant break in the year 1993. We can conclude that under Chow's procedure, the public investment growth series shows a significant structural break in the year 1993

***$p < 0.01$; **$p < 0.05$; *$p < 0.1$

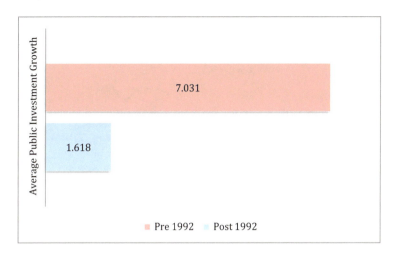

Fig. 7.9 Two-sample t test for growth in public investment. (Note: The average public investment growth rate is 5.4 percentage points higher pre-1992 as compared to post-1992. The difference in the average values between pre-1992 and post-1992 is significant at the 0.05 level. Standard errors given in parentheses. ***$p < 0.01$; **$p < 0.05$; *$p < 0.1$)

Figure 7.9 shows the results of the two-sample t test. The test is run separately to compare the average growth rates of both public and private investment pre-1992 and post-1992. Of the two demand-side determinants, the results for public investment are significant. They show that, on average, the public investment growth rate was 5.4 percentage points significantly higher pre-1992 than post-1992. This result supports Proposition (5b) that public investment growth was significantly lower post the break date of 1992/93, matching the direction of change in the investment growth variable.

7.9.2 Trend Analysis for the Shares of Demand-Side Variables in Output

We then move from examining growth in the macro aggregates to shares in the output of the macro aggregates. Given the confirmation of Proposition (5) in favour of the public investment growth variable, we now expect symmetry between the shares of public investment and investment. Having seen a declining trend in the investment share in output

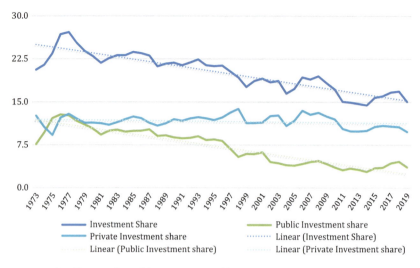

Fig. 7.10 Shares of total investment, public investment and private investment as percentage of GDP

over time in Essay 5, we move on to Proposition (6), testing for a decline in the trend in the shares of our demand-side variables in output—the public investment share and private investment share post-1992/1993.

Figure 7.10 plots total investment, public investment and private investment as shares in total output (GDP) for 1973–2019. Recalling that we observed the investment share in output decline over time in Essay 5, we now spot a smoking gun: the public investment share in output declining over time while the private investment share remains approximately constant. This implies that the declining investment share can be explained by the declining public investment share over time. It also implies that the declining investment share will not be explained well by the constant private investment share over time.

Regarding the shares, a non-rigorous test observing the time plots in Fig. 7.10 shows that the share of public investment declines over time. However, the share of private investment remains constant and does not increase. This provides some confirmation of the Keynesian hypothesis that pre-1992, when the public investment share in output was high, the total investment share in output was also high, while the private investment share in output was constant. However, post-1992, when the public investment share in output fell, it did not increase the private investment share in output. Thus, the total investment share in output also fell. This points to a refutation of the Ricardian hypothesis of public investment crowding out private investment, favouring the Keynesian hypothesis of public investment crowding in total investment.

Next, we proceed to test the statistical significance of the trends and relationships observed in Fig. 7.10 in the form of trend regressions for each of the total investment, public investment and private investment shares in output, following the empirical methodology in Box 7.9.

Figure 7.11 shows the trend regression result for the share of total investment in output. The left-hand-side variable is the share of investment in output and the right-hand-side variable is the time trend (t). The significant coefficient of trend variable (t) of -0.212 for the overall sample clearly shows a declining linear trend over time. In addition, the coefficient significantly declines post-1992 and the change between the two coefficients, pre-1992 and post-1992, differ significantly between the two periods.

The trend regressions for the public investment share in output are shown in Fig. 7.12. The left-hand-side variable is the share of public investment and the right-hand-side variable is the time trend (trend). For the overall sample, the significant coefficient of -0.204 for the time trend variable shows a declining trend over time. For the subsamples, pre-1992

Box 7.9 Using Trend Regressions to Examine the Shares of the Demand-Side Variables in Output

We run a regression equation for the investment and demand-side variables. The coefficients of the following equation with some statistical significance are used to analyse whether the share variables have a declining or increasing trend. The regression equation is specified as:

$$\text{share}_{kt} = \alpha_0 + \alpha_1 \text{trend}_{kt} + e_{kt} \quad (\text{Proposition 6})$$

share_{kt} represents the share of variable (k) in period (t) and $\alpha 1$ is the coefficient representing the linear trend.

Two-sample t tests for the equality of means

(*continued*)

Box 7.9 (continued)

We calculate the average share value for each variable for the yearly observations pre-1992 and post-1992. Our sample ranges from 1973 to 2019. We then test the difference in the average values using a *t* test, which allows us to test the following propositions:

$$\text{Ha}: \mu i1 = \mu i2 \qquad (\text{Proposition 6 i})$$

$$\text{Ha}: \mu i1 < \mu i2, \text{and} \qquad (\text{Proposition 6 ii})$$

$$\text{Ha}: \mu i1 > \mu i2 \qquad (\text{Proposition 6 iii})$$

$\mu i1$ is the average share value of the *i*th variable pre-1992, and $\mu i2$ is the average share value of the *i*th variable post-1992. To support Proposition (6), that there is a declining trend in the shares of the demand-side variables post-1992, we expect Proposition (6 iii) to hold. Proposition (6 iii) tests for the alternative hypothesis that the average value of the demand-side share in output pre-1992 is significantly greater than the average value of the demand-side share in output post-1992.

Our analysis of shares is limited to studying them as time plots or analysing them in trend regressions to see if a particular share variable has an increasing or declining trend. However, our primary purpose is to identify the determinant that explains the declining trend in the investment share in output post-1992. Therefore, running a regression with the investment share as a function of the public investment share and private investment share is not econometrically correct because, per our theoretical model, the three variables are governed by an additive macroeconomic accounting relationship:

Investment share = public investment share + private investment share

However, it would be econometrically correct if we ran the above equation in the form of growth rates.

Fig. 7.11 Trend regression of share of investment as percentage of GDP. (Note: The change between the two coefficients pre-1992 and post-1992 differs significantly between the two periods. For the overall sample, the coefficient of the trend variable −0.212 is significant at the 0.01 level, showing a declining linear trend over time. Standard errors given in parentheses. ***$p < 0.01$; **$p < 0.05$; *$p < 0.1$)

Fig. 7.12 Trend regression of share of public investment. (Note: For the sub-sample pre-1992, the coefficient value of −0.116 is significant at the 0.1 level. Post-1992, the coefficient value of −0.189 is significant at the 0.01 level. The coefficients show a declining trend in public investment over time. For the overall sample, the share of public investment coefficient −0.204 is significant at the 0.01 level. Standard errors given in parentheses. ***$p < 0.01$; **$p < 0.05$; *$p < 0.1$)

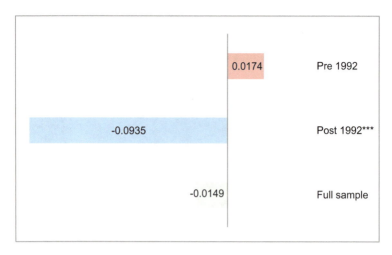

Fig. 7.13 Trend regression of share of private investment. (Note: For post-1992, the trend coefficient of −0.0935 is significant at the 0.01 level, showing that the trend of the private investment share has declined significantly post-1992 compared to pre-1992. Standard errors given in parentheses. ***p < 0.01; **p < 0.05; *p < 0.1)

and post-1992, the share of public investment in output consistently shows a significant declining trend in both periods. However, the negative trend for the share of public investment in output is higher in the post-1992 period than in the pre-1992 period.

The trend regression for the private investment share in output is insignificant (Fig. 7.13).

Figure 7.14 shows the results of the two-sample *t* tests for the share of public investment in output pre-1992 and post-1992. Of the two demand-side determinants (the public and private investment shares in output), only the results for the public investment share are significant. The result for the public investment share in output is 5.03 percentage points higher pre-1992 than post-1992. The difference in the average values between the two periods is statistically significant.

These empirical results for Propositions (5) and (6) show that the public investment share in output is a significant determinant of the investment share in output. However, we need to further investigate the demand-side variables of public investment and private investment jointly.

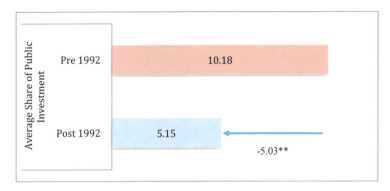

Fig. 7.14 Two-sample *t* test for share of public investment. (Note: The average public investment share is 5.03 percentage points higher pre-1992 compared to post-1992. The difference in average values between pre-1992 and post-1992 is significant at the 0.01 level. Standard errors given in parentheses. ***$p < 0.01$; **$p < 0.05$; *$p < 0.1$)

7.9.3 Investment Growth and Demand-Side Growth

We then proceed to test Proposition (7), which specifies that investment growth is well explained by the growth in public and private investment. For concreteness, Fig. 7.15 provides the multiple linear regression results for the specification in Box 7.10.

The left-hand-side variable is investment growth and the right-hand-side variables are public investment growth and private investment growth. For the full sample, investment growth is significantly correlated with both public investment growth and private investment growth. Pre-1992, investment growth is better correlated with public investment growth. Post-1992, the coefficient for public investment growth drops significantly. This means that post-1992, investment growth is better than public investment growth.

Our analysis for the demand side infers the following:

- Pre-1992, on average, growth in investment (6.3 per cent) and the share of investment in output (23 per cent) are higher compared to post-1992. This is explained by the growth in public investment (7.03 per cent) and the share of public investment in output (10.1 per cent) being significantly higher compared to the post-1992 period.

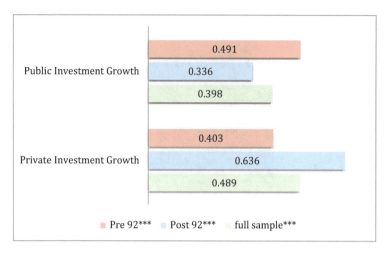

Fig. 7.15 Regression of growth of investment, growth in public investment and growth in private investment. (Note: For subsamples pre-1992 and post-1992, the coefficients of investment growth are significantly correlated with both public investment growth and private investment growth at the 0.01 level. For the full sample, investment growth is significantly correlated with both public investment growth and private investment growth at the 0.01 level. Standard errors given in parentheses. ***$p < 0.01$; **$p < 0.05$; *$p < 0.1$)

- Post-1992, on average, growth in investment (2.8 per cent) and the share of investment in output (17.9 per cent) declines significantly compared to pre-1992. This is explained by the share of public investment dropping by 5 per cent, while, on average, the share of private investment in output remains constant.
- Growth in investment is significantly correlated with growth in both public and private investment for the entire period and subperiods.
- Pre-1992, growth in public investment is better correlated with growth in investment.

Post-1992, the correlation of growth in public investment with investment growth drops significantly. Therefore, Proposition (7) holds that the drop in investment growth post-1992 is significantly associated with the drop in the growth of public investment post-1992.

Box 7.10 Analysis of the Investment Growth Variable in Relation to Demand-Side Growth Variables

An empirical model of investment growth based on a linear regression model is specified to explain the drop in investment growth. This makes investment growth (g_t^I) a function of public investment growth (g_t^{IG}) and private investment growth (g_t^{IP}), and is written as:

$$g_t^I = f\left(g_t^{IG}, g_t^{IP}\right) \text{(Proposition 7)}$$

We run specifications for investment growth as a combined function of public investment growth and private investment growth in a multiple linear regression framework. The specifications are run independently for pre-1992 and post-1992. The coefficients of the model are then tested for equality across the two periods.

$$g_t^I = \delta_0 + \delta_1 g_t^{IG} + \delta_2 g_t^{IP} + \epsilon_t \text{ (Proposition 7)}$$

g_t^I represents investment growth, g_t^{IG} represents public investment growth and g_t^{IP} represents private investment growth.

We aim to explain the drop in investment growth, and since we have established the methodology to test the break in investment growth coinciding with the break in the demand-side growth variables, we want our demand-side growth variables to significantly explain the drop in investment growth variables. Therefore, while testing Proposition (7) using the above specification of investment growth, we expect that:

> The public investment growth coefficient will be positive and significant for both phases, pre-1992 and post-1992, but higher in the former period.

7.9.4 Relationship Between the Demand-Side Determinants (Public Investment and Private Investment)

Our last set of empirical tests for Proposition (8) is based on the two testable hypotheses mentioned in the literature—the Keynesian crowding-in hypothesis and the Ricardian crowding-out hypothesis. The two

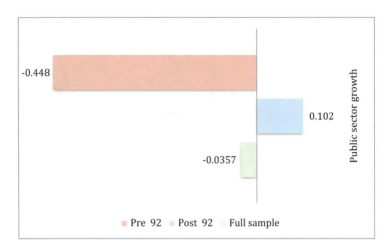

Fig. 7.16 Regression showing relationship between growth of private investment and growth of public investment. (Note: Pre-1992, the coefficient of the private investment growth variable −0.448 is correlated with public investment growth at a significance level of 0.1. Private investment has no significant correlation with public investment in the full sample and post-1992. Standard errors given in parentheses. ***$p < 0.01$; **$p < 0.05$; *$p < 0.1$)

hypotheses test the relationship between the demand-side determinants themselves, public investment and private investment.

The results are presented in Fig. 7.16 based on the empirical methodology explained in Box 7.11. The left-hand-side variable is private investment growth and the right-hand-side variable is public investment growth. For the full series, the relationship between public investment and private investment is not significant. Pre-1992, the coefficient is negative and marginally significant. Post-1992, the coefficient is insignificant.

We find that private investment has no significant correlation with public investment in the full sample. This implies a rejection of the Ricardian hypothesis that public investment crowds out private investment. The decreasing share of public investment over time also rejects the Ricardian hypothesis because, as the public investment share drops, it should have crowded in, increasing the private investment share. Instead, the private investment share remains constant at a very low level of approximately 12 per cent of GDP and the reduction in public investment over time accounts

> **Box 7.11 Empirical Model to Test the Relationship Between Public Investment and Private Investment**
>
> To test the two possibilities, Propositions (8a) and (8b), we specify the relationship between public investment and private investment as:
>
> $$g_t^{IP} = \alpha_0 + \alpha_1 g_t^{IG} + \epsilon_t \text{ (Proposition 8)}$$
>
> g_t^{IP} represents growth in private investment, and g_t^{IG} represents growth in public investment.
>
> The model is run independently for pre-1992 and post-1992. The model coefficients are then tested for equality across the two periods. The nature of the relationship between public and private investment depends on the sign of the coefficient (α_1). If α_1 is significant and positive, the relationship favours the first argument, that there is crowding in. On the contrary, a significant and negative α_1 favours the alternative, that there is crowding out.

for the drop in total investment over time. In turn, this accounts for the drop in GDP over time. This is a qualified acceptance of the Keynesian hypothesis that public investment in Pakistan crowds in.

7.10 Conclusion

This essay has focused on explaining the observed drop in Pakistan's investment growth between two periods, 1973–1992 (pre-1992) and 1992–2019 (post-1992). It has done so by examining the impact of the macro aggregate determinants of investment growth (supply-and demand-side determinants) on investment. Our empirical results show some weak evidence of explaining the drop in investment growth in terms of its supply-side variables, savings and inflows. The results in the case of demand-side determinants explaining the drop in investment growth are strong and significant.

We conclude that the reduction in public investment over time accounts for the drop in total investment over time in Pakistan, which, in turn, accounts for the drop in Pakistan's GDP over time. This is a qualified acceptance of the Keynesian hypothesis that public investment crowds in aggregate investment. Therefore, Essay 6 suggests that the growth in demand-side determinants and declining share of public investment explain the drop in the growth of investment post-1992.

References

Amjad, R. (2014). Pakistan's growth spurts and reversals: A historical perspective. *Lahore Journal of Economics, 19*, 91–104.

Apergis, N. (2000). Public and private investments in Greece: Complementary or substitute 'goods'? *Bulletin of Economic Research, 52*(3), 225–234.

Bahal, G., Raissi, M., & Tulin, V. (2018). Crowding-out or crowding-in? Public and private investment in India. *World Development, 109*, 323–333.

Blanchard, O. J. (1991). Crowding out. In *The world of economics* (pp. 155–159). Palgrave Macmillan.

Burnside, C., & Dollar, D. (2000). Aid, policies and growth. *American Economic Review, 90*(4), 847–868.

Chenery, R. M., & Strout, A. M. (1966). Foreign assistance and economic development. *American Economic Review, 56*(4), 679–733.

Clift, B. (2019). Contingent Keynesianism: The IMF's model answer to the post-crash fiscal policy efficacy question in advanced economies. *Review of International Political Economy, 26*(6), 1211–1237.

Cwik, T., & Wieland, V. (2011). Keynesian government spending multipliers and spillovers in the euro area. *Economic Policy, 26*(67), 493–549.

Djankov, S., Montalvo, J. G., & Reynal-Querol, M. (2006). Does foreign aid help? *Cato Journal, 26*, 1.

Easterly, W. (2003). Can foreign aid buy growth? *Journal of Economic Perspectives, 17*(3), 23–48.

Edwards, S. (1995). *Why are saving rates so different across countries? An international comparative analysis*. Working Paper No. 5097. National Bureau of Economic Research.

Elakkad, R. M., & Hussein, A. M. (2021). The effect of official development assistance on domestic savings and economic growth in Egypt. *International Journal of Economics and Finance, 13*(12), 1–33.

Erden, L., & Holcombe, R. G. (2006). The linkage between public and private investment: A co-integration analysis of a panel of developing countries. *Eastern Economic Journal, 32*(3), 479–492.

Fasanya, I. O., & Onakoya, A. B. (2012). Does foreign aid accelerate economic growth? An empirical analysis for Nigeria. *International Journal of Economics and Financial Issues, 2*(4), 423–431.

Feldstein, M. (2009). Rethinking the role of fiscal policy. *American Economic Review, 99*(2), 556–559.

Fry, M. J. (1994). Malaysia's inverse saving-investment correlation: The role of public and foreign direct investment. In *The economics of international investment* (pp. 191–202). Baltimore University Press.

Griffin, K. (1978). Foreign capital, domestic savings and economic development. In *International inequality and national poverty* (pp. 57–80). Palgrave Macmillan.

Griffin, K. B., & Enos, J. L. (1970). Foreign assistance: Objectives and consequences. *Economic Development and Cultural Change, 18*(3), 313–327.

Gupta, K. L. (1992). Ricardian equivalence and crowding out in Asia. *Applied Economics, 24*(1), 19–25.

Hasan, M. S. (2002). Concessional foreign capital inflows and domestic savings across countries: Dependency hypothesis re-visited. *Journal of Economic Studies, 29*(6), 388–422.

Idrees, M. A., Khan, A., Khan, M. A., Raees, M. B., & Syed, M. (2020). Impact of foreign capital inflows on household savings in Pakistan. *European Journal of Business and Management Research, 5*(4).

Khan, N. Z., & Rahim, E. (1993). Foreign aid, domestic savings and economic growth Pakistan. *Pakistan Development Review, 32*(4), 1157–1167.

Khan, R. E. A., & Gill, A. R. (2009). *Crowding out effect of public borrowing: A case of Pakistan.* MPRA Paper No. 16292. University Library of Munich.

Looney, R. E. (1997). Infrastructure and private sector investment in Pakistan. *Journal of Asian Economics, 8*(3), 393–420.

Mankiw, N. G. (2008). *Economics: Principles and applications.* Cengage Learning.

Musgrave, R. A. (1987). US fiscal policy, Keynes, and Keynesian economics. *Journal of Post Keynesian Economics, 10*(2), 171–182.

Naqvi, N. H. (2002). Crowding-in or crowding-out? Modelling the relationship between public and private fixed capital formation using co-integration analysis: The case of Pakistan 1964–2000. *Pakistan Development Review, 41*(3), 255–276.

Oladipo, O. S. (2010). Does saving really matter for growth in developing countries? The case of a small open economy. *International Business and Economics Research Journal, 9*(4), 87–94.

Rashid, A. (2006). Public-private investment linkage in Pakistan: A multivariate co-integration analysis. *South Asia Economic Journal, 7*(2), 219–230.

Reinhart, C. M., & Talvi, E. (1998). Capital flows and saving in Latin America and Asia: A reinterpretation. *Journal of Development Economics, 57*(1), 45–66.

Ricciuti, R. (2003). Assessing Ricardian equivalence. *Journal of Economic Surveys, 17*(1), 55–78.

Romer, C. D., & Romer, D. H. (2007). *Reducing inflation: Motivation and strategy.* University of Chicago Press.

Seater, J. J. (1993). Ricardian equivalence. *Journal of Economic Literature, 31*(1), 142–190.

CHAPTER 8

The Role of Policy Reforms and the Regulatory Policy Environment in Explaining the Behaviour of Public Investment in Pakistan

8.1 Implications of the Argument Established in Essays 5 and 6

Essays 5 and 6 are Maynard redux, applying an adapted Keynesian mum equation to explain the trajectory of long-run gross domestic product (GDP) growth for Pakistan. Pre-1992, high GDP growth of 6 per cent per annum on the left-hand side of the equation is explained by the determinants on the right-hand side—of high investment growth paired with low consumption growth. This high growth of aggregate investment pre-1992 is in turn explained (by a derivative set of equations) by the high growth of public investment, paired with fairly constant growth in private investment. Post-1992, low GDP growth of 4 per cent per annum, on the left-hand side of the equation, is explained by the determinants on the right-hand side of the equation, of low investment growth, paired with high consumption growth. This low growth of aggregate investment post-1992 is then shown to be due to the low growth of public investment, still paired with constant growth in private investment.

The search for the last mile in causality implies explaining the behaviour of public investment—its high growth, boosting aggregate investment growth and output growth pre-1992, and its low growth, lowering aggregate investment growth and output growth post-1992. Essay 7 shows that this last mile in causality closes the Keynesian loop. It brings in a third determinant of output in the Keynesian mum equation—government expenditures. Public investment is related to government expenditures, in this essay in three parts.

In the first part of Essay 7, public investment is explained on the left-hand side of the equation by two of its components on the right. These explanatory variables are public investment in productive sectors and public investment in administrative services. The head under public investment, of productive sectors, can be broken down further into the sectors of the real economy, such as electricity and manufacturing, as can the head under administrative services.

In the second part of Essay 7, public investment is explained using the policy reforms of the 1990s. These reforms, based on privatization, led to the reallocation of resources from the public to the private sector, particularly in the electricity sector.

In the third part of Essay 7, public investment is taken as a function of aggregate government expenditure. Government expenditure from the Keynesian mum equation is then the variable to be explained on the left-hand side of the equation. Its determinants on the right-hand side are taxation—including all government revenues as elaborated in the essay—and the budget deficit. This equation is taken as additive in nominal terms. The budget deficit becomes a key variable reflecting the liberality or austerity of the country's regulatory environment—Pakistan having been under 22 International Monetary Fund (IMF) loan agreements over the 50 years examined here, with increasing austerity over time.

The results from running government expenditures as a function of taxation and budgetary deficits show that pre-1992, high government expenditures are based on high deficits. On the other hand, in the post-1992 period, low government expenditures are based on low budget deficits. Meanwhile, tax revenues remain constant over both periods. The drop in government expenditures after 1992 is based on a drop in the development component of this expenditure, which is consistent with the first result of the drop in public investment in productive sectors.

The Government of Pakistan appears to have been unable to raise tax revenues over this long-run period of the past 50 years. So, it has based high-GDP growth pre-1992 (6 per cent per annum) on the high growth of aggregate investment, based on high public investment, based, in turn, on high budgetary deficits. Post-1992, lower growth (4 per cent per annum) has been based on the lower growth of aggregate investment, based on the lower growth of public investment, based, in turn, on lower budgetary deficits. Under IMF conditionality, the post-1992 regulatory environment appears to have reduced targeted deficits—and observed deficits.

The Keynesian general equilibrium model allows this complex and nested causality, which also clearly identifies three policy needs. Private investment has flatlined over this very long run of the past 50 years, as have tax revenues. Policy sequencing is all-important here. Tax revenues are the amenable variable for the short-run policy here. They need to be raised to allow higher-financed public investment to raise GDP growth while waiting for policy incentives for private investment—the amenable variable for the long-run policy here—to pick up significantly.

This essay proceeds in the following manner. Section 8.2 reviews the literature on the determinants of public investment and the role of the regulatory policy environment in shaping public investment behaviour in developed and developing countries. Section 8.3 presents the data. Section 8.4 presents the empirical results of the first part, explaining public investment behaviour over time in terms of its components and sub-sectors. Section 8.5 presents the empirical results of the second part, explaining the impact of policy reforms in the 1990s on shaping public investment behaviour. Section 8.6 presents the empirical results of the third part, explaining the impact of the regulatory policy environment on government expenditures. This still leaves the stationarity of private investment over this whole long-run period of 1973–2019 to be explained, especially for post-1992, when public investment dropped but private investment failed to substitute for it. Section 8.7 explains this behaviour of private investment as a classic case of policy mis-sequencing. Policy reforms to reduce budgetary deficits simultaneously liberalized the capital account, leading to significant and mounting capital outflows. Section 8.8 then concludes by summing up the argument of the book, followed by some summary policy implications in Sect. 8.9.

8.2   Literature Review

Essays 5 and 6 argue that a drop in investment growth post-1992 explained the drop in GDP growth in the same period. In turn, investment was explained by its two components: public investment and private investment. In our case, although we see that growth in public investment crowds in private investment, it [public investment] dropped post-1992, explaining the drop in aggregate investment. Our empirical arguments support the studies showing a positive relationship between GDP growth, investment and public investment (Caballero, 1999; Chirinko, 1993; Hashmi et al., 2012; Bivens, 2012). In this essay, we examine the behaviour of public investment.

We now examine the literature on the role of public goods, the declining trend in public goods and the determination of public goods by the regulatory policy environment.

8.2.1 The Role of Public Goods

There is some consensus in the literature that public investment in both developing and developed countries has played a role in raising GDP growth. The literature shows a strong positive correlation between GDP growth and public sector investment (Aschauer, 1989; Cullison, 1993; Barro, 1989; Ramirez, 2000; Papagni et al., 2021). Particularly, the scaling up of public investment in infrastructure, construction, transport and energy has significantly contributed to GDP growth. Further, in low-income economies with deficiencies in public investment in energy and infrastructure, the loss of productivity levels has been observed to be detrimental to GDP growth (Straub, 2008; Briceño-Garmendia et al., 2008).

There are significant simulations estimating the growth impact of infrastructure spending. Using physical indicators of infrastructure, Calderón and Servén (2008) show that if low-income countries halved their infrastructure gap, reaching the level of middle-income countries, their annual GDP growth rates would increase by 2 per cent. If low-income countries in sub-Saharan Africa were to reach the infrastructure level of their regional leader, Mauritius, their GDP growth could increase by 2.3 per cent per annum. If the infrastructure levels were to catch up with countries like South Korea, GDP growth could increase by 2.6 per cent per annum. Therefore, public investment in infrastructure has a well-observed and significant impact on output growth, while constraints on such public goods can be detrimental to output growth.

However, there is a declining trend in the provisioning of public goods. Low-income countries suffer from an infrastructure deficit compared to middle-income countries, but the gap is widening over time (Briceño-Garmendia et al., 2008). The drop in public investment growth is not specific to low-income countries; its growth in advanced and emerging economies seems to be on a downward trend as well (Breunig & Busemeyer, 2012), and the reason is episodes of fiscal consolidation (Välilä & Mehrotra, 2005).

8.2.2 The Role of Government Expenditure

The literature discusses the specific and overlapping reasons. It finds one of the reasons for the drop in public sector investment growth in advanced-, middle- and low-income countries to be the effect of the regulatory policy environment in shaping public investment behaviour. The regulatory policy environment can be based on the country's internal public sector policies or external advocacy.

The importance of public policy has been recognised by the public-policy endogenous growth models of Barro (1990), Barro and Sala-i-Martin (1992), Sala-i-Martin and Barro (1995) and Mendoza (1997), which provide mechanisms by which fiscal policy can determine the level of investment and output and the steady-state growth rate. Kneller et al. (1999) strongly support Barro's (1990) model for a pooled cross-section of countries. Specifically, productive government expenditure on health, education and infrastructure enhances growth, while non-productive expenditure does not. Thus, productive government expenditures are seen to be critical to a country's fiscal policy.

However, the need for fiscal probity has been manifest. The literature regarding achieving fiscal discipline suggests that the capacity of governments to shift resources towards soft public investment decreases as pressures for fiscal consolidation increase. In most economies, rich or poor, there is always a tendency for discretionary expenditures by the government to shrink. Most of these discretionary expenditures come under the category of public investment expenditures (Streeck & Mertens, 2011; Breunig & Busemeyer, 2012). Other evidence suggests that policymakers usually cannot resist spending more on current expenditures in good times but only pick capital expenditures to adjust during bad times (Ardanaz & Izquierdo, 2017).

Martner and Tromben (2005) show that from 1998 to 2003, when Latin American countries had to implement fiscal reforms embedded in IMF programmes, the governments postponed public investment projects rather than cutting current expenditures. For advanced economies, Delgado-Téllez et al. (2022) argue that public investment has also been at historical lows since the 1980s. The major reason is rigid fiscal rules putting downward pressure on public investment.

Fedelino and Hemming (2005) discuss proposals to modify the traditional fiscal policy framework by examining fiscal indicators and targets that may be better suited to safeguarding public investment. They conclude that public investment needs to be financed from public resources but that borrowing for public investment should be delinked from overall borrowing or public debt.

For a panel of advanced and emerging economies, Ardanaz et al. (2021) show that a fiscal consolidation of at least 2 per cent of GDP is associated with an average 10-per cent reduction in public investment in countries with either no fiscal rule or with a rigid fiscal rule. Conversely, under flexible fiscal rules, the negative effect of fiscal adjustments on public investment disappears. Therefore, fiscal rules have a significant impact on GDP growth.

So, the literature shows that the level of public investment has significantly dropped over the past few years in both developed and developing countries. However, the effect associated with the drop in public sector investment has been found to be more detrimental to developing countries than developed ones. The regulatory policy environment's role is one of the major reasons cited for the fall in public sector investments. This role is shaped by multilateral institutions, which, in turn, has a significant negative effect on a country's fiscal variables, particularly on development and public investment expenditures.

8.3 Data

This essay uses the same macroeconomic aggregate data series used for the empirical Essays 5 and 6 for internal consistency.

For the first and second parts of this essay, the component analysis of public investment, we construct a real series for the components and sub-sectors of public investment at constant prices (2005–2006). This data is taken from the Pakistan National Income Accounts and is consistent with the real series constructed for Essays 5 and 6. The data on the electricity sector is taken from multiple government sources, including the Central Power Purchasing Agency (CPPA), state of industry reports by the National Electric Power Regulatory Authority (2006–2023) (NEPRA) and the National Transmission and Distribution Company (NTDC).

The third part of this essay is on the role of the regulatory policy environment. The data for the fiscal variables is taken from the Ministry of Finance's budgetary plans. The data for the key policy variable, the targeted fiscal deficits under the IMF programme, is extracted from the letters of agreement between Pakistan and the IMF since 1973, which the IMF graciously provided to us. The list of variables used and their definitions and data sources are given in Appendix.

8.4 Part 1: Explaining the Behaviour of Public Investment Over Time

We seek to explain the discrete drop and declining trend in public investment observed in Essay 6. The two major components of public investment are productive sector investment and administrative services sector investment. So, public investment equals productive sector investment plus administrative services sector investment. The sectors comprising each of these components, productive investment and administrative services, are given in Box 8.1. The box shows that productive investment comprises all the real sectors of the economy, majorly agriculture, industry, services, energy, trade and housing. Administrative investment is mainly in public services, health, education, defence and social protection.

The components of public investment and further their sectors are examined as growth in real variables and as shares in output (GDP). The objective is to test which of the two components of public investment—productive or administrative investment—has contributed to the declining trend in public investment over time, further testing which of the sectors comprising productive investment and administrative investment may have contributed to their decline.

Box 8.1 Classification of Productive Sector and Administrative Services Investments

Productive sector investments are classified into investments in the following subsectors based on economic activity on the production side:

1. Agriculture
2. Construction
3. Transport
4. Mining and quarrying
5. Large-scale manufacturing and small and household manufacturing
6. Electricity generation and distribution, and gas distribution
7. Wholesale and retail trade
8. Financial institutions
9. Housing services and real estate, including ownership of dwellings

(continued)

> **Box 8.1 (continued)**
> Administrative services sector investment is classified into the following subsectors based on economic activity on the administrative and services side:
>
> 10. General public services
> 11. Defence
> 12. Public order and safety
> 13. Economic affairs
> 14. Environmental protection
> 15. Housing and community amenities
> 16. Health
> 17. Recreation, culture and religion
> 18. Education
> 19. Social protection

8.4.1 The Behaviour of Public Investment Explained in Terms of its Components: Productive Investment and Administrative Investment

We begin by explaining the drop in public investment in terms of its components. Figure 8.1 shows the time plots for the share of public investment in GDP and its two components: the shares of productive sector investment and administrative services sector investment in GDP. The figure shows that the share of public investment in GDP significantly declines post-1992. The share of productive sector investment follows a similar declining pattern, while the share of administrative and services sector investment shows an increasing trend post-1992.

We further examine growth in productive sector investment (Fig. 8.2). Pre-1992, the average growth rate of productive sector investment is 10 per cent. Post-1992, this average growth rate flatlines. So, the observed drop in public investment post-1992 is well-explained by the drop in productive sector investment post-1992. The drop in productive sector investment needs to be explained further in terms of which of its sectors contributed to the drop.

8 THE ROLE OF POLICY REFORMS AND THE REGULATORY POLICY... 187

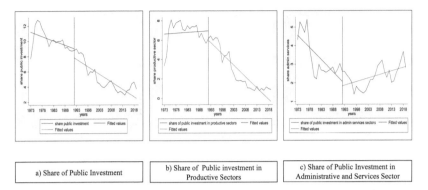

Fig. 8.1 Time-series plot and trend break in public investment, productive sector investment and administrative services sector investment as share of output (GDP)

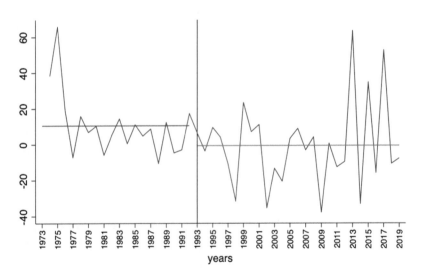

Fig. 8.2 Growth of productive sector investment, 1973–2019

8.4.2 The Behaviour of Productive Sector Investment in Terms of Its Sectors

Based on the relative share value and fluctuations of each sub-sector in total productive sector investment, we select the four major productive sectors from Box 8.1 in terms of their shares in productive investment, that is, manufacturing, electricity, construction and transport. The real values of public investment in these sectors over time are shown in Fig. 8.3. The two major sectors that seem to explain the drop in public investment in the productive sectors around 1992 are electricity and manufacturing. Public investment in electricity and manufacturing peaks around 1993 and 1994, respectively, before declining drastically.

We now examine public investment in these productive sectors in terms of their growth rates. Plotting this growth in public investment in electricity over time in Fig. 8.4 shows a significant decline around 1992. However, the growth of public investment in electricity picks up slightly after 2012. Econometric tests strongly support these plotted trends in the growth of public investment in the productive sectors. Box 8.2 elaborates on these econometric tests.

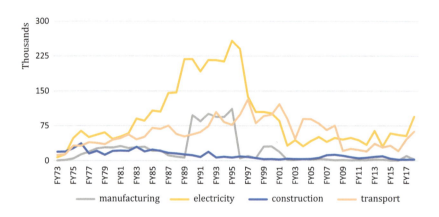

Fig. 8.3 Public investment, by sector (PKR million)

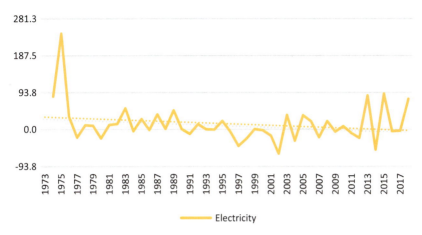

Fig. 8.4 Growth in public investment in electricity

> **Box 8.2 Econometric Tests in Essay 7**
> The econometric tests used in Essay 7 are given below:
> *Test A: Trend analysis using time plots*
> The time-series plots of variables are graphed to observe the trend.
> *Test B: Trend analysis using regressions*
> The trend regressions of the following form will be run on the share of variables.
>
> $$\text{share of variable}_t = \alpha_0 + \alpha_1 \text{trend}_t + e_t \qquad (8.1)$$
>
> The trend variable represents the time-trend variable. We run the above regressions for the entire period and separately for the two periods, pre-1992 and post-1992.
> *Test C: Structural break analysis*
> The structural break analysis is performed in two steps:
>
> - A structural break test at a known break date
> - A dummy regression to know the direction of change

(continued)

Box 8.2 (continued)

To test our explanatory variables series for the single mean shift at a known break date, we use the structural break model specified to test for the break at a known break date:

$$y_{it} = \beta_{ij} + \epsilon_t, \text{where} \beta_{i1} \neq \beta_{i2} \tag{8.2}$$

Where y_{it} represents the growth in the variable i in period t and β_{ij} is the mean shift parameter for the growth rate of variable i. This model allows the coefficient β_{ij} to change after the break. If TB is the break date, the model is

$$y_{it} = \begin{cases} \beta_{i1} + \epsilon_t \text{ if } t \leq \text{TB} \\ \beta_{i2} + \epsilon_t \text{ if } t > \text{TB} \end{cases} \tag{8.3}$$

The known break date TB is taken as the year 1992 ± 1 or the year 1993 in our case. We run the above model to test the break in the components.

The dummy regression will help us test the direction of change in the average growth rates. The regression can be specified as

$$g_{it} = \beta + \theta \text{DU}_t + u_t \tag{8.4}$$

where g_{it} represents growth of variable i and DU_t represents the break dummy variable. The break dummy variable takes the following values $\text{DU}_t = 1$ if $t > 1992$ and $\text{DU}_t = 0$ otherwise. The dummy regression allows us to test whether on average the specified growth drops or increases post-1992.

Test D: Regression analysis

The growth contribution regression specifies the growth of any variable A as a function of the growth in its explanatory variables. The regression equation of the following form is estimated:

$$\text{Agrowth}_t = \alpha_0 + \alpha_1 \text{growth} x_t + \alpha_2 \text{growth} y_t + \alpha_3 \text{growth} z_t + \epsilon_t \tag{8.5}$$

(continued)

> Box 8.2 (continued)
> Where Agrowth$_t$ represents the growth of variable A, growthx represents the growth of variable x, growthy represents the growth of variable y and growthz represents the growth of variable z. We run this equation independently for pre-1992 and post-1992. The coefficients of the model are then tested for equality across the two periods, pre-1992 and post-1992.

Table 8.1 Structural break test for break date in year 1992 ± 1

	Results: Test for known structural break			
Variable description	Break at year 1992 ± 1	Tests and probability		
		Test	Statistics	p value
Real public investment growth	1993	$\chi^2(1)$	4.72*	0.091
Real public investment growth by sectors	1993	$\chi^2(1)$	3.22*	0.072
Growth in electricity	1991	$\chi^2(1)$	3.40*	0.064

* = signficance level at 10 percent

The Wald test for a known break date using Chow's procedure to determine a structural break shows that of the two components of public investment, growth in productive sector investment has a significant break in 1993 (Table 8.1). Subsequently, of the sectors of productive sector investment, investment growth in electricity has a significant break in 1991. Additionally, the results of the dummy regression in Fig. 8.5 show that after 1992, on average, the growth of productive sector investment drops by 11 per cent. Furthermore, on average, after 1992, the growth of public investment in the electricity sector drops by 24 per cent.

We proceed to test whether the growth of public investment in the electricity sector is well correlated with the growth of productive sector investment in both phases, pre-1992 and post-1992. The results of the growth regression shown in Fig. 8.6 bear this out well. Only the growth of public investment in the electricity sector variable consistently explains the growth of public sector investment in the productive sectors across the two periods.

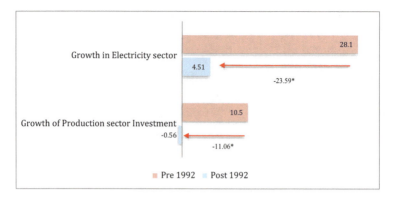

Fig. 8.5 Dummy regression to identify direction of change. (Note: For growth in the electricity sector, the coefficient of the break dummy variable θ takes the value −23.59 and is significant at the 0.01 level, showing a drop of 23.59 per cent post-1992. For the growth of productive sector investment, the coefficient of the break dummy variable θ takes the value −11.06 and is significant at the 0.1 level, showing a drop of 11.06 per cent post-1992. Standard errors given in parentheses. ***$p < 0.01$; **$p < 0.05$; *$p < 0.1$. Dummy92$t' = 1$ for $t > 1992$, Dummy92$t = 0$ otherwise)

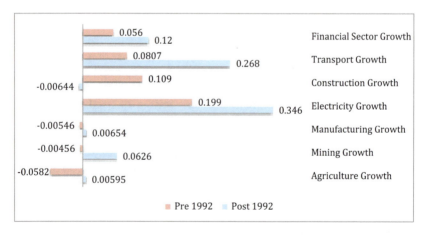

Fig. 8.6 Growth contributions using growth regression. (Note: Electricity growth impact has the highest coefficient pre-1992 and post-1992. The growth in electricity variable pre-1992 coefficient of 0.199 is significant at the 0.01 level, whereas the post-1992 coefficient of 0.346 is significant at the 0.01 level. Standard errors given in parentheses. ***$p < 0.011$; **$p < 0.05$; *$p < 0.1$)

The electricity coefficient shows that a 1 per cent increase in the growth of public investment in the electricity sector is associated with a 0.19 per cent increase in the growth of public sector investment in the productive sectors pre-1992. It is associated with a 0.34 per cent increase in the growth of public sector investment in the sector post-1992. The coefficients are significant and positive for both periods. Therefore, we can say that the drop in productive sector investment is significantly correlated with the drop in the growth of public investment in the electricity sector post-1992.

This turn of events post-1992 (the drop in GDP growth based on the drop in public sector investment, based, in turn, on a drop in public investment in the productive sectors, particularly electricity) needs to be explored further through the impact of power sector policy reforms enacted in the 1990s, and then through the broader regulatory policy environment that has since prevailed.

Part 2 of this essay examines the impact of the policy reforms on the power sector. Part 3 then examines the broader regulatory policy environment to explain the drop in public investment. This regulatory policy environment is seen to be governed by the IMF's loan conditionality to reduce budgetary deficits, which the Pakistan government enacted through a drop in government expenditures rather than an increase in revenues. Further, the curtailing of government expenditures has been at the expense of development expenditures rather than current expenditures. The drop in development expenditures is a drop in investment in expanding new capacity—this explains the drop in public investment. But this does not explain the failure of private investment to pick up and substitute for the drop in public investment at the very least.

What this essay proceeds to show is that policy has been mis-sequenced. There has been an unfortunate simultaneity between two sets of policies in the 1990s. The domestic economy was liberalized through privatization and reduction of public deficits. On the external economy, the capital account was opened up, allowing private capital outflows, which never substituted for the drop in public investment. This finally explains the drop in aggregate investment post-1992 and the fall in the GDP growth rate from 6 per cent to 4 per cent.

Had the capital account not been liberalized to such an extent, the counterfactual argument is that private capital would not have flowed out and would instead have been invested in the domestic economy. Thus, the Keynesian model would have remained investment-led, as in pre-1992, rather than switching to being consumption-led post-1992.

8.5 Part 2: The Impact of the Policy Reforms of the 1990s on the Power Sector

The drop in public investment in the productive sectors, particularly electricity, can be examined further. The causal factor is the policy reforms of the 1990s for the power sector. Their impact on the power sector has not been an unmitigated good, with unintended consequences for consumer welfare. The broader regulatory policy environment and changes to it from the 1990s onwards are examined further in Part 3 of this essay. However, spearheading the policy reforms of the 1990s were those for the power sector, which had grave outcomes for electricity and consumer welfare.

The policy reforms were kicked off by the IMF structural adjustment programme entered into by the Pakistan government in 1988 (Anwar, 1996; McGillivray, 2003; Jafarey, 1992). The gist of the programme was public sector privatization and the deregulation of economic structures and institutions.

The primary focus was the power sector, with a policy shift in the early 1990s for the withdrawal of public investment, mainly from the electricity sector. In its stead, the energy policies of 1994 and 1998, developed in collaboration with the World Bank and Asian Development Bank, aimed to increase private sector involvement in energy through the establishment of independent power plants. These plants were to generate electricity, while the public sector was to purchase that electricity and transmit and distribute it to consumers (Parish, 2006).

The institutional change these policy reforms took was to unbundle the vast public sector entity, the Water and Power Development Authority. The economic efficiency hypothesis argued that a significant programme of privatization in the power sector would usher in private sector involvement. This economic efficiency hypothesis had several implications:

1. Private sector capacity for power generation would substitute public sector capacity.
2. Adding private sector capacity for power generation would increase the rate of capacity growth.
3. Private sector capacity would be more efficient in production costs than public sector capacity.
4. The gains from cheaper production costs by private sector capacity would be passed on to the consumer, enhancing welfare.

5. The increase in investment in more efficient private sector capacity would at least compensate for the drop in investment in less efficient public sector capacity.

Privatization in the power sector was accomplished (but none of the others have followed).

Tables 8.2 and 8.3 show the gradual substitution of public sector capacity by private sector capacity for power generation. Table 8.2 shows that total electricity generation had increased from 14 GWh in 1981 to 141 GWh by 2021, a ten-fold increase in 40 years. All generation was by the public sector until 1995 when the first private sector generation came online. A gestation period of four to five years implies that it was around 1992 that the first investment in private sector capacity for power generation took place, with the first reduction in public sector investment in capacity. By 2022, private sector electricity generation stood at 62 per cent against the public sector's 38 per cent. Table 8.2 shows that most private sector electricity generation has been through thermal sources.

The substitution of public sector investment by private sector investment in electricity generation should have raised the growth rate of total electricity generation. However, Table 8.2 shows the opposite. The growth rate of total electricity generation pre-1992 was 8 per cent per annum. This figure halved to 4 per cent per annum in the post-1992 period. Figure 8.7 shows that the break in the growth rate of electricity came in at about 1991. This broadly coincides with the breaks in public investment and public investment in the productive sectors observed around 1992–2093.

The raison d'être of privatization is the efficiency argument—that private-sector electricity generation will be cheaper than public-sector generation. This has also not been borne out. Given data limitations, Table 8.4 and Fig. 8.8 estimate a shorter series of comparative electricity production costs between the public and private sectors for 2006–2023. In 2006, the public sector cost of electricity generation was PKR 2 per kWh. By comparison, the private sector, which had been online for a decade (sufficient to reap economies of scale), was generating electricity at PKR 8 per kWh, higher by a factor of four. In 2023, the public sector cost of electricity generation had inflated to PKR 17 per kWh. Unfortunately, the corresponding private sector figure had now risen to PKR 31 per kWh.

We now have a three-agent game, with possible welfare gains for consumers and public and private sector producers. However, there have been

Table 8.2 Public and private source-wise energy generation (GWh)

	Public		Private		Total
Year	GWh	Percentage (%)	GWh	Percentage (%)	GWh
1981–1982	14,186	100%	0	0%	14,186
1982–1983	15,920	100%	0	0%	15,920
1983–1984	17,559	100%	0	0%	17,559
1984–1985	18,152	100%	0	0%	18,152
1985–1986	20,465	100%	0	0%	20,465
1986–1987	22,309	100%	0	0%	22,309
1987–1988	25,704	100%	0	0%	25,704
1988–1989	25,751	100%	0	0%	25,751
1989–1990	29,078	100%	0	0%	29,078
1990–1991	31,951	100%	0	0%	31,951
1991–1992	34,657	100%	0	0%	34,657
1992–1993	36,268	100%	0	0%	36,268
1993–1994	36,930	100%	0	0%	36,930
1994–1995	40,016	100%	0	0%	40,016
1995–1996	41,663	100%	161	0%	41,824
1996–1997	37,926	78%	10,740	22%	48,666
1997–1998	37,260	73%	13,580	27%	50,840
1998–1999	36,217	70%	15,326	30%	51,543
1999–2000	38,352	69%	17,418	31%	55,770
2000–2001	35,559	61%	22,836	39%	58,395
2001–2002	39,223	65%	21,573	35%	60,796
2002–2003	43,209	68%	20,755	32%	63,964
2003–2004	49,943	72%	19,036	28%	68,979
2004–2005	50,064	68%	23,316	32%	73,380
2005–2006	55,400	68%	26,639	32%	82,039
2006–2007	55,377	63%	32,259	37%	87,636
2007–2008	51,488	60%	34,570	40%	86,058
2008–2009	48,262	57%	35,887	43%	84,149
2009–2010	30,587	34%	58,084	66%	88,671
2010–2011	34,920	39%	55,386	61%	90,306
2011–2012	33,015	37%	56,369	63%	89,384
2012–2013	33,656	38%	53,948	62%	87,604
2013–2014	36,504	39%	58,227	61%	94,731
2014–2015	37,578	39%	59,359	61%	96,937
2015–2016	38,168	38%	63,381	62%	101,549
2016–2017	37,960	35%	69,140	65%	107,100
2017–2018	37,368	31%	82,357	69%	119,725
2018–2019	41,616	34%	79,984	66%	121,600
2019–2020	48,961	40%	72,077	60%	121,038
2020–2021	50,002	39%	79,252	61%	129,254
2021–2022	54,127	38%	87,161	62%	141,288

Source: NEPRA and NTDC

Note: In 1997, public sector generation constituted 78 per cent of all energy generation compared to 22 per cent by the private sector. In 2022, the public sector accounted for 38 per cent of energy generation compared to 62 per cent by the private sector. This clearly shows that the energy mix has changed from public to private

Table 8.3 Source–wise energy generation (GWh)

Year	Public Hydro	Public Thermal	Public Nuclear	Total public	Private Hydro (IPPs)	Private Thermal	Private Solar	Private Wind	Total private	Public and private total
1981–1982	9526	4660	0	14,186	0	0	0	0	0	14,186
1982–1983	11,366	4554	0	15,920	0	0	0	0	0	15,920
1983–1984	12,822	4737	0	17,559	0	0	0	0	0	17,559
1984–1985	12,245	5907	0	18,152	0	0	0	0	0	18,152
1985–1986	13,804	6661	0	20,465	0	0	0	0	0	20,465
1986–1987	15,251	7058	0	22,309	0	0	0	0	0	22,309
1987–1988	16,689	9015	0	25,704	0	0	0	0	0	25,704
1988–1989	16,196	9555	0	25,751	0	0	0	0	0	25,751
1989–1990	16,925	12,153	0	29,078	0	0	0	0	0	29,078
1990–1991	18,298	13,653	0	31,951	0	0	0	0	0	31,951
1991–1992	18,647	16,010	0	34,657	0	0	0	0	0	34,657
1992–1993	21,111	15,157	0	36,268	0	0	0	0	0	36,268
1993–1994	19,436	17,494	0	36,930	0	0	0	0	0	36,930
1994–1995	22,858	17,158	0	40,016	0	0	0	0	0	40,016
1995–1996	23,206	18,457	0	41,663	0	161	0	0	161	41,824
1996–1997	20,858	17,068	0	37,926	0	10,740	0	0	10,740	48,666
1997–1998	22,060	15,200	0	37,260	0	13,580	0	0	13,580	50,840
1998–1999	22,448	13,769	0	36,217	0	15,326	0	0	15,326	51,543
1999–2000	19,288	19,064	0	38,352	0	17,418	0	0	17,418	55,770
2000–2001	17,196	16,798	1565	35,559	63	22,773	0	0	22,836	58,395
2001–2002	18,941	18,620	1662	39,223	115	21,458	0	0	21,573	60,796
2002–2003	22,253	19,570	1386	43,209	97	20,658	0	0	20,755	63,964
2003–2004	27,372	21,012	1559	49,943	105	18,931	0	0	19,036	68,979
2004–2005	25,588	22,181	2295	50,064	83	23,233	0	0	23,316	73,380
2005–2006	30,751	22,479	2170	55,400	104	26,535	0	0	26,639	82,039
2006–2007	31,846	21,587	1944	55,377	96	32,163	0	0	32,259	87,636
2007–2008	28,536	20,497	2455	51,488	131	34,439	0	0	34,570	86,058

(continued)

Table 8.3 (continued)

Year	Public Hydro	Public Thermal	Public Nuclear	Total public	Private Hydro (IPPs)	Private Thermal	Private Solar	Private Wind	Total private	Public and private total
2008–2009	27,636	19,568	1058	48,262	547	35,340	0	0	35,887	84,149
2009–2010	27,927	565	2095	30,587	19,632	38,452	0	0	58,084	88,671
2010–2011	31,685	305	2930	34,920	13,044	42,342	0	0	55,386	90,306
2011–2012	28,166	436	4413	33,015	12,652	43,711	0	6	56,369	89,384
2012–2013	29,326	662	3668	33,656	13,838	40,072	0	38	53,948	87,604
2013–2014	31,084	989	4431	36,504	14,248	43,721	28	230	58,227	94,731
2014–2015	31,525	1020	5033	37,578	14,223	44,441	231	464	59,359	96,937
2015–2016	33,151	1132	3885	38,168	17,294	44,650	657	780	63,381	101,549
2016–2017	31,084	1016	5860	37,960	19,821	47,316	664	1339	69,140	107,100
2017–2018	27,431	1137	8800	37,368	17,087	62,487	665	2118	82,357	119,725
2018–2019	31,146	1432	9038	41,616	13,590	62,571	657	3166	79,984	121,600
2019–2020	37,431	1795	9735	48,961	8205	60,753	662	2457	72,077	121,038
2020–2021	37,144	1922	10,936	50,002	7079	68,896	727	2550	79,252	129,254
2021–2022	33,449	2374	18,304	54,127	6596	76,154	0	4411	87,161	141,288

Source: NEPRA and NTDC

Note: The energy mix has changed from public to private and from hydro to thermal. Pre-1982, there was no private energy generation. Post-1997, private energy generation was three fourths of total energy generation in Pakistan

8 THE ROLE OF POLICY REFORMS AND THE REGULATORY POLICY… 199

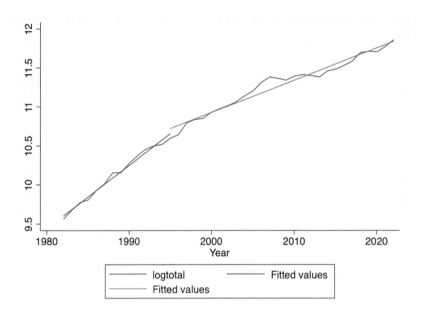

Fig. 8.7 Log total energy generation GWh (public + private). (Note: Pre-1996: log total = −150.77 + 0.08 year. Post-1996: log total = −69.80 + 0.04 year)

no efficiency gains to pass on to enhance consumer welfare because the private sector's generation cost was consistently above the public sector's and almost twice the cost in 2023.

Given data availability, Fig. 8.9 then estimates gains for public- and private-sector electricity producers for a short series from 2014 to 2025. It does this through the methodology in Box 8.3. Total power purchase price (PPP) is decomposed into energy purchase price (EPP) and capacity purchase price (CPP). The EPP is essentially the cost of production, while the CPP is the price the Pakistan government pays the private sector for the installed capacity, regardless of how much of the capacity has generated electricity over a period. So, the CPP becomes a gain for the private producer. Figure 8.9 shows that the capacity producer price in 2014 was a small fraction of the EPP. By 2025, this capacity producer price will have become twice the EPP. So, gains for private electricity producers have come to double.

Table 8.4 Estimated average generation cost for public versus private sectors, 2006–2023

Year	Public average generation cost (PKR/kwh)	Private average generation cost (PKR/kwh)
2006	2.2	7.9
2007	2.7	6.8
2008	3.3	11.9
2009	4.4	8.2
2010	5.2	7.7
2011	6.1	9.2
2012	6.9	11.2
2013	5.8	11.9
2014	6.9	12.6
2015	6.6	10.7
2016	7.4	7.8
2017	7.4	7.3
2018	8.9	8.4
2019	8	12.2
2020	9.7	13.7
2021	17	12.5
2022	14.1	22.5
2023	17.2	30.7

Source: Authors' calculations based on data from *State of Industry Report* (2006 to 2023), NEPRA; and *Power System Statistics* (48th to 38th edition), NTDC

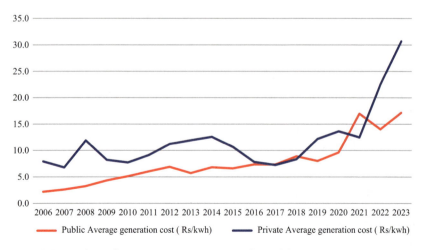

Fig. 8.8 Estimated average generation cost for public versus private sectors, 2006–2023

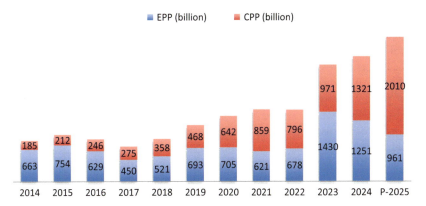

Fig. 8.9 EPP, CPP and PPP. (Source: Ministry of Energy, Government of Pakistan. Note: PPP = EPP + CPP. The share of the CPP increases relative to the share of the EPP, resulting in a sharp increase in the PPP)

Box 8.3 Components of CPP and EPP

The CPP comprises:

- Project debt payments (inclusive of interest and principal)
- Return on equity over the project life
- Fixed element of the operating and maintenance cost
- Insurance cost for the plant.
- Foreign exchange risk insurance cost, which is the cost of hedging loans against foreign exchange risk.

The EPP comprises:

- Fuel cost, which is set by the Government of Pakistan and is above world oil prices by an amount of a surcharge
- Variable element of the operating and maintenance cost
- PPP = EPP + CPP

Note: Definition from the CPPA's PPP forecast

There are two parts to the private efficiency argument. First, the more efficient private sector should be allowed to substitute for the less efficient public sector, enabling cheaper costs of production and welfare gains for consumers. This has not happened in power generation in Pakistan. Second, the private efficiency argument is that public investment crowds out private investment. Again, this did not happen, as shown in Essay 6. Public investment dropped post-1992, but private investment did not substitute for this drop, reducing aggregate investment and GDP growth—which begs the question: why not?

The answer lies in the regulatory policy environment developed from the 1990s onwards. It has been strongly influenced by multilateral advice, particularly from the IMF, under a series of loan agreements to reduce the budgetary fiscal deficits. These agreements would have been fine in and of themselves if not for another set of policy reforms on the external economy: opening up the capital account. This mis-sequencing of policy led to the advent of increased capital outflows, explaining private investment's inability to compensate for the drop in public investment. This is examined in Part 3 of this essay.

8.6 Part 3: The Role of the Regulatory Policy Environment in Explaining the Drop in GDP Growth and Aggregate Investment

Pakistan's GDP growth dropped by 2 per cent on trend, irrevocably, after 1992 because aggregate investment dropped significantly after 1992 by 3 per cent. A Keynesian investment-led model explains Pakistan's high GDP growth pre-1992, and a Keynesian consumption-led model explains lower GDP growth post-1992. Thus, the fall in aggregate investment was based on a significant drop in public investment by 5 per cent, in turn, due to a drop in public investment in productive sectors, particularly power generation.

This drop in public investment was argued for by a private sector efficiency argument, which did not work well for the power generation sector. However, the broader regulatory policy environment shaped under the aegis of a succession of IMF loans, which set increasingly stringent budget deficit targets, does appear to explain the drop in public investment. This is examined in the next section.

However, that still begs the bigger question of why private investment did not step in to substitute for the drop in public investment, especially when this essay showed substantive gains for private power producers. The answer lies in another part of the regulatory policy environment—policy reforms for opening up the capital account, which increased capital outflows significantly. This explains why private investment did not pick up to substitute for the drop in public investment.

This simultaneous enacting of policy reforms—budgetary deficits and opening up the capital account—was a huge case of policy mis-sequencing. On the one hand, it discouraged public investment through budgetary policy. On the other hand, it allowed capital outflows, which kept private investment from picking up and substituting for the drop in public investment (through opening up the capital account). The last section of this essay, and indeed this book, examines the argument being made for policy mis-sequencing.

8.6.1 The Impact of Domestic Policy Reforms on Public Investment

8.6.1.1 Conceptual Framework

Public investment is now examined as a part of the general equilibrium of Keynesian aggregate demand as a continuation of this conceptual framework adopted in the book. This is a conceptual framework of macro aggregates of consumption (C), investment (I), government expenditures (G) and net exports (NX), determining aggregate output (Y) as set out in Eq. (8.6) in Box 8.4. Government expenditures (G), on the left-hand side of Eq. (8.7), are now defined as comprising on the right-hand side, a component financed by tax and nontax revenues (T),[1] plus a component unfinanced by any revenues—which becomes the budgetary deficit (D). Or, taking the deficit on the left-hand side in Eq. (8.8), the deficit is determined on the right-hand side by government expenditures (G) minus tax revenues (T). Another way to slice the government pie (G) on the left-hand side is to decompose it on the right-hand side into two government expenditures—recurrent and development expenditures, as in Eq. (8.9).

---

[1] For simplicity, we refer to both tax and nontax revenues as tax revenues.

> **Box 8.4 The Aggregate Demand Equation Recalled**
> Recalling the aggregate demand equation:
>
> $$Y = C + I + G + NX \qquad (8.6)$$
>
> where:
>
> $$G = T + D \qquad (8.7)$$
>
> Or
>
> $$D = G - T \qquad (8.8)$$
>
> Total government expenditures can also be decomposed into two elements: recurrent expenditures and development expenditures.
>
> $$G = \text{Recurrent expenditures} + \text{development expenditures} \qquad (8.9)$$

We now seek to explain public investment as a component of government expenditure (G), where government expenditures (G) are a function of tax revenue (T) and the budget deficit (D), as in Eq. (8.8).

Equation (8.8) captures the proposition that government expenditure will be subject to the regulatory policy environment. A liberal regulatory policy environment will allow a high government expenditure (G) uncovered by taxes (T) through a higher budget deficit (D). A tighter regulatory policy environment will permit only a lower government expenditure (G) covered more by higher taxes (T) and a lower budget deficit (D). Further, the proposition is that if the regulatory policy environment becomes austere, reducing government expenditure (G) and the budget deficit (D), the government has two choices.

Total government expenditure (G) has also been decomposed into two elements: recurrent and development expenditures, as in Eq. (8.9). Both recurrent and development expenditures determine total government expenditure (G), but the major difference between the two budgetary components is that recurrent expenditures maintain the existing capacity of public goods while development expenditures expand the capacity of public goods. Therefore, recurrent expenditures keep the provision of public investment constant. Development expenditures allow for the expansion of public investment. Ergo, an expansionary development budget will expand public goods capacity and therefore public investment. Conversely, a decreasing development budget will reduce the rate of expansion of public goods capacity and therefore public investment.

Using this conceptual framework, we now hypothesise that the observed reduction in public investment will be explained by the regulatory policy environment working through two key variables: an observed fiscal deficit and an agreed fiscal deficit. The observed fiscal deficit is the prevalent deficit in the economy, and the agreed fiscal deficit is the agreed deficit under, say, a multilateral funding programme.

The regulatory policy environment is based on a country's independence in formulating its macroeconomic policies. However, these have been strongly influenced by multilateral organizations for several decades, with mixed results for many developing countries (Simmons et al., 2008; Shaffer, 2015; Križic, 2019; Abbott & Snidal, 2013). One case of regulatory ambiguity in outcomes is IMF lending programmes, which require countries to implement a series of targeted economic reforms in exchange for loans (Reinsberg et al., 2021). Let us consider the case of Pakistan.

Pakistan has entered into 23 loan agreements with the IMF since 1953. Figure 8.10 shows the number and size of these lending arrangements. In keeping with the period of our analysis, we consider the 14 agreements during 1973–2018. In each agreement, Pakistan was given loans subject to economic conditionalities. These economic conditionalities have been mainly targeted towards curtailing the fiscal deficit, increasing the interest rate ceilings and or liberalising the exchange rates. We are however interested in looking at a particular economic conditionality that imposed a restriction on fiscal outlays. So, the key policy variable we wish to examine is the targeted fiscal deficit agreed under the IMF agreement.

We wish to explain the observed significant drop in the share of public investment and its components post-1992, underlying the drop in aggregate investment, and therefore GDP growth. Our conceptual framework posits that the observed reduction in public investment in sectors observed post-1992 will be based on a drop in government expenditure. We now hypothesise that the targeted fiscal deficit agreed upon under the IMF conditionality will explain the drop in government expenditure.

Accordingly:

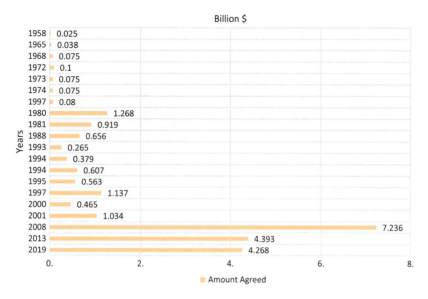

Fig. 8.10 Loans taken by Pakistan from IMF

- H1: An observed reduction in the budget deficit will lead to a drop in government expenditure post-1992.
- H2: An observed reduction in development expenditures, which expand the capacity of public goods, will lead to a drop in government expenditure post-1992.
- H3: The observed drop in the budget deficit will be influenced by the liberality or austerity of the regulatory policy environment, captured by the variable of the agreed budget deficit decided between the IMF and Pakistan government.

To test these hypotheses, we proceed empirically in the following way. First, we analyse the behaviour of the fiscal variables (Box 8.5) as shares of GDP over time. We then analyse the behaviour of fiscal variables under the regulatory policy environment.

> **Box 8.5 Fiscal Variables as Shares of Output**
> The following set of fiscal variables as shares of output (GDP) are used:
>
> - Observed fiscal deficit, measured as a percentage share of output (GDP).
> - Total expenditures, current expenditures and public investment expenditures or development expenditures, measured as a percentage share of output (GDP).
> - Total revenues, measured as a percentage share of output (GDP).
> - Targeted fiscal deficits as agreed under the IMF programmes.

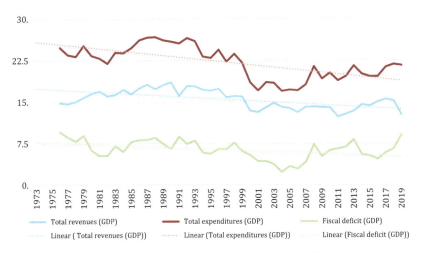

Fig. 8.11 Observed fiscal deficits, revenues and expenditures as percentage of GDP

8.6.1.2 Explaining the Behaviour of Fiscal Variables

The behaviour of government expenditures, revenues and fiscal deficits, and the shares of government expenditures, revenues and fiscal deficits in GDP are shown in Fig. 8.11. Overall, government expenditures have a declining trend over time. The trend however differs between the pre-1992 and post-1992 periods. Pre-1992, the trend is positive, peaking around

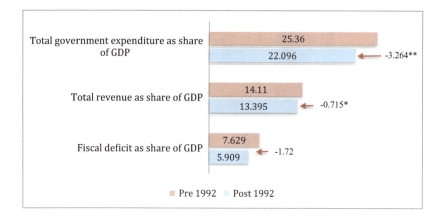

Fig. 8.12 Dummy regression to identify direction of change. (Note: The share of total expenditures drops on average by 3.2 per cent of GDP and is significant at the 0.05 level. The coefficient for the share of revenues is insignificant. The share of fiscal deficits drops on average by 1.7 per cent of GDP. Standard errors given in parentheses. ***$p < 0.01$; **$p < 0.05$; *$p < 0.1$. Dummy92$t' = 1$ for $t > 1992$, Dummy92$t = 0$ otherwise)

1992. Post-1992, the trend significantly declines. Revenues, too, show an increasing trend pre-1992 but decline post-1992. Fiscal deficits follow the same pattern as government expenditures, showing an increasing trend to peak in 1992 and then drop considerably post-1992.

Overall, the deficit seems to be more expenditure-driven than revenue-driven. Figure 8.12 validates the results using dummy regressions. Controlling for the trend, the results suggest that government expenditures fall significantly post-1992, on average, by 3.2 per cent of GDP. Fiscal deficits also drop significantly post-1992, on average, by 1.7 per cent of GDP, whereas revenues remain constant over the whole period. The coefficient for the share of revenues came out insignificant. Theoretically, this drop in the deficit can be associated with two changes—increases in revenues or a fall in government expenditures. In this case, government expenditures have fallen while revenues have remained constant.

These results support hypothesis 1, showing that fiscal deficits have been curtailed in Pakistan, particularly in the post-1992 period. The reduction in fiscal deficits is mainly expenditure-driven and not revenue-driven.

Since we have seen a drop in total government expenditures, we now proceed to analyse the two components of total government expenditures: current and development expenditures.

8.6.1.3 The Behaviour of Total Government Expenditures, Current Expenditures and Development Expenditures

Total government expenditures can be expressed in terms of current expenditures and development expenditures, as in Eq. (8.9) in Box 8.4. Development expenditures in Fig. 8.13 declined on trend over the entire period, but the dummy regression in Fig. 8.14 shows that the decline is significantly steeper by −3.2 per cent post-1992. Current expenditures slightly increase on trend over the whole period, remaining high even after 1992. Total government expenditures drop by 3.3 per cent post-1992.

Correlating the trends of total government expenditure to its two components gives a nuanced picture. The increase in total government expenditures till 1992 appears to have been enabled by the increasing trend in current expenditures. However, the sharp fall in total government expenditures post-1992 (3.3 per cent) is explained entirely by the sharper decline in development expenditures post-1992 (3.2 per cent) because current expenditures post-1992 remained high with no significant fall. The results support hypothesis 2, which is that the reduction in total government expenditures is mainly based on the reduction in development expenditures.

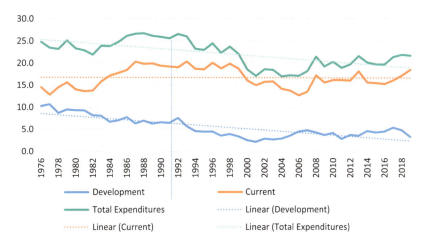

Fig. 8.13 Development, current and total expenditures as percentage of GDP

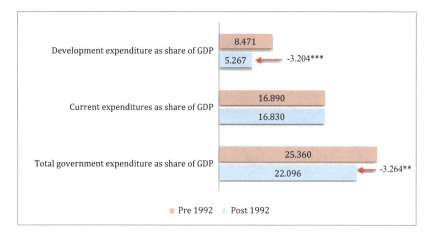

Fig. 8.14 Dummy regression to identify the direction of change. (Note: The share of development expenditures on average falls significantly by 3.2 per cent post-1992 and is significant at the 0.01 level. The share of current expenditures remains constant. The share of total government expenditure as a share of GDP drops on average by 3.2 per cent of GDP and is significant at the 0.05 level. The share of current expenditures remains constant. Standard errors given in parentheses. ***$p<0.01$; **$p<0.05$; *$p<0.1$. Dummy92t' = 1 for $t > 1992$, Dummy92$t = 0$)

In sum, it is evident that observed fiscal deficits have been curtailed in Pakistan, particularly in the post-1992 period. The drop in fiscal deficits resulted from a drop in government expenditures rather than an increase in revenues, supporting hypothesis 1. This drop in government expenditures was based, in turn, mainly on development expenditures being significantly cut and not current expenditures, supporting hypothesis 2.

Having observed that fiscal deficits have declined, we proceed to test the role of the regulatory policy environment that might affect the observed fiscal deficits. To test this posit in hypothesis 3, we examine the behaviour of fiscal variables under the regulatory policy environment.

8.6.1.4 Explaining the Behaviour of Fiscal Variables under the Regulatory Policy Environment

We now proceed to test whether the regulatory policy environment has determined the behaviour of fiscal variables. We are measuring the role of the regulatory policy environment through the introduction of a key policy variable, which is the 'targeted and agreed fiscal deficit under the fund programme'. Theoretically, we are positing that targeted fiscal deficits, as conditionality in the Pakistan-IMF agreements, affect the determination of observed fiscal deficits, as in hypothesis 3, which affects total government expenditures, whose downturn is largely explained by development expenditures. Since development expenditures expand the capacity of public goods, their drop explains the observed drop in public investment, particularly in the productive sectors.

Now, to test the impact of the regulatory policy environment on these fiscal variables, we assume that the tighter the targeted fiscal deficit, the lower the observed fiscal deficit, and the greater the cut in government expenditures, development expenditures and government investment. Therefore, we proceed in a sequential manner to empirically observe the relationship between targeted and observed fiscal deficits.

8.6.1.5 The Behaviour of Targeted and Agreed Fiscal Deficits Under the IMF's Programmes

Figure 8.15 illustrates the relationship between the targeted and observed fiscal deficits. Pakistan has been part of IMF programmes at various times since 1973. We have plotted the agreed targeted fiscal deficits under IMF programmes and the observed fiscal deficits on the y-axis. The x-axis shows episodes in which Pakistan has been part of IMF programmes during 1973–2018. However, we will have to base our analysis on the period in which targeted fiscal deficits were enacted, which is from the Extended Fund Facility of 1981 onwards.

First, analysing the trend of the targeted fiscal deficits till the Enhanced Structural Adjustment Facility (ESAF) of 1991, the targeted fiscal deficits increase on trend to peak at 7 per cent of GDP. However, post-1991, the targeted fiscal deficits decline, that is, they become tighter after 1991. Second, analysing the trend of the observed fiscal deficits, Fig. 8.15 shows that till ESAF 1991, the observed fiscal deficits increase on trend to peak at 9 per cent of GDP. However, post-1991, the observed fiscal deficits fall on trend. Therefore, observed fiscal deficits appear to be correlated with targeted fiscal deficits—both deficits followed an increasing trend till 1991 and a decreasing trend after 1991.

Thus, we can suggest that the targets have put pressure on observed fiscal deficits, which were quite high before 1991 when no targets or relaxed targets were placed by the IMF programmes. However, the conditionality becomes tighter after 1991, which means that the targeted

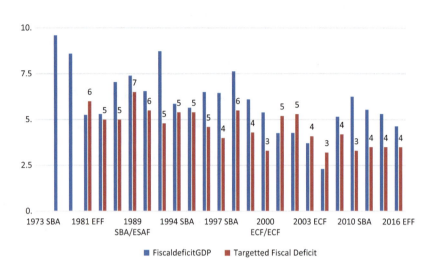

Fig. 8.15 Targeted fiscal deficit by IMF versus observed fiscal deficit, 1980–2016. (Note: The figure plots targeted fiscal deficits as *red bars*. The targeted fiscal deficits only appear in the years that Pakistan was part of an IMF programme from 1980 to 2016. The *blue bars* represent Pakistan's observed fiscal deficits)

deficits have been considerably lowered. Figure 8.15 further shows that the trend of our observed fiscal deficits is clearly in line with the targeted fiscal deficits.

Although Pakistan's observed fiscal deficit was higher than the ambitiously agreed-upon targeted fiscal deficit in most cases, it remained on a downward trend. This means that the drop in fiscal deficits post-1992 observed earlier can be significantly attributed to the regulatory policy environment. If this is the case, we should observe a significant reduction in targeted fiscal deficits post-1992, and the targeted deficits should be correlated with observed fiscal deficits.

Figure 8.16 validates the trend results using a dummy regression (Box 8.2). The result shows that the targeted fiscal deficits drop significantly, on average, by 1.2 per cent of GDP post-1992. This result provides statistical significance for our argument that the targeted deficits have declined, becoming tighter post-1992. Figure 8.16 also shows that the observed

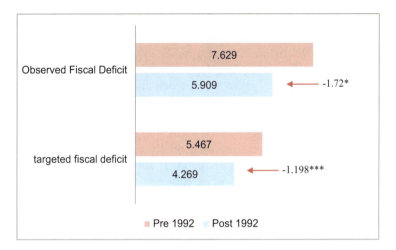

Fig. 8.16 Dummy regression to identify direction of change. (Note: The observed fiscal deficits dropped on average by 1.7 per cent post-1992 and the coefficient is significant at the 0.1 level. The dummy regression for the targeted fiscal deficits agreed under IMF programmes dropped significantly on average by 1.1 per cent post-1992 and the coefficient is significant at the 0.01 level. Standard errors given in parentheses. ***$p < 0.01$; **$p < 0.05$; *$p < 0.1$. Dummy92$t' = 1$ for $t > 1992$. Dummy92$t = 0$ otherwise)

fiscal deficits dropped, on average, by 1.7 per cent post-1992, confirming the pressure of the targeted fiscal deficits on the observed fiscal deficits—a good confirmation of hypothesis 3.

We can now trace back one chain of causality explaining the observed 2 per cent drop in GDP growth post-1992. This was observed to be correlated to the drop in investment post-1992, transforming Pakistan's growth model from investment-led to consumption-led, in Keynesian terms. This drop in investment was further observed to be due to a drop in public investment post-1992 in productive sectors, especially power generation.

The regulatory policy environment explains the drop in public investment through a drop in government expenditures post-1992. Tighter targets for fiscal deficits under sequential IMF loan agreements from 1991 onwards pressured observed fiscal deficits to also drop significantly post-1991. The decrease in observed fiscal deficits comes entirely from reduced government expenditures rather than increased revenues. Thus, as government expenditures came down post-1992 due to the pressures of the regulatory environment, so did public investment.

A parallel decomposition of government expenditures into recurrent and development expenditures provides an additive explanation for the drop in public investment. Recurrent public expenditures maintain existing capacity in public goods. Development expenditures expand capacity in public goods. Hence, development expenditures enable public investment, especially in productive sectors like power generation, allowing capacity expansion. The drop in government expenditures to meet tighter fiscal deficits under pressure from the regulatory environment of IMF programmes has been observed to be met entirely through a drop in development expenditures. This explains the drop in public investment, particularly in productive sectors like power generation.

However, this still begs a second chain of causality. If total investment dropped significantly post-1992 due to an observed drop in public investment, why was private investment not observed to go up to compensate for the drop in public investment? Indeed, private investment remained constant in its share of GDP over the entire period examined, pre-1992 and post-1992. So, the Ricardian hypothesis did not work, and private investment was not being crowded out any more post-1992, but it chose not to increase its share in GDP. The question is why.

The explanation for why private investment did not increase post-1992, despite the retreat of public investment, appears to lie in a second set of policy reforms on opening up the capital account. Two sets of policy reforms coincided: 1) domestic policy reforms to reduce the fiscal deficit, which the Pakistan government chose to achieve by reducing government expenditures, especially development expenditures, which enable public investment; and 2) exogenous policy reforms to open up the capital account, which significantly increased capital outflows from the country.

Ergo, while public investment retreated post-1992, private investment did not substitute for it because of the increased option of flowing out of the country. This was a case of policy mis-sequencing and is examined in the last part of this essay and this book.

8.7 Policy Mis-sequencing as an Explanation for the Behaviour of Private Investment to Substitute for Public Investment

Policy reforms should improve outcomes for the growth of output and welfare. Policy reforms should be sequenced and piecemeal to be able to observe that the outcomes are foreseen and intended, which implies the sequencing of reforms. If there is simultaneity of two sets of policy reforms, their interactive impact on the economy increases the probability of unforeseen and unintended consequences.

The literature on the sequencing of policy reforms is myriad. Instances of the mis-sequencing of policy reforms are instructive.

Mahmood (2005) shows the simultaneity of policy reforms having grave unintended consequences in Nepal. The country liberalized domestic price structures, which weakened returns to the main sector's (agriculture) small-farmer incomes. Simultaneously, external tariff policy was also liberalized, lowering tariff barriers on imports, which flooded in cheaper and subsidized agricultural imports from the larger neighbour India, pauperizing Nepal's small farmers. This may have driven the impoverished peasantry into the ongoing Maoist insurrection, which eventually reached Kathmandu.

Pakistan's regulatory policy environment has been subject to two major sets of policy reforms over the long-run period examined here (1973–2019), that is, domestic policy reform to reduce the fiscal deficit and exogenous policy reform—opening up the capital account (KA). The sequencing of each set of policy reforms becomes critical for their macro outcomes.

8.7.1 Domestic Policy Reforms

Up to 1990, Pakistan had a large public sector inherited from the Bhutto nationalization of the 1970s, with high public investment in state-owned enterprises (SOEs). Development expenditure approximated 10 per cent of GDP in the 1970s but had crept down to 7 per cent by the end of the 1980s. The fiscal deficit was high, financed through non-bank borrowing. Interest payments on the borrowing had risen to 4 per cent of GDP by 1999. Haque and Montiel (1993) found that Pakistan's per-capita GDP growth was higher than a band of developing countries, with price inflation lower and current account (CA) deficits approximating 2.5 per cent of GDP—just about sustainable.

Albeit on multilateral advice, especially from the IMF, at the turn of the decade to 1990, the government liberalised the economy, reducing government subsidies and the fiscal deficit. A privatization commission set up in 1991 privatized 50 of 115 SOEs. A new regime for private investment was ushered in, and new sectors opened up for it, leading with power generation and including banking, telecommunications, airlines and shipping.

The cutting edge of these domestic policy reforms however was deficit reduction, which had peaked at 8.5 per cent of GDP by 1988. Haque and

Montiel (1993) simulated a deficit reduction of 10% per year for the IMF through a reduction in public investment. Successive iterations found the only benefit to be a reduction in the CA deficit, but, importantly, with GDP growth falling.

Nevertheless, the IMF loan agreements from 1991 onwards reduced the agreed targeted fiscal deficits, bringing down the observed deficits, as has been well-observed above. The fiscal deficits were lowered by the Pakistan government through a reduction in public expenditure, especially development expenditure, both of which explain the observed drop in public investment—bringing down total investment and GDP growth post-1992.

That bit of causality has been reasonably demonstrated over the course of this book. However, that still begs the second causality as to why private investment did not step in to at least compensate for the drop in public investment. Domestic policy reforms liberalized the economy with huge gains demonstrated here for the private sector in power generation. Yet, recalling the shares of public and private investment, total investment drops from 22 per cent of GDP in 1992 to 15 per cent by 2019 (Fig. 8.17). Public sector investment explains the entire drop in total investment (5 per cent of GDP), because private sector investment remains constant on trend at 10 per cent of GDP throughout this period.

So, the elephant in the economy is why private sector investment has never risen above 10 per cent of GDP. The answer arguably lies in a second set of policy reforms enacted simultaneously with domestic policy reforms—to wit, the opening up of the capital account.

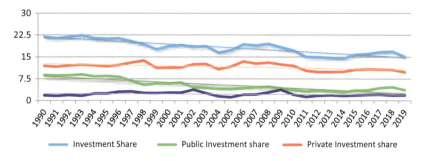

Fig. 8.17 Impact of capital outflows on savings and investment (as percentage of GDP)

8.7.2 Opening Up of the Capital Account

The capital account (KA) is the transfers of assets into and out of the country by residents and non-residents, as defined by the State Bank of Pakistan (SBP). There have been two policy reforms affecting the capital account over the period examined (1973–2019).

First, and as a precursor to the opening up of the capital account, the rupee was unpegged from the US dollar in 1982 and put into a managed float. So, the SBP allowed some market forces to determine the exchange rate, but it also bought and sold forex to currency dealers and commercial banks to manage the exchange rate. This allowed step devaluations. The SBP's objective was to trade off a weaker rupee for the competitiveness of exports against a stronger rupee to ward off imported inflation.

The actual opening up of the capital account came in 1991 with the deregulation of foreign currency deposits. This allowed residents and non-residents, like foreign companies, to open forex accounts and transact forex. This was followed by de jure capital account liberalization in 1994, with:

- Convertibility of rupees into forex.
- No restrictions on the repatriation of capital and profits by non-residents like foreign direct investment and portfolio investors.
- Residents being allowed to transfer forex abroad from their foreign currency accounts in Pakistan.

The result has been periodic forex crises in 1993, 1995 and 1998, with reserves falling below USD 1 billion, requiring successive bailout loan agreements with the IMF.

The graver result for the economy has been the onset of capital outflows, which were negligible pre-1990. Mahmood and Chaudry (2020) estimate a series from 1990 to 2022, showing that capital outflows rose above USD 1 billion in 1990 and doubled to USD 2 billion in 1994 with the full opening up of the capital account. They rose consistently in nominal terms to reach USD 9 billion in 2022. Adjusting for GDP, this series of capital outflows had risen from 1 per cent of GDP in 1991 to approximately 3 per cent by 2022 (Fig. 8.17).

This implies that while private investment has remained constant on trend at about 10 per cent of GDP over the period 2017–2019, private capital has gone out of the country from 1990 onwards, rising from under

1 per cent of GDP to about 3 per cent of GDP by 2022. So, the drop in public investment from 1992 onwards (5 per cent of GDP by 2019) has been accompanied by an increase in private capital (rising to 3 per cent of GDP), but which has not been invested in the domestic economy. Ergo, capital outflows, enabled by the opening up of the capital account from 1991 onwards, explain why private investment in the domestic economy did not pick up to compensate for the drop in public investment from 1992 onwards.

The simultaneity of two sets of policy reforms had an unplanned outcome. Domestic policy reforms for deficit reduction reduced public investment. However, the simultaneous opening up of the capital account allowed capital outflows, keeping private investment in the domestic economy constant. The unplanned outcome was a drop in total investment and GDP growth.

8.8 Summing Up the Book's Theory and Empirics

This has been a book about explaining the behaviour of output. The book deliberated over three fundamental models to explain this behaviour—the neoclassical, Harrod-Domar and Keynesian, to choose one fit for purpose.

The criteria for goodness of fit were four mathematical properties of these growth models. The first desirable property is a notion of general equilibrium based on multiple markets rather than partial equilibrium based on just one market. The second desirable property is theoretical consistency. The third useful property is the need for an equilibrium solution that is not an extreme corner solution with a low probability of occurring. The fourth property entails giving a non-corner equilibrium solution through an equilibrating relationship within the model.

These mathematical properties are not posited as desirable in economic models for mathematical rigour but for economic intuition—to give results that track and explain the behaviour of macro variables better. However, some mathematical rigour has had to be contended with in the course of this deliberation on modelling.

The model chosen for meeting these four mathematical properties is the Keynesian model—it is just slightly better on all four counts. The proof of the pudding and the model is in the number that it comes up with. Its credibility lies in its explanation of observed behaviour. In this sense, this has been a modeller's and certainly not a mathematician's book—the search for a better number that explains observed behaviour better, and perhaps, too, Popperian for pure theorists. Nonetheless, this is how we have chosen to argue.

The Keynesian model of aggregate demand has been used to explain the observed behaviour of Pakistan's long-run growth of GDP in the period 1973–2019. Prior to 1972, the country comprised another part, now Bangladesh. A more consistent set of national income accounts and macro aggregates becomes available only after 1972.

Pakistan's GDP growth over the long run between 1973 and 2019 is observed here to be marked by a statistically significant hiatus at approximately 1992. Pre-1992, GDP growth on trend approximates 6 per cent per annum. Post-1992, GDP growth drops on trend to approximately 4 per cent per annum. These observed trends require an explanation. An adapted Keynesian model explains this observed hiatus in GDP growth very well. The Kahn-Keynes multiplier explains output growth on the left-hand side of an equation as a function on the right-hand side of the macro aggregate of investment times a multiplier k. The multiplier k is given by the marginal propensity to consume (MPC) and therefore ultimately by the macro aggregate of consumption.

However, the two macro aggregates of investment and consumption are not simply additive complements as the national income identity seems to present them because investment for Keynes is a function not of the rate of interest but of the supply of loanable funds (savings). So, if investment goes up, savings go up, and savings plus consumption are equal to income. Then, if savings go up, consumption must come down. Therefore, given the multiplier k, investment and consumption become trade-offs, not complements.

This theoretical model then says that output on the left-hand side of the equation will be determined on the right-hand side by both investment and consumption, but as trade-offs rather than complements because if investment goes up, consumption will go down. Therefore, the impact of investment going up on output will be traded off by the multiplier k going down because consumption and the MPC will go down. Conversely, the impact of investment going down on output will be traded off by the multiplier k going up because consumption and the MPC will go up.

Applied to the hiatus in Pakistan's GDP growth after 1992, this model shows pre-1992 high GDP growth to be explained by high investment growth paired with a low MPC. Conversely, in the post-1992 period, lowered GDP growth is explained by lowered investment growth paired with a higher MPC. So, Pakistan's higher GDP growth pre-1992 has been investment-led, while lower GDP growth post-1992 has been consumption-led.

The book then traces the causality of these trends in investment and consumption. It finds that high total investment pre-1992 has been due to high public investment. So, the drop in total investment in 1992 was due to a significant drop in public investment, which is further tracked to a drop in the productive sectors, particularly power generation. However, private investment is observed to remain fairly constant over the entire two sub-periods, pre-1992 and post-1992. This begs the Ricardian hypothesis: if public investment was high pre-1992 and private investment was crowded out by public investment, then post-1992, as public investment dropped, why did private investment not rise to substitute for it?

This requires two causal chains to be pursued: one to explain the drop in public investment and another to explain private investment's inability to substitute for public investment. The causal chain to explain the drop in public investment, especially in productive sectors like power, is sought in a set of domestic policy reforms to the regulatory policy environment. These have been to reduce the fiscal deficit. The causal chain to explain private investment's inability to rise and substitute for the drop in public investment is sought in a simultaneous set of exogenous policy reforms to the regulatory policy environment. These have been to open up the capital account, giving a case of policy mis-sequencing and leading to unplanned outcomes.

The drop in public investment post-1992 is explained through government expenditures. Government expenditures are a function of revenues and budget deficits set out in a Keynesian analytical macro framework. Government expenditures are observed to drop significantly post-1992. This drop is based on a significant drop in fiscal deficits post-1992, while tax revenues remain constant between the pre-1992 and post-1992 periods.

Clearly, the Pakistan government was forced by the need to reduce the budget deficit and did so by reducing government expenditures rather than raising tax revenues. The reduction in budget deficits leading to a reduction in government expenditures is further based on a cut in government development expenditures rather than a cut in government recurrent expenditures. Since development expenditures expand the capacity for public goods while recurrent expenditures are on existing capacity, the drop in development expenditures enables the observed drop in public investment in productive sectors like power generation.

The fundamental question then becomes what kind of regulatory policy environment influenced the observed drop in budget deficits. Pakistan has seen a succession of loan agreements with the IMF whose conditionality appears to have become tighter over time, particularly after 1991. This has been the impetus for domestic policy reforms to reduce runaway fiscal deficits.

The liberality or austerity of the regulatory policy environment is captured well by the size of the agreed budget deficit decided between the IMF and the Pakistan government. These agreed-upon budget deficits are seen to drop after the 1991 agreement and for all subsequent agreements. In addition, the agreed budget deficits are seen to be well correlated with the observed budget deficits. So, the regulatory policy environment, heavily influenced by domestic policy reforms to reduce fiscal deficits, became significantly more austere post-1992, leading to the chain of causality through reduced government expenditures to reduced public investment.

However, these domestic policy reforms to the regulatory policy environment of cutting the budget deficit explain only the drop in public investment. They do not explain why private investment did not pick up post-1992 to compensate for the drop in public investment. To explain why private investment remained constant over the entire period examined (1973–2019) and did not pick up post-1992, a second set of policy reforms to the regulatory policy environment is invoked—exogenous policy reforms to open up the capital account. Enacted simultaneously with the domestic policy reforms, the opening up of the capital account in 1991, and more fully by 1994, led to significant capital outflows.

Beginning at about 1 per cent of GDP, these capital outflows had risen to about 3 per cent of GDP by 2022. Public investment dropped by about 5 per cent of GDP post-1992 coming up to 2019. With private investment fairly constant on trend at about 10 per cent of GDP over the whole long-run period, the drop in public investment reduced total investment by 5 per cent of GDP. Private investment did not fill this gap of 5 per cent of GDP because, by 2022, it was sending nearly 3 per cent of GDP into capital outflows.

8.9 Policy Implications

This is not a book about policy. Being preoccupied with explaining the behaviour of macro aggregates based on a picky search for models that might serve better, there are some logical implications of the causality that explain the drop in GDP growth in Pakistan post-1992. There are two causal chains, one each for public and private investment. One clear policy option is to fund an increase in public and productive sector investment to enhance total investment and output growth.

Theoretically, this first policy option should be based on enhancing tax revenues to enhance public investment without raising the observed fiscal deficits. Pakistan has not followed this option as tax revenues have fallen. The second policy option is to raise private investment. In the short to medium term, this can only be done by reducing capital outflows by closing the capital account.

The existential question for Pakistan's economy is how to raise its low investment as a share of GDP, which has now slumped to 15 per cent. A balanced growth path is clearly needed—one that incentivizes private investment and increases public investment to enhance total investment. Therefore, if private investment is shy in the shorter run, public investment must be increased to increase total investment. Again, balance is a need in funding public investment both from increasing revenues and prudent increases in the public deficit.

Appendix: Definitions of Variables

Variables	Definition	Data source
Public investment	Public investment is the value of the gross fixed capital formation (GFCF) carried out by the government. According to the national income accounts, GFCF is measured by the total value of a producer's acquisitions less disposal of fixed assets during the accounting period plus certain specified expenditure on services that adds to the value of non-produced assets. GFCF may also take the form of improvements to existing fixed assets, such as buildings or computer software that increase their productive capacity, extend their service lives or both	National income accounts, Pakistan Bureau of Statistics

(continued)

(continued)

Variables	Definition	Data source
Public investment in sectors	Public investment in commodity-producing sectors and services sector	National income accounts, Pakistan Bureau of Statistics
General government	Public investment in services sector, mainly public administration and defence and other social services	National income accounts, Pakistan Bureau of Statistics
Fiscal deficit	Total expenditure minus total revenues	Ministry of Finance, Pakistan
Total expenditures	Current expenditures + development expenditures	Ministry of Finance, Pakistan
Current expenditures	Expenditures (nondevelopment) relating to the ongoing costs of government, such as salaries and contingent expenditures	Ministry of Finance, Pakistan
Development expenditures	Development expenditure component of fiscal outlays equals net investment by the public sector in Pakistan	Ministry of Finance, Pakistan
Total revenue	Inflow of cash arising as a result of collections received in a given reporting period	Ministry of Finance, Pakistan
Targeted fiscal deficit	The targeted fiscal deficit agreed on between the Pakistan government and IMF on the approval of a loan	IMF archival database. Letter of Intent/Agreement between Pakistan and IMF, 1973–2018. Provided bilateral to researcher
PPP	The generation cost and transmission cost to be worked out and allocated from the CPPA/NTDC pool to distribution companies in accordance with the transfer price mechanism approved by the authority plus power purchase by distribution companies through bilateral contracts duly approved by the authority	PPP forecast, CPPA, Pakistan
CPP	The fixed cost of generation. This constitutes fixed operation and maintenance, return on equity, return on equity during construction, the cost of working capital, insurance and debt servicing. Typically, the loan needs to be repaid in the first ten years of the project	PPP forecast, CPPA, Pakistan
EPP	The price associated with dispatch, comprising variable operation and maintenance costs and fuel costs, etc	PPP forecast, CPPA, Pakistan

References

Abbott, K. W., & Snidal, D. (2013). Taking responsive regulation transnational: Strategies for international organizations. *Regulation and Governance, 7*(1), 95–113.

Anwar, T. (1996). Structural adjustment and poverty: The case of Pakistan. *Pakistan Development Review, 35*(4), 911–926.

Ardanaz, M., Cavallo, E., Izquierdo, A., & Puig, J. (2021). Growth-friendly fiscal rules? Safeguarding public investment from budget cuts through fiscal rule design. *Journal of International Money and Finance, 111*, 102–319.

Ardanaz, M., & Izquierdo, A. (2017). *Current expenditure upswings in good times and capital expenditure downswings in bad times? New evidence from developing countries.* Working Paper No. IDB-WP-838. Inter-American Development Bank.

Aschauer, D. A. (1989). Public investment and productivity growth in the Group of Seven. *Economic Perspectives, 13*(5), 17–25.

Barro, R. J. (1989). *Economic growth in a cross section of countries.* Working Paper No. 3120). National Bureau of Economic Research.

Barro, R. J. (1990). Government spending in a simple model of endogenous growth. *Journal of Political Economy, 98*(5), 103–125.

Barro, R. J., & Sala-i-Martin, X. (1992). Public finance in models of economic growth. *The Review of Economic Studies, 59*(4), 645–661.

Bivens, J. (2012). *Public investment: The next 'new thing' for powering economic growth.* Briefing Paper No. 338). Economic Policy Institute.

Breunig, C., & Busemeyer, M. R. (2012). Fiscal austerity and the trade-off between public investment and social spending. *Journal of European Public Policy, 19*(6), 921–938.

Briceño-Garmendia, C. B., Smits, K., & Foster, V. (2008). *Financing public infrastructure in Sub-Saharan Africa: Patterns and emerging issues.* Report No. 71815. The World Bank.

Caballero, R. J. (1999). Aggregate investment. In Handbook of macroeconomics: *Volume 1B* (pp. 813–862). Elsevier.

Calderón, C., & Servén, L. (2008). *Infrastructure and economic development in Sub-Saharan Africa.* Policy Research Working Paper No. 4712). The World Bank.

Chirinko, R. S. (1993). Business fixed investment spending: Modelling strategies, empirical results, and policy implications. *Journal of Economic Literature, 31*(4), 1875–1911.

Cullison, W. (1993). Public investment and economic growth. *FRB Richmond Economic Quarterly, 79*(4), 19–33.

Delgado-Téllez, M., Gordo, E., Kataryniuk, I., & Pérez, J. J. (2022). The decline in public investment: 'Social dominance' or too-rigid fiscal rules? *Applied Economics, 54*(10), 1123–1136.

Fedelino, A., & Hemming, R. (2005). *A fiscal policy framework to safeguard public investment*. SSRN.

Haque, N., & Montiel, P. (1993). Fiscal adjustment in Pakistan: Some simulation results. *IMF Economic Review, 40*, 471–480.

Hashmi, M. H., Akram, W., & Hashmi, A. A. (2012). Role of investment in the course of economic growth in Pakistan. *International Journal of Academic Research in Economics and Management Sciences, 1*(5), 48–61.

Jafarey, V. A. (1992). *Structural adjustment and macroeconomic policy issues*. International Monetary Fund.

Kneller, R., Bleaney, M. F., & Gemmell, N. (1999). Fiscal policy and growth: Evidence from OECD countries. *Journal of Public Economics, 74*(2), 171–190.

Križic, I. (2019). *The international politics of public procurement*. Unpublished doctoral thesis. Université de Genève.

Mahmood, M. (2005). *Poverty reduction strategy paper for Nepal*. International Labour Office.

Mahmood, M., & Chaudry, S. (2020). Pakistan's balance-of-payments crisis and some policy options. *Lahore Journal of Economics, 25*(2), 55–92.

Martner, R., & Tromben, V. (2005). *Public investment and fiscal adjustment in Latin American countries*. SSRN.

McGillivray, M. (2003). Policy-based lending, structural adjustment and economic growth in Pakistan. *Journal of Policy Modeling, 25*(2), 113–121.

Mendoza, E. G. (1997). Terms-of-trade uncertainty and economic growth. *Journal of Development Economics, 54*(2), 323–356.

Papagni, E., Lepore, A., Felice, E., Baraldi, A. L., & Alfano, M. R. (2021). Public investment and growth: Lessons learned from 60 years' experience in southern Italy. *Journal of Policy Modeling, 43*(2), 376–393.

Parish, D. (2006). *Evaluation of the power sector operations in Pakistan*. Asian Development Bank.

Ramirez, M. D. (2000). The impact of public investment on private investment spending in Latin America: 1980–95. *Atlantic Economic Journal, 28*, 210–225.

Reinsberg, B., Stubbs, T., & Kentikelenis, A. (2021). Compliance, defiance, and the dependency trap: International Monetary Fund program interruptions and their impact on capital markets. *Regulation and Governance, 16*(4), 1022–1041.

Sala-i-Martin, X. X., & Barro, R. J. (1995). *Technological diffusion, convergence, and growth*. Center Discussion Paper No. 735. Economic Growth Center, Yale University.

Shaffer, G. (2015). How the World Trade Organization shapes regulatory governance. *Regulation and Governance, 9*(1), 1–15.

Simmons, B. A., Dobbin, F., & Garrett, G. (2008). Introduction: The diffusion of liberalization. In *The global diffusion of markets and democracy*. Cambridge University Press.

Straub, S. (2008). *Infrastructure and growth in developing countries: Recent advances and research challenges.* Policy Research Working Paper No. 4460. The World Bank.

Streeck, W., & Mertens, D. (2011). *Fiscal austerity and public investment: Is the possible the enemy of the necessary?* MPIfG discussion paper.

Välilä, T., & Mehrotra, A. (2005). *Evolution and determinants of public investment in Europe.* Economic and Financial Report No. 2005/01. European Investment Bank.

Index[1]

A
Advanced economies, 101–103, 183
Aggregate investment, 6, 7, 23–25, 138–142, 147, 176, 179–181, 193, 202–214
Asian financial crisis, 100, 101

B
Behaviour of public investment, 6, 179–222

C
Cambridge capital controversy, 14, 15, 45–46, 48, 64, 66
Capital account (KA), 3–5, 7, 36, 116, 123, 144, 181, 193, 202, 203, 214–218, 220–222
Capital market for investment, 19, 36
Capital-output ratio, 16, 17, 47, 50, 66–69, 73, 74, 79, 80, 88, 90, 93
Capital reversing, 49–50, 56
Classical-cum-neoclassical argument, 41, 43
Classical-cum-neoclassical function, 37, 40
Classical-cum-neoclassical model, 32, 33, 38, 41, 42, 44, 62
Competitive market economy, 30, 62
Consumption-driven growth, 21, 113, 121, 133
Corner solution/corner solutions, 1, 13, 15–18, 62, 66, 83, 84, 86–92, 218
Covid-19 pandemic, 100, 102, 103
Crowding-in hypothesis, 147, 173
Crowding-out hypothesis, 147, 173

D
Demand for employment, 33, 37–41, 63
Demand-side variables, 161–170

---

[1] Note: Page numbers followed by 'n' refer to notes.

228 INDEX

Determinants of growth, 6, 22, 115, 119, 123, 137
Developing countries, 23, 114, 138–140, 142, 181, 184, 205, 215
Disequilibrium, 69, 71–77, 79–81, 83
Drivers of growth, 104, 124

E
Enhanced Structural Adjustment Facility (ESAF), 211
Equilibrium solution, 1, 5, 13, 15–17, 20, 29, 32, 33, 45, 61–96, 218
European Central Bank, 102, 103

F
Factor price equalization, 80, 81
Federal Reserve Bank, 102
Feldman-Mahalanobis model, 16–18
Fiscal deficit/fiscal deficits, 3–5, 116, 184, 202, 205, 207, 208, 210–216, 220–222
Flexibility of the money wage, 31, 62
Frankenstein model/'Frankenstein' model, 16, 17
Full employment, 30–33, 38, 62, 65–67, 77–80, 100, 107–109

G
General equilibrium, 1, 5, 6, 13–14, 17–26, 29–58, 61–63, 85, 87–89, 96, 113–133, 181, 203, 218
General Theory of Employment, Interest and Money, The, 30, 62, 85, 99, 103, 104, 107–109
Global financial crisis, 100, 102, 117
Gosplan Committee, 81
Great Depression, 100, 101
Griffin-Enos hypothesis, 149, 159, 160

Growth of output, 5, 6, 14, 16, 18–26, 29, 45, 61, 63, 64, 66–70, 78, 79, 84, 85, 88, 90–92, 113, 115–133, 141, 149, 214
G20 countries, 103

H
Haq, Mahbub ul, 115, 215
Haq, Zia-ul, 116
Harrod-Domar model, 1, 11–19, 45, 63–72, 74, 76–81, 83, 84, 88, 90–93, 96

I
IMF programmes, 183, 184, 207, 211–214
International Monetary Fund (IMF), 4, 7, 25, 114, 116–118, 125, 133, 180, 181, 183, 184, 193, 194, 202, 205–207, 211–217, 221
Investment-driven growth, 21, 113, 121, 133
Investment growth, 3, 6, 21–24, 113, 123, 124, 126–133, 137–176, 179, 181–183, 191, 219

K
Kahn-Keynes model, 121, 123
Kahn-Keynes multiplier, 2, 18, 21, 22, 93–96, 107, 113, 119–121, 133, 137, 219
Keynesian conceptual framework, 93
Keynesian economics, 17
Keynesian general equilibrium, 6, 18–26, 37, 42, 44, 96, 113–133, 181
Keynesian hypothesis, 166, 167, 175, 176

Keynesian model, 1–7, 11–14, 16–19, 21–23, 30, 32–33, 35, 37, 38, 42, 44, 45, 62–64, 85, 89–96, 99–103, 107, 109, 137–139, 141, 142, 147, 193, 218, 219
Keynesian model of aggregate demand, 2, 11–14, 16–19, 32–33, 35, 45, 63, 64, 102, 103, 219
Keynesian 'mum' equation, 6, 18–20, 22, 24, 36, 42–44, 99–109, 137, 179, 180
Keynesian notion of aggregate demand, 33
Khan, Ayub, 115, 116, 118, 142, 143
Knife edge/knife edge of equilibrium, 70–74
Kuzarbeit, 103

L

Labour market, 19, 30–34, 37–42, 45, 62, 63, 102, 103
Lahore School of Economics Modelling Lab, 16, 85, 86, 88, 89
Latin American crisis, 100, 101
LEETS, 53
Long-run GDP growth, 19–21, 24, 45, 63, 113–119, 130, 132, 133, 140, 179, 219

M

Macro goods market, 37, 38
Market for global capital flows, 14, 19, 42, 99–100
Marshall and Walras's rate of interest, 76
Mathematically equilibrating model, 5, 13, 17–20, 29, 45, 61–96
Mathematical properties (of growth models), 1, 96, 218

Multiple markets, 1, 13, 14, 17, 18, 30, 33–39, 42, 44, 45, 63, 218
Mum equation, 18–22, 24, 36, 42–44, 94, 96, 99–109, 119, 120, 128, 137, 144, 179, 180
See also Keynesian 'mum' equation
Musharraf, Pervez, 117

N

Neoclassical conceptual framework, 47, 48
Neoclassical models, 1, 30–31, 58, 62
Neoclassical production function, 11, 46–49, 57, 66
Non-equilibrating model, 89

O

Oil price shock, 116
Okun's law, 19, 106

P

Pakistan, 1–7, 13, 19–26, 109, 113–133, 137–176, 179–222
Paradox of thrift, 91, 92
Partial equilibrium, 1, 13, 18, 31, 34, 35, 37–40, 42, 44, 62, 63, 118, 218
Policy mis-sequencing, 3, 7, 181, 203, 214–218, 220
Power sector, 193–202
Private goods market, 14, 19, 36
Private investment, 3–7, 19, 23–26, 108, 120–122, 138–143, 146–148, 161–163, 165–168, 170–175, 179, 181, 193, 202, 203, 214–218, 220–222
Privatization, 117, 180, 193–195, 215
Production possibility frontier, 32
Properties of growth models, 5, 11–26, 29–58, 61–96

Public goods market, 14, 19, 36, 62, 63
Public investment, 3–7, 23–26, 138–143, 147, 161–176, 179–222

R
Regulatory environment, 7, 24, 25, 116, 180, 181, 213, 214
Regulatory policy environment, 3, 4, 179–222
Re-switching, 49–51, 53–57
Ricardian equivalence, 23, 24, 138, 139
Ricardian hypothesis, 3, 167, 174, 214, 220
Ricardian model, 141, 142, 147
Robinson, Joan, 11, 12, 15, 16, 46, 48, 49, 53, 67, 77, 81
Roosevelt, Franklin D., 101, 108

S
Samuelson-Swan-Solow production function, 11–15, 17–19, 45, 46, 49, 58, 63, 66, 96
Say's law, 30–32, 62
Single market, 13, 18, 44, 63
Soviet economy, 81, 83
Sraffian pricing, 50–52
Structural break, 125, 126, 150–153, 161–165, 189–191
Supply-side variables, 150–152, 154–156, 158, 175

T
Theory of income distribution, 17
Tradeables market, 14, 19, 36, 99, 115
Trade-off between investment and consumption, 2, 18, 22, 89, 90, 92, 93, 95, 96, 120, 121, 137, 143, 219

W
Wage bill, 39, 40, 85, 88, 89
Wicksell effects, 15
Workhorse models, 11, 12, 14, 20, 45, 63, 64, 99